Women's Lives and the Eighteenth-Century English Novel

A young woman of the upper middle class, or gentry. Collet. Engraving by Pranker. Reproduced by courtesy of the Trustees of the British Museum.

WOMEN'S
LIVES

AND THE

18TH-CENTURY
ENGLISH NOVEL

Elizabeth Bergen Brophy

University of South Florida Press/Tampa

The University of South Florida Press is a member of University Presses
of Florida, the scholarly publishing agency of the State University System of Florida. Books are selected for publication by faculty editorial
committees at each of Florida's nine public universities: Florida A & M
University (Tallahassee), Florida Atlantic University (Boca Raton), Florida International University (Miami), Florida State University (Tallahassee), University of Central Florida (Orlando), University of Florida
(Gainesville), University of North Florida (Jacksonville), University of
South Florida (Tampa), and University of West Florida (Pensacola). The
activities of the University of South Florida Press are supported in part
by the University of South Florida Research Council.

Orders for books published by all member presses should be addressed
to University Presses of Florida, 15 Northwest 15th Street, Gainesville,
Florida 32611.

Library of Congress Cataloging-in-Publication Data

Brophy, Elizabeth Bergen, 1929–
    Women's lives and the eighteenth-century English novel / Elizabeth
Bergen Brophy.
    p.   cm.
    Includes bibliographical references and index.
    ISBN 0-8130-1036-5
    1. English fiction—18th century—History and criticism.   2. Women
and literature—Great Britain—History—18th century.   3. Women—
Great Britain—Books and reading—History—18th century.   4. English
letters—Women authors—History and criticism.   5. Women—Great
Britain—History—18th century—Sources.   6. Autobiography—
Women authors.   7. Women in literature.   I. Title.
PR858.W6B76 1991
820.9'352042'09033—dc20   90-47980

FOR

Christopher, Siobhan, Prudence, and Caleb

CONTENTS

ACKNOWLEDGMENTS

WOULD LIKE to express my gratitude to the American Council of Learned Societies for the grant which enabled me to begin this work and to the National Endowment for the Humanities for a grant which enabled me to complete it. I am also grateful for a Faculty Fellowship from the College of New Rochelle for additional support. I thank Josephine Asaro Manning who told me about the Mary Martin Rebow letters she discovered in the Washington State University Library. Through the kindness of Washington State University photocopies of these letters have been deposited in Colchester, England, where I read them. I am most grateful to those who aided me at the Victoria and Albert Museum, the Historical Manuscripts Commission, the Williams Library, the Friends' Library, and the British Library, all in London, as well as the public record offices both for Greater London and Middlesex County.

I am indebted to Timothy F. Beard and Frank Bradley of the New York Public Library, both specialists in the Genealogy Room, for first telling me about the wealth of material held by the county record offices, and to John Gillis for alerting me to the records of the Foundling Hospital. I thank Betty Rizzo for sharing her detailed knowledge of the period and James Griffith for informing me about eighteenth-century fainting. I thank Katherine Henderson for her criteria for feminist criticism. I especially thank all of the archivists in the county public record offices who so generously responded to my inquiries and shared detailed knowledge of their collections. My thanks also to those who assisted me at the Morgan Library, the New York Public Library's Berg Collection, the Beinecke Library at Yale, especially John Riely and his wife, Elizabeth, together with Stephen Parks who gave me access to the Osborn Collection and helpful information about its holdings. I thank the trustees of the British Museum, the British Library, and the Friends' Library for the photographs used as illustrations. I am grateful also for the unfailing helpfulness of the librarians at the College of New Rochelle, and especially to Patricia Rader who was indeed a friend in need.

I owe a very great debt to those hundreds of women in the eighteenth century who recorded their thoughts and deeds, never thinking of what interest their private writings would be to an eavesdropper from the twentieth century who could by this means learn of their intimate lives and daily concerns. But as always, my greatest debt is to my husband for his unfailing encouragement and support, not only in this, but in all endeavors.

Introduction

D R. SAMUEL JOHNSON declared in *Rambler* number four that "The works of fiction, with which the present generation seems more particularly delighted, are such as exhibit life in its true state." He then went on to demand a special moral responsibility from the novel because it was "realistic" and therefore provided a model of behavior for its readers which was much more likely to inspire emulation than were the actions of characters in improbable romances. Generations of readers and critics have accepted his assumption that the novels of the eighteenth century are basically realistic.

This book began with my own questioning of Johnson's assertion, not from the viewpoint of modern critics for whom such a statement is virtually meaningless, but in its own terms. How do we know that this is what everyday life—the chief province of the novel—was like? And, as my question started to focus more precisely, how do we know, especially, whether these works give us an accurate portrayal of the normal, everyday woman of the century? I realized that we, in fact, know too little about women in the eighteenth century except for the famous or notorious. What was it like to be an *average* eighteenth-century woman? The answer to this question, aside from its intrinsic interest, would help to assess the question of "realism" in eighteenth-century fiction.

Another related question arose. Since the relationship between a society and its art is usually a complex interaction, how might the depiction of women in fiction have influenced the women of the time? What attitudes, what modes of behavior are suggested as admirable and what characteristics are depicted as dangerous or, perhaps, ludicrous? This study presents eighteenth-century women themselves in their various roles and examines novels of the period to assess both the accuracy of their portrayal of women and the influence they might have had upon their women readers.

I have based the description of eighteenth-century women entirely on their own writings—personal revelations in letters, diaries, and journals. I have not used published diaries or collections of letters because these were too often edited by pious relatives and are therefore not reliable. Unfortunately, while families tend to save wills, deeds, and legal papers, the kinds of manuscripts I was seeking are often discarded as either too trivial or too revealing. However, during a year's residence in England I succeeded in finding thousands of letters and dozens of journals written by more than 250 women who constitute, I believe, as representative a group as it is possible to find. They range from upper servants (the usual lower range of literacy) to the upper gentry and lower nobility. I have avoided court memoirs and those journals and letters which reflect a life too exalted to bear comparison with the life depicted in most eighteenth-century fiction. Some of the letters to the Foundling Hospital also reflect the problems of the illiterate who found scribes to write for them. To round out the picture, I have consulted printed materials as well—especially the conduct books of the century.

Rather than range over a large body of fiction for examples, I have chosen to focus on seven novelists in this study, chiefly so that their entire corpus could be considered. The former practice, I feared, too easily leads to choosing material to fit a thesis. I also decided to consider only novelists who were writing in the mode of responsible realism made newly respectable by Samuel Richardson. All of the writers explored in this study, no matter how different their approach to the art of fiction, would have agreed to two basic tenets: they were presenting real life and they had a moral purpose. The choice of Richardson and Henry Fielding needs no defense, but the omission of Daniel Defoe, Tobias Smollett, and

Laurence Sterne requires an explanation. Defoe, although he indeed depicts lively heroines, preceded the period considered here, that of realistic fiction as established by Richardson and Fielding. His fictions, indeed, were probably accepted by some of his readers as true accounts rather than novels. Furthermore, his heroines are outside the bounds of ordinary, largely middle-class life and unlikely to be thought of as exemplary. Smollett and Sterne, in the greater part of their work, offer difficulties of tonality which would make the kind of analysis attempted here subject to tedious qualification. The complex irony of Sterne's narrative is a critical commonplace, while Smollett's leaning toward the picaresque and toward caricature offers almost equally difficult problems. It is also true that few eighteenth-century women would have turned to their work seeking models of behavior.

I chose the other writers using three criteria: first, each was writing in the tradition of realistic fiction established by Richardson and Fielding; second, each published at least three novels and considered herself a serious novelist; third, each wrote novels that give women a substantial role. The third criterion might seem to prejudge the case, but, in fact, it would be useless to examine in detail novels that deal with almost entirely male environments—war, the sea, societies of rakes—and one can suppose that such novels, while they might have been read by women for the same reasons they were read by men, would have had little influence on women's perception of themselves, except, perhaps, to arouse envious interest in worlds that were closed to them. It happens that the five other novelists selected are all women. This resulted from the criteria cited above, not from deliberate policy. The result is not altogether surprising. A large percentage of eighteenth-century novelists were women because the new genre, still rather far down the literary hierarchy, was considered to be one from which women were not debarred by the lack of a classical education. The five writers examined in addition to Richardson and Henry Fielding are Sarah Fielding, Charlotte Lennox, Sarah Scott, Clara Reeve, and Fanny Burney. The novels discussed all appeared between 1744 and 1799. Burney's *The Wanderer* is omitted because its publication date, 1814, places it outside the period.

Quotations confront one with the problem of whether to reproduce the sources or to regularize spelling and grammar. A good argument can always be made for preserving the original form. However, I decided in reading these diverse letters and diaries that the original spelling puts barriers between the reader and the writer that are not justified. In the early part of the century spelling is very uncertain. Later, uniformity of spelling gains ground, but the orthography of any given writer is influenced by age, by distance from London (old habits last longer in the country), and by other factors such as the local school. A twentieth-century reader can receive a quite unjustified impression of the writer's degree of literacy unless all these circumstances are understood. Furthermore, while it is worthwhile to preserve original spelling if one is dealing at length with a single figure, it is confusing and tedious for the reader to have to adjust to a series of new modes in numerous short excerpts. I have, therefore, regularized the spelling to conform to modern British usage. I have followed the same policy in quoting from the novels and from printed works. Where italics were used simply as a printing convention, such as italicizing all proper names, I have omitted them. Where emphasis is indicated here, however, it always exists in the original.

To avoid excessive documentation, I have identified the writer of each passage in the text. The location of the document cited can then be found by consulting the bibliography at the end of the book. The bibliography also indicates the date of the documents. Since the record repositories have varying methods of identifying items, and since both letters and journals are often unpaged, heavy annotation with an apparatus which is useless unless one has access to the documents seemed pretentious and futile. Citations from printed works are followed by the page number in parentheses. Again, the edition used can be found in the bibliography. I have generally used first editions except where accurate modern texts would be more available to the reader. I have therefore used the Oxford English Novel texts when possible. I have used the Everyman edition of *Pamela* and *Clarissa,* and the Wesleyan edition of the works of Fielding.

The framework chosen to unify a large collection of primary materials must always be somewhat arbitrary. I have used the stages of a woman's life—daughter, wife, widow, or spinster—chiefly because this arrangement best permits the reader to gain some sense of the women letter writers and journal keepers as individuals. I have included certain thematic topics in the chapter which seemed most relevant, placing women's education, for example, with daughters, even though the issues of women's intellectual capacity naturally affected women of all ages. In a final chapter I address the overall effect that reading novels might have had on the self-perceptions of eighteenth-century women.

I have refrained from complicating this work with extensive references to modern criticism on the literary texts and to modern scholarship on the feminist movement in the eighteenth century. This study is not intended as a social history of the period, although it deals with some of the materials of interest to the social historian, nor is it intended as a critical assessment of the novels in esthetic terms. Its aims are much more modest—to try to create a picture of the actual lives of real women, and then to examine the novels in terms of their depiction of these women and of their possible influence on them.

CHAPTER I

"Made He a Woman"

E VERY AGE gives signals about what is considered acceptable, desirable, and worthy of praise. Cultural formation comes from many sources, including such apparently frivolous pastimes as reading novels as well as more overt forms. This chapter will discuss some of the more obvious general influences on the way in which an eighteenth-century woman would see herself, such as conduct books, collections of essays designed for women, the Bible, and, last but certainly not least, the actual law of the land. It will also consider the way in which novelists either tended to reinforce the dominant cultural forces of the time or to question them, providing an alternative view of women for their readers.

The eighteenth century's ideal view of the nature of woman, her purpose in creation, and the roles proper to her was most clearly set forth in the conduct books which were popular and pious reading during the period.[1] The reading and re-reading of such books was considered an integral part of an individual's devotional practices and essential to proper moral formation. *The Ladies Calling,* conventionally attributed to Richard Allestree, is typical of the

6

genre. Its frequent reprinting is testimony to its popularity and in-fluence; by 1720 it was already in its eleventh printing. Steele's *Ladies Library,* itself an influential publication, is largely plagiarized from the earlier work. *The Ladies Calling* is by no means extreme in its attitudes. In fact, some might have regarded its position on the education of women as a bit revolutionary.

The same author had previously written *The Gentleman's Call-ing,* and a comparison of the table of contents of the two books is in itself instructive. *The Gentleman's Calling* lists:

    I Of Business and Callings in General
    II Of Varieties of Callings
    III The Particulars of the Gentleman's Advantages above
        Others
    IV The Branches of His Calling Founded in the First
        Advantage, that of Education
    V Of the Second Advantage, Wealth
    VI Of the Third Advantage, that of Time
    VII Of the Fourth Advantage, that of Authority
    VIII The Last Advantage, that of Reputation
    IX The Conclusion

The Ladies Calling has the following table of contents:

Part I: I Of Modesty
           II Of Meekness
           III Of Compassion
           IV Of Affability
           V Of Piety
Part II: I Of Virgins
           II Of Wives
           III Of Widows

The Gentleman's Calling's concern is the proper Christian use of privilege. It notes that, in contrast to the gentleman, "the poor man's authority is bounded within the narrow circuit of his little cottage, being in effect no other than the propagation of that power nature hath given him over his own body to those branches that spring from it, his children; and to that scion which is engrafted into it, his wife" (16). The book directed toward the gentleman has no discussion of marriage at all.

In the preface to *The Ladies Calling,* the writer explains that the purpose of the work is to hearten women: "The world is much governed by estimation; and as applause encourages and exalts, so a universal contempt debases and dejects the spirit." The author worries that "if it can once pass into a maxim that women are such silly and vicious creatures, it may put fair for making them so indeed," and that, having imbibed the common opinion, women will "charge all their personal faults on their sex. . . . It may therefore upon this account be a necessary charity to the sex to acquaint them with their own value, and animate them to some higher thoughts of themselves." Women are encouraged "not to yield their suffrage to those injurious estimates the world hath made of them" nor "from a supposed incapacity of nobler things to neglect the pursuit of them" but to realize that from this endeavor "God and Nature have no more precluded the Feminine than the Masculine part of mankind." The writer declares that it will be "no absurd attempt to decipher those excellencies which are the genuine and proper ornaments of women," noting that "in some instances they may perhaps prove consistent with those of men" but cautioning that "by the divine command" they "have some additional weight on the female side, in respect of decency, fame, or some other (not despisable) consideration" (I, 4). The excellencies, of course, are those of the chapter headings—modesty, meekness, compassion, affability, and piety.

Women of honor must be always concerned "to vindicate their sex" (I, 28), and this can be done "by making their own virtue as illustrious as they can," so that "By the bright shine" they "draw off men's eyes from the worser prospect," presumably the majority of women. To accomplish this "there is required not only innocence but prudence"; one has "to abstain, as from all real evil, so from the appearance of it too," and women are enjoined "to deny themselves the most innocent liberties when any scandalous inference is like to be deduced from them." After the primary virtue of modesty, the writer places meekness, which "even nature seems to teach." Nature "abhors monstrosities and disproportions" and since she has "allotted to women a more smooth and soft composition of body, infers thereby her intention that the mind should correspond with it" (I, 29). In the preface, the writer acknowledges that "men have their parts cultivated and improved by eduction, refined and subtilized by learning and arts." They are compared to "an enclosed piece of the common which by industry and husbandry becomes a different thing from the rest, though the natural turf owned no such inequality." It is conceded that "truly had women the same advantage, I dare not say but they would make as good returns of it," and that "some of those few that have been tried have been eminent in several parts of learning," although women must have "ballast to their sails, have humility enough to poise them against the vanity of learning." With this caution, the author does not see "why they might not more frequently be intrusted with it," keeping in mind "that in respect to their intellects they are below men." Offered as comfort is the thought that "in the sublimest part of humanity," women are men's equals: "they have souls of as divine an original," and these souls will have "as endless a duration" and be "as capable of infinite beatitude." In this one sense, then, "There is neither male nor female, but all are one."

In discussing young women in "Of Virgins," the writer identifies "the two grand elements essential to the virgin state" as "modesty and obedience" (II, 5). Virgins must guard against curiousity, ill company, and idleness (II, 7). Therefore, pursuits are desirable to "fill up the vacancies of their time: such are the acquiring of any of those ornamental improvements which become their quality, as writing, needleworks, languages, music or the like." Furthermore, the author suggests, "If I should here insert the art of economy and household managery, I should not think I affronted them in it, that being the most proper feminine business from which neither wealth nor greatness can totally absolve them" (II, 8). The writer's interest in women's education rapidly veers away from learning when an actual program is prescribed.

In the same vein, *The Ladies Calling* cautions that it is "the most important concern of all" for women to guard the ear and "to fortify that so assailable part." This is true of all, "but 'tis especially so of women not only in respect of that natural imbecility which renders them liable to seducement, but also because the opinion of their being so makes them particularly aimed at by seducers," since "these sophisticators of Divinity desire the most undiscerning auditors" (I, 33). The reference here is to theological, not sexual, seduction. In addition to this "natural imbecility" women are afflicted with "passions naturally the more impetuous" (I, 39), and therefore must be "the more strictly guarded" and "kept under the severe discipline of reason." Since this is the distinctive quality of men, "God's assignation has thus determined subjection to be the women's lot," and "there needs no other argument of its fitness, or for their acquiescence" (I, 40).

In this state of acquiescent subjection, the book recommends "affability and courtesy," which are "amiable in all" but "singularly so in women" and "more universally necessary in them than in the other sex." The author explains that "men have often charges and employments which do justify, nay perhaps require, somewhat of sternness and austerity, but women ordinarily have few or no occasions of it" (I, 73).

As daughters, women, in addition to practicing modesty and obedience and guarding against idleness, curiosity, and ill company, are also to avoid gaming, reading romances, undue attention to dress, and masks and revels. Daughters are above all to be submissive to parents, especially in the question of marriage (II, 8–22). Older spinsters are pitied, and the convenience of sending them to nunneries somewhat regretfully forfeited (II, 40); England had no convents from the time of Henry VIII until the nineteenth century.

In marriage, a woman functions in three capacities—as wife, as mother, and as the mistress of a household. She also owes a duty to her husband in three aspects: "to his person, to his reputation and to his fortune." Love is most important, especially in the first aspect, and jealousy is to be avoided above all else. If the husband should prove unfaithful, he is to be treated with patience and gentleness; if he should unjustly suspect her, again the wife should respond with submissive meekness. *The Ladies Calling* emphasizes that fidelity is an absolute duty for wives and agrees that death is the fit punishment for adultery in women. Obedience is second only to fidelity as a wifely obligation, and it extends to all her husband's wishes and commands. She must be careful to guard his reputation both by her own prudent conduct and by never saying anything which might detract from him. She must be thrifty and manage well, although "the management of [his fortune] is not ordinarily the wife's province" (II, 23).

Her duties as a mother are love and care, but overfondness is cautioned against. The upbringing of children should not be left to servants. As the mistress of the household she is responsible for the moral welfare of all in it; she must see that the servants are properly instructed and that they regularly practice pious observances— prayer, church attendance, and so on. The writer notes that this also has practical benefits, for servants will then be more honest and faithful. Widows are advised to retire from the world and devote themselves to their children's welfare and to works of charity. Ideally "the conjugal love transplanted into the grave (as into a finer mold) improves into piety" (II, 68). Remarriage is discouraged, and stringent conditions are laid down regarding equality of fortune and of age. The widow is expected to always regard her children's welfare, not her own happiness.

In all her roles, then, as spinster, wife, or widow, a woman is expected to live in a submissive selflessness consonant with her congenital incapacities. As a daughter she obeys her parents, as a wife she obeys her husband, as a widow she practices pious self-sacrifice. In each of these roles there is no promise of reciprocity, especially for wives. While a wife must be above reproach, she must tolerate, even expect, a much lower order of conduct from her husband, both in sexual promiscuity and in other masculine prerogatives such as drunkenness.

The views of *The Ladies Calling* were echoed in many other manuals, and remained the standard, even the enlightened, view of the century, as the wholesale plagiarism in Steele's *The Ladies Library* indicates. Another work, *The Whole Duty of a Woman* by "a Lady," proclaims, "It is not for thee, O woman, to undergo the perils of the deep, to dig in the hollow mines of the earth, to trace the dark springs of science, or to number the thick stars of the heavens." Rather, "Let the wise men and counsellors enact laws and correct them; the policy of government is a hidden thing, like a well of water in the bottom of a deep pit." For woman, "thy kingdom is thine own house, and thy government the care of thy family." Therefore, "let the laws of thy condition be thy study, and learn only to govern thyself and thy dependents." The author cautions against even the least semblance of intelligence: "Discover not the knowledge of things, it is not expected thou shouldst understand, for as the experience of a matron ill becometh the lips of a virgin, so a pretended ignorance is often better than a show of real knowledge" (16).

The Whole Duty of a Woman consists of "directions how women of all qualities and conditions ought to behave themselves in the various circumstances of this life for their obtaining not only present, but future happiness." The book begins by instructing women "how to obtain the divine and moral virtues of piety, meekness, modesty, chastity, humility, compassion, temperance, and affability with their advantages, and how to avoid the opposite vices." While lip service is given to the idea that these are Christian virtues "recommended to all," the writer does stress that meekness is valuable "particularly to women, as a peculiar accomplishment of the sex" (6). As to the relations between men and women, according to the writer, "Our sex wants the other's reason for our conduct and their strength for our protection. Theirs want our gentleness to soften and entertain them" (69). This view is echoed in *The Ladies Magazine, or Polite Companion for the Fair Sex,* in an article titled "Of the Duties of the Fair Sex in Society." "It is in this manner that the sexes should endeavour to perfect each other," the writer explains. "The masculine courage of the one is tempered by the yielding softness of the other, which in its turn borrows some degree of constancy from that courage it serves to restrain" (214). For instance, "the ideas of the men assume a more agreeable ease in mixed society, while those of women lose all their lightness and inconstancy," and "the different qualities of both are thus balanced against each other." Women are counselled to rule through their charm and clever persuasiveness: "It is true that the administration of affairs, and the different departments of government are in the hands of the men," yet "men may reign, but women command, and where the first are clad in the ensigns of power they are most commonly nothing more than a sort of second causes, and receive all their motives to action from the latter" (216).

The Polite Lady: or, A Course of Female Education in a Series of Letters from a Mother to her Daughter even more vigorously eschews any participation in politics and worldly power. "With regard to the former [politics]," writes the mother, "I shall only observe that it is a subject entirely above your sphere." She continues, "I would not willingly resign any of the privileges that properly belong to our sex, but, I hope I shall have all the sensible part of it on my side when I affirm that the conduct and management of state affairs is a thing with which we have no concern." This results not from mere custom or convention, but from constitutional incapacity, one feature of which is women's lack of reason and temperance. "Besides, my dear," she writes her daughter, "our passions are much more keen and violent than those of the other sex, or, which is the same thing, we are less capable to check and restrain them" (277).

The Female Guardian also stresses the private and domestic as women's proper role. The "Lady" who is its author quotes Mrs. Montagu as having said that "examples of domestic virtues would be more particularly useful to women than those of great heroines." She agrees, having "often wished" for "a collection of examples of excellence in pure and genuine female characters, such examples as are imitable by every woman who is blessed with a common degree of understanding." She wishes specifically for "such as should exhibit a woman acting with propriety in her particular province, the domestic circle; to show her performing her duty as a daughter, wife, mother, mistress, friend and nurse" (34–35). *The Ladies Complete Pocket Book* adopts a more censorious tone in a prefatory essay, "A Serious Address to the Ladies of Great Britain": "It is by no means to be denied that in this gay and voluptuous age many of you have given yourselves up a great deal too much to the heightened pleasures of theatrical and musical entertainments, to the neglect not only of all that is spiritual and sacred, but also of those domestic cares which are your proper province." The essayist then admonishes, "For believe me, my dear countrywomen, whenever you aim at anything else than to be dutiful daughters, loving wives, tender mothers, prudent mistresses of families, faithful friends and pious christians you aim at somewhat that is quite out of nature, and set aside the intention of heaven in making you rational creatures" (15). Books for children, almost universally thinly disguised conduct books, also discourage any energy or curiosity on the part of girls.[2] For example, *May Day; or, Anecdotes of Miss Lydia Lively, Intended to Improve and Amuse the Rising Generation* tells about the adventures of Lydia who in trying to be good learns that she must not be lively.

"The Character of My Dearest Mother," written by Arabella Dighton just after her mother's death, is no doubt a sincere tribute; it is also a telling portrait of the ideal woman. "She was always a devout Christian, a most incomparable wife, an excellent kind and tender mother, a constant friend, a discreet and prudent mistress and generous to the utmost of her power, the good of her husband and children being always in her thoughts." Further, "She was a lady of great beauty and good understanding and of the greatest sweetness of temper." We are told that she was "well educated under a kind and careful father and mother and according to their examples she excelled in goodness and prudence and was perfectly instructed in all parts of housewifery and in the skill of management of a great family." The next sentence begins, "She was of a very good quality," but the writer thought better of this phrase, crossed it out, and instead listed her mother's descent on both sides without qualifying comment. Dighton concludes, "She had the best inclinations to all that was good and virtuous which made my best of fathers rejoice in her, and all her children love and adore her and above all her most dutiful daughter, Arabella." One cannot doubt that the dutiful daughter did indeed see her mother as an exemplar—she was the very model held up by the conduct books.

With intellect both unnatural and undesirable in a woman, and with pleasing males one of her highest callings, beauty assumed

AFFECTION.

Figure 1. Affection. Miss Hodgson. Engraving by Miss Keate. This charming work of two amateur artists is evidence of "female accomplishments." Reproduced by courtesy of the Trustees of the British Museum.

exaggerated status as a feminine attribute. Therese Parker, writing during pregnancy, confides, "I wish very much for one girl at least, and think beauty of such infinite consequence to a woman, that if it was not the first thing I should ask of la Fée Bienfaisante, it should certainly be the second. A little attention to her education will prevent her making a bad use of it."

An anecdote told by Caroline Powys reflects the amazement, verging on incredulity, with which she discovers that a homely woman can actually be agreeable. While at a house party, she records in her journal, it was announced that a Miss Strahen would stop for one night on her way to the Shrewsbury races. She was "a

14

ATTENTION.

Figure 2. Attention. Affection's companion piece depicts boys paying close heed to a schoolmaster holding a book. The two engravings illustrate the pervasive sexual stereotyping of emotion as the domain of women and intellect as that of men. Reproduced by courtesy of the Trustees of the British Museum.

proverb for plainness," and the story was told of her that once two gentlemen laid a wager that each could name the ugliest woman in London and Miss Strahen was named by both. Therefore, "you may suppose those who had not seen her of our party were pleased to find she was expected." At dinner she was seated next to Miss Connynham, noted for her beauty, and Powys, sitting opposite, observes, "It was really hardly possible to suppose those two of the same species." However, she found the lady "so agreeable, so exceedingly clever, so everything but handsome that before she left Court of Hill the next day, I had lost the idea of her bad person." Powys assumes that "with so excellent an understanding she must have been sensible in her youth that her chance for society was the cultivation of her mind." She has succeeded and "no one's company is more sought after," but for Powys lack of beauty obviously remains a dreadful handicap. She observes, not unkindly, that age will aid Miss Strahen since beauty is expected in youth, "while even a remarkable plainness in persons of years, if not overlooked, is at least by the young and gay thought to be a thing of course attendant on the decline of life." Meanwhile, "I fancy if *Miss* Strahen would take a more matronly title, as her person is genteel she'd soon pass for a good 'Comely Woman,' an excellent exchange for that of an Ugly Miss, in my opinion."

Sarah Fox, a far from frivolous Quaker, betrays a similar bias in her journal: "I experienced the truth of an observation which has often been made, that there is something more attracting in a pleasing manner joined to real worth than in a mere pretty face." She describes "two young women—one pretty, the other disgustingly ordinary at first sight" but "so sensible, so engaging in conversation that before the end of the day, she not only ceased to be disagreeable but became really agreeable and greatly eclipsed her pretty friend." That a woman whose appearance is described as "ordinary" is also immediately perceived to be "disagreeable" speaks eloquently of the age's attitude toward feminine beauty.

While fictional heroines are almost uniformly beautiful, novelists did also stress that mindless beauty was no match for the liveliness of beauty animated by wit. Charlotte Lennox's heroines are beautiful but the narrative always stresses that intelligence is their chief charm. A character in the novel *Harriot Stuart* is described as very pretty, but "her eyes were not animated by anything but motion," and "no woman could ever look well that did not think well" (II, 111). In *Sophia,* the virtuous and intelligent heroine is contrasted with her spoiled and shallow sister, Harriot (curiously given the same name as the exemplary heroine of *Harriot Stuart.*) Harriot, the elder, is the beauty of the family and therefore is the favorite of their silly mother. Money is lavished on her finishing-school education and clothes and when the family is in financial distress a good match for Harriot is seen as the solution to their problems. However, the wealthy man she covets is immediately attracted to Sophia because of her wit and learning. Harriot, encouraged to regard beauty as all-important, is an easy prey to flattery and falls into a life of vice.

The title of *Agreeable Ugliness,* by Sarah Scott, suggests that the work will contradict the idea that beauty is a woman's most important attribute. This theme is presented, however, with curious ambivalence. The heroine, who tells her own story, is the younger of two daughters in a middle-class French merchant family. Her beautiful sister, always known as the "Fair Villiers," is her mother's pampered favorite, while she herself is never called anything but "Shocking Monster." The heroine comments that "an ugly face reduces a woman to a kind of non-existence" (3). Her father takes a kinder attitude toward his homely daughter, and, encouraging her to acquire charms "more valuable and lasting," instructs her "in all the useful knowledge which he possessed." Still, "he would often say he did not wish to make me learned; his principal endeavour was to form my heart and understanding" (14). In contrast, her sister becomes an empty-headed, vain coquette.

The moral of the tale—that ugliness can be agreeable—is weakened by the lack of convincing evidence that the heroine is truly ugly. Unlike Fanny Burney's *Camilla,* in which Eugenia is jeered at by children because of her appearance, the heroine in Scott's novel is liked wherever she goes. A noble lady remarks that "if she is not as handsome as her sister, the sweetness of her countenance, and the sense and spirit in her eyes, make full reparation for what may be wanting in the regularity of her features" (54). Curiously, Dorigny, her first husband, falls in love with her not because of her intelligence, learning, or virtue, but because, before he actually sees her, he is enchanted by the emotive power of her voice as she sings an affecting aria. Even more curiously, her chief objection to him as a husband is his looks; "as for his person," she complains, "I see it is impossible for me to like it" (70). Her father has reassured her that "in marriage beauty has less power over the hearts of men than you imagine," while "understanding and goodness of heart and temper" (63) create a lasting passion, but this precept seems to have little influence on the daughter when she judges a suitor. In fact, *Agreeable Ugliness* counsels daughterly obedience fully as much as the futility of empty-headed beauty.

Fanny Burney's *Camilla* contrasts the cousins Indiana, an empty-headed but very beautiful young woman, and Eugenia, Camilla's sister, maimed by a fall and disfigured by smallpox. Indiana is encouraged by her foolish governess to believe that any cultivation of the intellect is not only useless but harmful. Eugenia, on the other hand, becomes truly learned and has a sweet, unselfish disposition. Unlike Scott, Burney does make it clear that Eugenia is truly ugly. Indiana describes her as "the ugliest little fright . . . a short dumpty, hump backed, crooked, limping figure" (568), and a group of children burst into laughter when they see her. That her lack of beauty is a great disadvantage to Eugenia is never denied, but finally Melmond, her true love, realizes her worth and proposes. Then he finds in her "a companion delighting in all his favorite pursuits, and capable of joining even in his severer studies" (912). Like Scott's "Shocking Monster," "Eugenia once loved, was loved forever."

The beautiful Indiana causes every head to turn, but the more discriminating are soon discouraged by her shallowness. When Mrs. Tyrold, Camilla's mother, thinks that Edgar, whom Camilla loves, is in love with Indiana, she asks indignantly, "What will he find in Indiana but a beautiful doll?" Her husband points out that "many wives of this description are more pleasing in the eyes of their husbands than women who are either more informed in intellect or more alive in conversation," for "it is not an uncommon idea amongst men, that where, both in temper and affairs, there is least participation, there is most repose" (221). Mrs. Tyrold replies that she feels "indignant at such a triumph of mere external beauty." And, in fact, Edgar finds Camilla more attractive. "Her face, her form, however penetrating in loveliness, aid, but do not constitute her charms," he declares: "'Tis the quick intelligence of soul that mounts to her eyes, 'tis the spirit checked by sweetness, the sweetness animated by spirit, the nature so nobly above all artifice, all study." He rhapsodizes that "one single look, one single word, one sweet beaming smile" from Camilla is worth more than "all of beauty . . . in some wonderful aggregate could oppose to her" (174). The contrast between mindless beauty and intelligent charm is the same as that in the works of Lennox and Scott. Eugenia, of course, can make no claim at all to beauty, but, in the eyes of a discerning observer, makes up for this by other qualities: "Where her countenance was looked at, her complexion was forgotten; while her voice was heard, her figure was unobserved; where her virtues were known, they seemed but to be enhanced by her personal misfortunes." When he finally sees rightly, Melmond finds in her "a charm to beguile from him all former regret" (912).

Samuel Richardson's heroines are all beautiful. It is always insisted, however, that mere physical beauty is not their main attraction. In *Pamela* Mr. B. says, "I do assure you my Pamela's *person,* all lovely as you see it, is far short of her *mind*" (I, 364). He admits that it was her beauty "that indeed first attracted my admiration and made me her *lover,*" but "the beauties of her mind . . . made me her *husband.*" While in *Clarissa* even the rake Lovelace says of Clarissa, "It was her character that drew me to her; and it was her beauty and good sense that riveted my chains" (II, 38). Similarly, in *Sir Charles Grandison* Greville, a rakish suitor of Harriet, confesses that once he thought beauty the only attraction in a woman, but, he asks, "Who . . . can describe the person of Miss Harriet Byron, and her person only; animated as every feature is by a mind that bespeaks all human excellence?" (I, 9). Sir Charles declares that if anyone would "leave *mind* out of the description of Miss Byron, that *they* art not to describe her" (I, 424).

In contrast, Henry Fielding's heroines are chiefly praised for beauty. Sophia is introduced in *Tom Jones* with "a short hint of what we can do in the sublime" (154). She is "adorned with all the charms in which nature can array her; bedecked with beauty, youth, sprightliness, innocence, modesty, and tenderness, breathing sweetness from her rosy lips, and darting brightness from her sparkling eyes" (155). An even more extensive catalogue of her physical attributes follows, concluding with "her mind," which "was every way equal to her person" (157). In *Joseph Andrews* Fanny's beauty attracts all who see her, joined with "a sensibility . . . almost incredible; and a sweetness, whenever she smiled, beyond either imitation or description" (153). No claim is ever made for Fanny's mind.

In Fielding's *Amelia* the heroine is so lovely that "nothing almost can add to or diminish" her "exquisite beauty" and even when disguised in rags she "looked scarce less beautiful than . . . at a ball or an assembly" (85). Nevertheless, when a coaching accident injures her nose, she bears the misfortune "with dignity, with resignation, without complaining, almost without a tear." Booth, her future husband, marvels at this heroism, exclaiming, "With what astonishment ought we to behold, with what praises to honour, a young lady who can submit to the loss of exquisite beauty, in other words to the loss of fortune, power, glory, everything which human nature is apt to court and rejoice in" (67). Booth's telling "in other words" certainly reveals the high place of feminine beauty in his own scale of values. Fortunately, Amelia's beauty is not lost, and the incident seems to serve principally to illustrate the cattiness of Amelia's women friends.

There is a certain irony in the fact that although women were looked upon as deficient in intellect and reason, given over to passion and caprice, a higher standard of conduct was uniformly expected of them. This double standard was most obvious and most rigorously exacted in sexual behavior, but it extended to all areas of life. As Sarah Chapone noted, acceptance of conduct varied greatly with sex, and what was called "obstinacy and perverseness" in women was transmuted into "fortitude and resolution" in men. Sarah Cowper records a discussion of "which was most desirable to have—sons or daughters"—in which "specious reasons were given both ways." For instance, "a worthy lady said she least desired girls for fear of the disgrace which attends their misbehaviour and ill conduct, whereas boys could scarcely do anything the world esteemed a fault." Cowper agrees that "at first sight this seemed plausible," although she quarrels with the basic morality implied in the position, since "the sins of both sexes are equal in the sight of God whose honour should be more regarded than the shame and disrepute we incur from men." Unchallenged goes the assertion that in the eyes of the world scarcely anything men did was esteemed a fault.

In most of the novels written by women, the hero is conventionally described as "virtuous" and the details of his past are not closely examined. When the heroine marries a man known to have been a rake, reformation is insisted upon and happy marriages are always characterized by faithful husbands, again sometimes reformed by loving wives, such as Sarah Fielding's Mrs. Bilson. The double standard is never expressly tolerated. Lennox's virtuous Sophia, for example, is rewarded by marriage to the man who planned to debauch her sister but Sir Charles is shown as reformed by his love for her, and his former transgressions are excused by the mores of society. In Lennox's *Henrietta,* however, the heroine rejects this lenient attitude. When Lord B., who had first tried to seduce her, finally offers marriage, Mrs. Willis, a worthy lady who has befriended Henrietta, declares, "But surely, my dear, your gratitude would be engaged, should Lord B., in the present inequality of your circumstances, make you an offer of his hand." "Not at all," Henrietta replies with warmth, "no man has a right to the love or esteem of a woman on whom he has entertained dishonorable designs, and, failing in them offers marriage at last." This shows "just as much generosity as the highwayman who leaves a traveller in possession of his money because he is not able to take it from him" (II, 103).

Henry Fielding takes a much more tolerant view of masculine lust. The sexual adventures of *Amelia*'s Booth and of Tom Jones are not lauded, but they are seen as evidence of virility rather than as grave faults. The narrator of *Amelia* is also willing to excuse Booth's affair while married to the ideal Amelia, asking the reader to "set before his eyes a fine young woman . . . let him consider

20

time and place; let him remember that Mr. Booth was a young fellow in the highest vigor of life; and lastly . . . that the parties were alone together" (154). Men's transgressions are, in fact, implicitly laid at the door of women: "I am firmly persuaded that to withdraw admiration from exquisite beauty or to feel no delight in gazing at it, is as impossible as to feel no warmth from the most scorching rays of the sun." Furthermore, "the admiration of a beautiful woman, though the wife of a dearest friend, may at first perhaps be innocent, but let us not flatter ourselves it will always remain so; desire is sure to succeed" (232). Since it is impossible not to admire beauty, and admiration always becomes desire, some form of purdah (perhaps the actual rationale behind the male club, an eighteenth-century innovation) seems the only solution. Certainly, social interchange between the sexes, in Fielding's view, is always highly charged with sexuality, making purely intellectual conversation difficult and leading to the use of an appropriated language with women which effectually destroys any assumption of equality.

The title character of *Joseph Andrews* is Fielding's only chaste hero, playing on the novel's parodic relation to *Pamela* and giving Fielding opportunities to ridicule the hypocritical lasciviousness of Lady Booby and Mrs. Slipslop. In *Tom Jones,* however, the libertine code is condemned when it harms the innocent. Nightingale, Tom's fellow lodger in London, has seduced the landlady's daughter, Nancy, by promising her marriage. When he discovers that she is pregnant, he hesitates to marry her, not because he no longer loves her, but because "her disgrace" is publicly known. He seeks Tom's advice: "Can I, after this publication of her disgrace, think of such an alliance with honour?" Tom is astounded and says that even if there has been no direct promise, Nightingale has implied one. When Nightingale confesses that he did, in fact, make an explicit promise of marriage, Tom tells him that "the very best and truest honour, which is goodness, requires it of you" (767). Tom continues with a catalogue of questions, each of which emphasizes the artificiality of the term "honour" as it is used by rakes. Nightingale agrees that "common sense, indeed, warrants all" Tom says but contends that "the opinion of the world is so contrary to it, that was I to marry a whore, tho' my own, I should be ashamed of ever showing my face again." Tom replies, "When you promised to marry her, she became your wife" (768). Pointing out that "she hath sinned more against prudence than virtue," Tom asks whether honor can "bear the thought, that this creature is a tender, helpless, defenseless young woman?" (767) and declares that he does not "pretend to the gift of chastity" more than his neighbors, but that he would never "to procure pleasure to myself, be knowingly the cause of misery to any human being" (755).

Adultery is always vigorously condemned by Fielding as well as by the other novelists. Dr. Harrison, who in *Amelia* is described as the embodiment of "the most consummate goodness" (357), writes a letter to Colonel James exhorting him to stop his campaign to seduce Amelia. He points out that adultery is condemned not only by Christianity but even in barbarous nations because "it includes in it almost every injury and every mischief which one man can do to, or can bring on, another. It is robbing him of his property—and of that property which, if he is a good man, he values above all others" (414). He goes on to list the consequences to the betrayed husband: "destruction of his peace of mind, and even of his reputation, . . . hatred and revenge, . . . despair and madness," until, finally, "murder and suicide often close the dreadful scene." Harrison next details the eternal punishments in store for the sinner, and, saving the most telling shot for last, assures James that he will never succeed because Amelia is strengthened by "that firm and constant affection of her husband which would guard a much looser and worse-disposed heart" (414). Harrison sees adultery almost entirely as an offense of one man against another man whose property is thereby damaged. Ironically, in Richardson's work this view is propounded by the rake, Lovelace, who declares that while women are fair game only the most abandoned rake will stoop to adultery. Moreover, Amelia's distress over the various unwelcome attentions she receives is never on her own account, but because of her fears that they will anger Booth, possibly provoking a duel.

In the novels of Richardson the double standard is always condemned, although Pamela does marry Mr. B. who has tried to seduce her and who has fathered an illegitimate child. It was this marriage, in fact, which prompted Henry Fielding's satire *Shamela* in which the opportunistic heroine declares, "I once thought of making a little fortune by my person. I now intend to make a great one by my vartue." Mr. B. is excused somewhat because he has acted honorably within the dubious ethics of his class—he supports his illegitimate child and has helped the mother start a new life—and because, despite ample opportunity, he never does rape Pamela. The seduction of a serving girl was well within the recognized code of conduct for gentlemen, as Sir Simon Darnford's comment shows: "Why, what is all this, my dear, but that our neighbour has a mind to his mother's waiting maid! And if he takes care she wants for nothing, I don't see any great injury will be done her" (116). Mr. Peters, the minister of the parish, refuses to intervene in "so common and fashionable a case" (116), declaring that "'tis what all young gentlemen will do." These spokesmen are, of course, portrayed as morally defective but they do put Mr. B.'s transgressions in context. Marriage to a woman so far beneath him socially is a great sacrifice to Mr. B.'s pride and signals the depth of his intention to reform. However, the marriage is not secure until Mr. B. becomes a true convert to religion and gives over the direction of his life to Pamela.

Richardson's most powerful condemnation of the code of the rake is his portrait of Lovelace. Indeed, one of his professed motives for writing *Clarissa* was to contradict the common notion that a reformed rake made the best husband. Lovelace, after he tricks Clarissa into running away with him, is confident that either his powers of seduction will quickly overcome her, giving him the triumph of a conquest, or that, failing to seduce her, he can still marry at will. "Marriage, I see, is in my power," he writes to Belford, "now *she* is so" (II, 42). He is wrong on both counts. Clarissa is indeed in many ways an unworldly innocent, and Lovelace has no difficulty in maneuvering her into taking rooms in Mother Sinclair's, an ostensibly respectable boarding house which is actually a brothel. He greatly underestimates her intelligence, however, and exaggerates his own sexual powers. For Lovelace, women are primarily goals of the chase, and it is the game of catching them which brings pleasure. "We begin, when boys, with birds," he says, "and, when grown up, go on to women" (II, 245). In both cases he finds "more pleasure in the contrivances than in the end of them" (II, 147), since just as a barnyard chick is apt to be better eating than the wild bird, so the sexual act itself is "a vapour, a bubble!" (II, 337), with joy to be found only in the conquest. Clarissa is not long in sensing that he is "*a hard-hearted man.*" Far from falling under his sway, she asks herself, "Am I not guilty of a punishable fault, were I to love this man of errors? And had not my own heart deceived me, when I thought I did not?", adding, "I hope my reason will gather strength enough from his imperfections to enable me to keep my passions under" (II, 438).

The duel between Lovelace and Clarissa, as he phrases it, is "whether I am to have her in *my own way,* or in hers?" (III, 92). Characteristically, he simplifies the issue, never supposing that she will not have him at all. From day to day, Lovelace vacillates in his intentions, sometimes genuinely planning marriage, then thinking, "What a figure should I make in rakish annals! The lady in my power" (II, 250), or "Then what a triumph would it be to the *Harlowe pride* were I now to marry this lady!" (II, 34). His insistence on pride and domination is inescapably reminiscent of the statements of the Harlowe family themselves. The reader becomes aware that the libertine code of the rake is simply an extension of the conventional attitude toward women in the century. Like Clarissa's family, Lovelace believes that women can be treated according to a different standard of behavior, one that would never be acceptable in dealing with men. "Men such as we are," Lovelace asserts, "consider all those of the [female] sex as fair prize over whom we can gain a power" (II, 158). He explains that "*our honour* and *honour* in the *general* acceptation of the word, are two things." The difference, of course, is the sex one is dealing with. "I never lied to man," Lovelace boasts, "and hardly ever said truth to woman" (IV, 445). Like Clarissa's family, Lovelace sees women only as possessions, actual or potential, of men. For this reason, "adultery is so capital a guilt, that even rakes and libertines . . . disavow and condemn it" (II, 332). Clarissa, who has had the strength to withstand her own family, now has only scorn for "the man, who has the assurance to think me, and to endeavour to make me, his *property*" (III, 17).

Declaring that "*wisdom* never entered into the character of a woman" (II, 273), Lovelace tries all "the delicacies of intrigue" without effect. Finally, in desperation, he rapes Clarissa, a deed that violates not only the warped honor of the rake but also Lovelace's own previous judgment: "Abhorred be *force*. . . . There is no triumph in *force*" (II, 398). He now uses this last measure because he trusts in "the libertine's creed, *that once subdued, is always subdued!*" (II, 363). Again, Lovelace resembles the Harlowes, with their confidence that Clarissa will be "easy and pacified" once she is married and her virginity is violated. He is confident that now he will at last have the upper hand: "She will not refuse me, I know . . . the haughty beauty will not refuse me when her pride of being corporally inviolate is brought down" (III, 190).

Once more, Lovelace is wrong. Far from the rape proving an ultimate assertion of male power, it is for Clarissa the final proof of Lovelace's baseness. He has expected her to be "abashed—conscious" while he will be "the most confident of men" (III, 218). The reality is different. "She entered with such dignity in her manner, as struck me with great awe" (IV, 219), he records, and as he stands with his "whole frame shaken," he asks, "Whose the triumph now! HERS, or MINE?" (IV, 221). When he offers his trump card, marriage, which he has always been sure will make amends for everything, she refuses: "*The man who has been the villain to me you have been, shall never make me his wife*" (IV, 222).

Clarissa never moves from this position. Richardson dramatizes the falseness of contemporary values through her rejection of Lovelace's offer of "respectability." Although by the hypocritical double standards of her society, it is Clarissa who needs vindication, not Lovelace, she sees that to marry him would be "to give . . . a sanction to the most premeditated baseness" (IV, 250). She asks Anna Howe, "Do you think your Clarissa Harlowe so lost, so *sunk,* at least, that she could [marry] for the sake of patching up, in the world's eye, a broken reputation?" (III, 519–20). To the end, Clarissa heeds her "own judgement of the *fit* and the *unfit,*" answering "*for* myself *to* myself, in the first place . . . and to the *world,* in the *second* only" (II, 306).

While the triumph is Clarissa's, the reader cannot help feeling a sense of waste. Not, certainly, because Clarissa does not marry the Lovelace we encounter in the novel—he is indeed love-less, as the eighteenth-century pronunciation of his name indicates—but because we see in him a man gifted with good looks, energy, intelligence, and, where women are not concerned, generosity who is trapped in a sterile, childish world that refuses to accept any mature relationship with one-half of humanity. Lovelace's own comparison of libertines to sportive boys is a telling one. Clarissa, at the end, pities rather than hates him. "Poor man, I once could have loved him," she says. "Would he have permitted me . . . I think I could have made him happy" (IV, 306). The waste is even more poignant when we realize that Lovelace's attitude toward women is in many ways only an intensified version of the general attitude of the century. Lovelace's denigration of women and his rhetoric of mastery and submission, while placed in an ostensibly different moral framework, are identical to the attitudes of the men in Clarissa's own family.

Richardson wrote *Sir Charles Grandison* with the avowed purpose of giving a picture of "the good man." He also presents a picture of the kind of society a good man could create—a utopian society which far from denigrating women accepts their values. Sir Charles always shows his complete acceptance of a single standard of judgment for men and women. In contrast to his age, he believes that "men and women are . . . much alike . . . put custom, tyrant custom, out of the question" (I, 455). Where the differences in his own society are sharpest, he finds in favor of women. He condemns the double standard in sexual behavior, asking, "How can that crime be thought pardonable in a man, which renders a woman infamous?" (II, 140). He derides duelling, the military, excessive drinking, and other masculine prerogatives. Richardson deliberately made the point that Sir Charles himself was chaste. Olivia, a beautiful and passionate woman, offers herself to him but is refused. When Richardson's friend Lady Bradshaigh protested this shocking scene, he made it clear to her that it was designed to demonstrate Sir Charles's sexual purity even in the face of great temptation.

The century's usual view of woman's purpose and role was grounded in and strongly supported by biblical authority. The Old Testament, especially, reflects a strongly paternalistic society, and provides a rich source for supporting citations. The chief text cited is Genesis—the story of the creation and the story of the fall. Woman was made to please man. "And the Lord God formed man of the dust of the ground, and breathed into his nostrils the breath of life; and man became a living soul. And the Lord God planted a garden eastward in Eden; and there he put the man whom he had formed" (2:7–8). The story continues, "And the Lord God said, It is not good that the man should be alone; I will make him an help meet for him" (2:18). After the creation of the animals, "the Lord God caused a deep sleep to fall upon Adam, and he slept: and he took one of his ribs, and closed up the flesh instead thereof; and the rib, which the Lord God had taken from the man made he a woman and brought her unto the man." The man who has named all the animals, now names this new creature: "This is now bone of my bones and flesh of my flesh; she shall be called woman because she was taken out of man" (2:23). Then, as now, the version of creation that occurs earlier, in Genesis 1:27, with its implications of parity, was largely ignored: "So God created man in his own image, in the image of God created he him; male and female created he them." The later version has its own implications—woman is a secondary creation, an afterthought, produced expressly for man, made from man (who is primary material), and given her identity, named, by him. The story is indeed familiar to us, but most of us today read the Bible less often and less seriously than our counterparts in the eighteenth century, when daily reading of the Bible, either alone or as a part of family prayers, was an accepted part of daily routine. The very language of the passage could not help but be a powerful influence from earliest childhood.

The second key text is the story of the fall. It was the woman who was tempted by the serpent, the woman who ate the fruit, "and gave also unto her husband with her; and he did eat" (3:6). When God accuses them of guilt, "the man said, The woman whom thou gavest to be with me, she gave me of the tree, and I did eat. And the Lord God said unto the woman, What is this that thou hast done? And the woman said, The serpent beguiled me, and I did eat" (3:12–13). God then tells the woman, "I will greatly multiply thy sorrow and thy conception; in sorrow thou shalt bring forth children; and thy desire shall be to thy husband and he shall rule over thee" (3:16). Once again the man names the woman, this time Eve. Again, the story is familiar to us, but the actual text would be read far more often and more literally by eighteenth-century readers. "He shall rule over Thee" was an unequivocal command, and the phrase "and thy desire shall be to thy husband" suggests that sexuality itself, with its consequences of pain in childbirth, is a punishment for women although a pleasure for men. This text was the basis for eighteenth-century conjugal relations; the husband was master by God-given command.

The Ladies Calling declares that wives are absolutely bound to obedience, "and that not only by their promise of it, though that were sufficient; but from an original of much older date, it being the mulct that was laid upon the first woman's disobedience to God, that she (and all derived from her) should be subject to the husband" (II, 33). Although women were expected to be more chaste by nature, the sexual double standard was also based in practical considerations. A promiscuous wife's offspring might inherit the family property, whereas a promiscuous husband was fathering a bastard in someone else's house. Nevertheless, the conduct expected of women as virgins, wives, and widows rested on the assumption that sexual desire was proper to the male and unbecoming to the female. At the same time, Eve's succumbing to temptation was constantly cited as typifying woman's frailty and her inherent lack of reason and intellectual capacity. Woman's bias toward the irrational and emotional, it was thought (somewhat contradictorily), made her especially vulnerable to sexual temptation. Woman, the actual name used in Genesis (the name "Eve" appears after the fall), is responsible for all humanity's unhappiness and is never to be completely relied upon again.

The force of religious belief in the eighteenth century should never be underestimated. Although in terms of the broad currents of intellectual history the century is seen as a period of deism, of growing rationalism, and of decline of faith, the average person was deeply religious. In letters and journals, even by women not overtly pious, there is constant reference to God and to religious doctrine, usually as a source of reassurance. Among other reasons for this, the high death rate, especially among the young, made faith and the Christian resignation demanded by faith a primary source of comfort to the bereaved. Ann Congreve writes in a letter of the death of her sister, "As there is no duty in religion more justly required by God Almighty than a perfect submission to his will in all things, I hope he will endue me with that disposition of mind of being satisfied with all he gives and contented with all he takes away." The sentiment is echoed often, and the virtues of submission and resignation were effective ways of coping emotionally with irrational evil. This attitude also encouraged acceptance of all parts of the divine order, one of which was the God-given authority of men set forth in the Bible.

The religious basis for the subjugation of women was occasionally argued. *The Ladies Magazine, or Polite Companion* printed "Freyjo's Defence of Women," which contends that "it is not as yet decided which of the two it was that committed the greatest sin, Adam or Eve, for the fathers are divided about it." For one thing, "the excuse which Cayetano makes in favour of Eve, that she was deceived by a creature of far superior understanding and sagacity, a circumstance which did not concur in Adam, abates a great deal, in respect to this of the sin of the other" (199). Furthermore, the contention that man is superior because created first is highly suspect because it is usually assumed that God created the inferior first and worked upwards. Freyjo's defence echoes the writings of earlier continental writers such as Henry Cornelius Agrippa. In some cases these arguments seem to have been exercises in rhetoric, demonstrations of the writer's ability to prove the most difficult cases, as much as they were feminist polemics. They did succeed, at least, in showing that scripture can be argued in more than one way.

The more usual protests, however, simply worked at establishing that women were designed to be companions rather than slaves. When the "Lady of Quality" who is the author of *The Female Advocate* cites the stricture from Genesis that "it is not good that the man should be alone," she interprets it to refer to "a creature that should be a social help not a servile one" (20, 21). The limited nature of her protest becomes evident as she begins to backpedal: "'Tis granted the woman was created for the man, but we deny that this is any pretence to use the limited power which Heaven has given him to the unhappiness and ruin of a creature that was made for him" (21). Finally, she qualifies even these mild statements: "It's true, a woman that abridges her husband of his reasonable authority, and has impudence enough to put on the breeches, does certainly pervert the end of her creation," and such women deserve "the discipline their husbands think fit to exercise upon them" (22).

An Essay in Defence of the Female Sex, most probably by Judith Drake, also uses the Bible to defend the capabilities of women. This essay is in the tradition of more radical feminist polemic stemming partly from the work of Christine de Pisan in fifteenth-century France and partly from the pamphlet writers of Renaissance England. The large claims these writers made for women's equality were not renewed in the eighteenth century, but their arguments occasionally surface, even if only for purposes of satire. In this seriously argued essay, the writer notes that it is often urged that women are not endowed by nature with the qualities—sense and good nature, fidelity and integrity—which would make them truly fit companions for men. The author, identified only as "a Lady," writes that she "might easily cut this part of the controversy short by an irrefragable argument which is that the express intent and reason for which woman was created was to be a companion and helpmeet to man, consequently those that deny them to be so must argue a mistake in Providence" (9). Although some "affirm that the propagation and continuance of mankind was the only reason for which we were made," she points out that "the Wisdom that first made man" could easily have continued the species by "any other method" (10). The writer is one of the most overtly feminist pleaders of this period, but in her dedication "To Her Royal Highness, the Princess Anne of Denmark," she is careful to explain that she has "only endeavoured to reduce the sexes to a level, and by arguments to raise ours to an equality at most with the men."

She takes a satiric look at the ruling sex in "the characters of a pedant, a squire, a beau, a virtuoso, a poetaster, a city-critic etc." Of the observations made by visitors from the continent upon the privileged position of women, especially upper-class women, in England, she notes that "fetters of gold are still fetters, and the softest lining can never make them so easy as liberty" (25). She remarks that in country people "the condition of the two sexes is more level than amongst gentlemen, city traders, or rich yeomen," and, arguing that inequality is culturally imposed, notices "that in brutes and other animals there is no difference betwixt male and female in point of sagacity, notwithstanding there is the same distinction of sexes that is between men and women" (14, 15). She rejects the evidence of history because "as men are parties against us, their evidence may justly be rejected, for if any histories were anciently written by women, time and the malice of man have effectually conspired to suppress them." Besides, "it is not reasonable to think that men should transmit, or suffer to be transmitted to posterity, anything that might show the weakness and illegality of their title to a power they still exercise so arbitrarily, and are so fond of" (23). The contemporary estimates written by men are equally false. Women's "company is generally, by our adversaries, represented as unprofitable and irksome to men of sense," she notes, "and by some of the more vehement sticklers against us, as criminal." These imputations, she declares, are both unjust and "savour strongly of the malice, arrogance and sottishness of those that most frequently urge them" (8).

Inevitably, however, despite such occasional protests, even intellectual women became imbued with a strong sense of diffidence. Catherine Talbot writes in her journal of her difficulty in discovering an acceptable tone and manner. After she "read or rather skimmed over some silly plays and petites pieces," she comments that "Phoebe Clinket (in a detestable foolish farce) is a character admirably drawn." Phoebe is a stereotyped character of the prating, learned female, and Catherine Talbot adds, "I live with the dread of her before my eyes." The next day, she records that company came to tea and "the whole was rather formal. I contributed my share to the conversation, but took care that it should be a mighty quiet one, and neither talked of books nor bel esprit nor said any one thing that could be remembered." Then she adds, "But though I have for many years tried to live like a plain commonsense creature, yet still I find the world will look upon me as a Phoebe Clinket."

On another occasion, she describes a discussion of Richardson's *Sir Charles Grandison*: "After prayers we resumed the book. The gentlemen have no patience with Harriet's vanity, and talkativeness." She concedes that Harriet "*does* agree too much with Mr. Walden" and reflects that "a long sentence never sounds well out of woman's mouth." Nevertheless, they "read, disputed, debated and after supper I came up full of wise references." Regretting her con-

Figure 3. Portrait of Catherine Talbot. Engraving by Hopwood. Catherine Talbot's journal illustrates the problems confronting an intellectual woman, such as feeling self-conscious about talking too much. Reproduced by courtesy of the Trustees of the British Museum.

versational boldness, she laments, "What can one do . . . to keep just the right medium and make a tolerable part of any company one respects without saying a word too much?"

Marthae Taylor, also an independent and intellectual woman, nevertheless felt compelled to remove herself from the ordinary category of the feminine. In a letter she reconfirms her refusal of a proposal: "My sentiment knows no variation in matters of this importance. Think you that I am so much the downright woman (as the phrase is) to say one thing today and another tomorrow, for which they are too oft but too justly reproached?" She continues, "No, sir, I disdain their weaknesses as well as their vices." She then implicitly removes herself to some asexual plane: "Nor concerns it me whether my soul animates a male or female body while it boast the dignity of human nature, nor will I by any persuasion demean it so far as to forfeit my pretentions to prudence."

Margaret Lucas, who became a Quaker minister, records in her autobiography the difficulties she experienced in following her call because of her feelings about the proper role of women: "The first time I ever heard a woman preach, from a prejudice imbibed from my companions and, probably, an aversion in my own nature, I thought it very ridiculous, and the oftener I had opportunities to witness it, the more I secretly despised it" (159). Her attitude was a difficulty in her conversion: "At the time that I joined with the Friends, this was one of my strongest objections to them" (159). Even after becoming a Friend, she narrates, "such was my perverseness that one day I had much difficulty to stay the meeting when a woman ministered though I could not help acknowledging within myself that it would have been acceptable testimony, had it come from a man" (160). Overcoming "this great prejudice" was her major struggle in accepting the call to the ministry. The Friends were almost unique in the eighteenth century in their belief in the intellectual and spiritual equality of women.

One tract proclaims forthrightly: *The Woman as Good as the Man: or the Equallity of Both Sexes.* Designated only as "by a Man" and translated from the French, the pamphlet is, in fact, a translation of François Poulain de la Barre's major treatise, *De l'egalite des deux sexes.* Poulain, who published his work in 1673, was that rarity, a cleric and academic who was also a radical, outspoken feminist. In the first part "is shown that the vulgar opinion is prejudiced; and that comparing (impartially) that which may be remarked in the conduct of men and women, we are obliged to acknowledge an entire equality between both sexes." In the second part tradition is attacked and it "is made to appear that the reasons which may be adduced against the opinion of the equality of the two sexes from poets, orators, historians, lawyers and philosophers are all idle and fruitless." The author demonstrates that "women (considered according to the principles of sound philosophy) are as capable as men of all sorts of sciences." He, in fact, gives them a slight edge in science, because their sense perceptions are more acute. He goes on to argue "that women are as capable of offices and employments in civil society as men are" and "that the true notions of perfection, nobility and honesty suit with them as well as men." Most of the proof rests upon assertion rather than demonstration, and the author concludes by observing that there is "no difference betwixt men and women with regard to vice and virtue: and that the temperament and constitution in general, in itself, is neither good nor bad," but that "the difference which is observed, between men and women, in regard of manners proceeds from the education which is given them."

The anonymous author of *Woman: Sketches of the History, Genius, Disposition, Accomplishments, Employments, Customs and Importance of the Fair Sex,* writing in 1790, demonstrates that the currents of radical feminism took little hold. He is considerably less strong in his claims, although described as "a Friend to the Sex." His views are far more typical of the period than the strongly feminist position of Poulain de la Barre. Of the "philosophical spirit" in women, he observes "more sallies than efforts. What they do not see at once they seldom see at all; they either disdain or despair to comprehend it" (119). Women are, in fact, firmly placed in the lower ranks of intellectuals because "they are not possessed of that unremitting assiduity which alone can pursue and discover important truths." As a compensation, the author suggests that "imagination seems rather to be their province." In the same vein, he asserts that "women of all countries and in all ages, know better how to paint a delicate and tender sentiment than a violent and turbulent passion" (121).

Preconceptions about women's limitations—their lack of true reason and of restraint—led to the opinion that learning was not only impossible for most women, but also that whatever learning women achieved would be turned to bad purposes. The predominance of women as writers of scandal novels, fictional memoirs, lurid gothics, and vapid romances seemed to give some support to this contention. (Since almost all fields of employment were closed to women, hack writing was one of the few ways a woman could earn a living, albeit a precarious one.) Sarah Chapone commented acidly in a letter in 1750, "Female authors seem at present to be debauching the taste and manners of the world." She was especially pleased, therefore, with a project of George Ballard to publish *Memoires of Several Ladies of Great Britain* which would record the lives of women distinguished for learning. George Ballard, a son of humble parents, was apprenticed to a dressmaker, but managed despite weak health to teach himself Old English. He attracted the attention of Lord Chedworth who made him an allowance of sixty pounds a year to live at Oxford where, at forty-four, he matriculated at Magdalen.

A feminist at Oxford was indeed an anomaly. Sarah Chapone wrote to Ballard: "I am glad my brother had the pleasure of your company in Oxford. He could have told you that the men there are not over acknowledging to our sex." She explained that "he heard a whole roomful of them deny that a thing was, or could be, written by a woman" when he knew it had been. "Oxford is the seat of liberal education, but they strongly imbibe some illiberal sentiments there, of which this is a specimen." Ballard's book consisted of 130 lives, including Catherine of Aragon, Margaret Roper, Queen Elizabeth, Mary Queen of Scots, Anne Killigrew, and Anne Countess of Winchilsea, as well as a host of unknowns, and coming up to the present day. The intention of the work was to demonstrate by example that women were not only capable of learning, but that they would put their learning to good use.

In the preface, Ballard "hopes these memoires will show the women of the present age, that instances of learning and piety in their sex have frequently been found together," and, a still stronger claim, "that great natural talents joined with high degrees of acquired knowledge have not yet (as far as he can inform himself) been misapplied to propagate or defend ill principles by any of the women eminent for those perfections, as they frequently are and have been by the other sex." From reading these lives "it is hoped the women of the present age may be animated with a desire of following such illustrious examples which at the same time show the use and excellence of such invaluable accomplishments and direct the proper methods of attaining them."

Sarah Chapone, in encouraging him, wrote that she believed, as Ballard asserted in his preface, that "it would be a difficult matter to find one single instance where a woman of real learning and knowledge has misapplied those talents." She conceded that "some few women of gay imaginations and who carried more sail than ballast have indeed fallen in with the enemy and joined the impious squadron, making shipwreck of their faith and modesty in the service," giving as examples, "the author of the *Atalantis* [Mrs. Manley] and the famous Mrs. Behn," the playwright and novelist. They did not disprove Ballard's premise, however, because "they, nor none of that slight sisterhood, were ever thought women of learning or had any pretence to be called women of knowledge." Chapone observed that "the other sex have a most inveterate and, I may add, illiberal dislike to intellectual improvements of any kind in ours" and hoped that Ballard's work would "obviate all objections and soften that dislike (if possible)." The parenthesis betrays her realistic estimate of the actual good the book would achieve; intellectual women continued to provoke the hostility of, as she phrased it in another letter, "a sex that have been long used to call fortitude and resolution in a woman by the names of obstinacy and perverseness."

Even a convinced feminist like George Ballard needed some reminding to correct conventional habits. In discussing the drafts of a dedication to Mrs. Delany (the volume was eventually dedicated to Mrs. Talbot) Sarah Chapone gently chided Ballard: "I showed them to Mr. Chapone and another friend; they are both of the opinion that Mrs. Delany is so eminently known that it will be looked upon as superfluous and indecorous to attempt to distinguish her by saying whose wife she is." She also took exception to a line in Ballard's printed inscription, "which adorn her sex," explaining that "it is the common expression in every newspaper when a bride is described" and pointing out that "all the cardinal virtues are neither masculine nor feminine, but common to both sexes."

Champions of the intellectual potentialities of women were justifiably defensive; they were running counter to the assumptions of the age. Sarah Talbot, to whom Ballard's book was dedicated, writes that she had "never fully considered a natural superiority in either sex, but wholly the understanding, disposition and heart." Later in the same letter she admits that "men, it is true, are called upon to fill up all the public offices in the world, and therefore they appear to do greater good or hurt according to how they act," but, she adds with apparent contentment, "let it not be forgot that the little circle women have to act in is not so trifling as may be imagined," because "their example and instructions will have some influence, and may be considered not improperly as the little wheel which sets larger ones in motion."

John Sprint, a conservative clergyman, in concluding his long discourse designed to teach wives how to behave, speaks for many of the age in his estimate of women's intellectual capacity: "I must forbear enlargement lest that, by overloading the memories of the women, I should cause them to forget their duty which has been set before them" (16). *The Female Jester; or, Wit for the Ladies* included this ironic "Humble Wish" by "a young lady":

I ask not wit, nor beauty do I crave,
Nor wealth nor pompous titles wish to have;
But since 'tis doomed, thro' all degrees of life,
Whether a daughter, sister, or a wife,
That females should the stronger males obey,
And yield implicit to their lordly sway;
Since this, I say, is every woman's fate,
Give me a mind to suit my slavish state. (148)

Not surprisingly, the legal codes of eighteenth-century England also recognized and sustained the superiority of men, especially as fathers and husbands.[3] It should also be remembered that the whole judicial system was comprised of men—judges, juries, lawyers, sheriffs, justices of the peace were all men. Women had no vote and no political power. They were barred from the universities and therefore from all learned professions. It seems inevitable, therefore, that the adjudication and enforcement of the existing statutes was biased in favor of men. At one point in *Clarissa,* Anna Howe suggests that Clarissa should try to gain financial independence by legally reclaiming the inheritance which she has given over to her father's custody. Clarissa demurs not only because it would be an unfilial deed but because she recognizes, pragmatically, that her suit would have almost no chance of success. In a legal action of a woman against a man, and, in this case, a daughter against a father, the scales would be heavily weighted regardless of the actual merits of the case. In a somewhat similar situation described in chapter 2, Isabella Eccleston's father did succeed in gaining control of her inheritance and depriving her of financial independence.

Under the law, both men and women were considered children until the age of twenty-one, and legal transactions were carried out through parents or legally constituted guardians. In most cases a woman became a substantial heiress only in the absence of male heirs. Estates were entailed, passing to the eldest male heir, and during the century these arrangements tended to become increasingly strict. The holder of a landed estate was often only a life-tenant, prevented from either disposing of it for income during his life or of distributing it after his death according to his wishes. Women did, however, sometimes become wealthy heiresses. In the rising merchant class, estates were less likely to be entailed, and daughters could become heirs. In the older landed classes there was sometimes enough money to go around, especially if an uncle or aunt were conveniently childless. The chief financial provision for women, however, was connected with dowries and marriage settlements. The unmarried daughter tended to remain dependent on her parents, and after their death dependent on the eldest brother. This was often a precarious and ungrateful role. A single woman who was fortunate enough to have property could, legally, hold it in her own name and enter into contracts, buy and sell, and engage in legal transactions. In practice, of course, she was dependent on males to execute all of this, and feminine temperament and capacities were considered unsuited to such activities.

A married woman had no legal status. The basis for this was the doctrine of coverture: when a woman married she and her husband became one person in law. It has been suggested that the historical basis for coverture rested in the feudal system, in which the duties owed to an overlord could only be performed by men, and therefore a woman always had to be represented by a man. Coverture was also based upon the biblical idea of husband and wife being "one flesh," and therefore in law a single person. In interpretation that one person was, in fact, the husband, and a wife therefore ceased to exist as a legal entity. In civil law she could not control property, make contracts, sue, or be sued. In criminal law spouses could not be found guilty of stealing from one another, and, curiously, all acts of a wife committed in a husband's presence were assumed to be under his command, exempting the wife from criminal responsibility.

Careful parents tried to protect daughters from the more unpleasant financial consequences of the absolute power given to husbands through stringent marriage settlements. A woman's "writings," the legal documents setting up the terms of her jointure or pension as a widow, and of her allowance for her own expenses while a wife, became her only protection against a spendthrift or penurious husband. The elaborateness of these arrangements varied, usually in proportion to the fortunes involved, ranging from verbal agreements to trusteeships that prevented the husband from ever gaining any control of his wife's assets. In all cases, however, the woman herself was a dependent ward with no more status than a child.

Sarah Chapone argued bitterly with a correspondent who claimed that this arrangement was to women's advantage: "I don't find that you have so much as softened, much less retracted that most surprising assertion, that it is not proper for any women, at any age, to be independent. Independent of whom? Why, of the other sex. Why so?" She quotes her opponent's answer: "Because they do not make so good bargains for themselves." She accuses her opponent of "begging the question. To deprive a woman of her natural liberty under pretence of keeping her out of harm's way is just such a favour as it would be to deprive a man of all pleasure and then, in return, graciously decree he should feel no pain. As such a deprivation would strike a man out of being as a human creature who has the image of God upon him, so such deprivation of liberty would strike a woman out of being as a member of civil society." Chapone goes on to argue for the natural rights of women, stating that "in religious points she must judge for herself. God has qualified her for it, and she must answer for the misapplication of her talents as men must answer for the misapplication of theirs." She concedes that "in the form of marriage the woman is given, but forms cannot destroy realities by depriving her of her Christian liberty, nay and her natural liberty too." She points out that "without law the whole species would be equally free" and paints this picture of the actual state of a woman in her society: "She must behold herself a puppet danced about by foreign impulses—a wooden thing upon wires, to be played off at the will and pleasure of (most likely) her more wooden director."

Once widowed, a woman regained the legal status of a person. She could again act for herself in civil transactions, and she could enter into marriage at her own volition. The actual freedom she gained was directly proportional to the financial independence she had, and this, in turn, depended both upon the settlements made at the time of marriage and the amount of the estate. The plight of a widow dependent on the generosity of the eldest son was often unenviable, and the dilemma of an impoverished widow with small children was even more difficult than that of an unmarried woman, since she could not become a servant, one of the few occupations open to women.

In general, then, women were seen as properly fulfilling a dependent and subservient role throughout their lives. This was indeed for their own good, because it suited their capacities. Weakness of intellect and "natural imbecility," especially in the faculty of reason, coupled with an inherent tendency to the uncontrolled, the passionate, and the impetuous meant that women should be under the care and guidance of the superior creatures, men, who were

gifted with wisdom, rationality, and strength. With glaring incon-
sistency, however, these august beings were permitted far greater
lapses from accepted moral and social codes, while any lapses in
women were further proof of the sex's frailty.

The novels of the period, in general, provided an alternate view.
Novels questioned the acceptance of the double standard of morality for men and women, though some realistically conceded that
men were held to a lower standard. While a man's previous sexual
adventures were sometimes excused, all of the novels by women
rejected the idea that a happy marriage is possible when the husband is unfaithful. Sarah Fielding, it is true, did depict Mrs. Bilson
cheerfully following the conduct book precept to ignore a husband's transgressions, but the result of this policy is his imprison-
ment for debt. In prison he becomes a reformed man and only then
will the couple's future, with Bilson thoroughly domesticated, be
happy.

Henry Fielding is the only author in this study who implicitly
suggests that sexual promiscuity is acceptable for men and, in fact,
a demonstration of virility. In *Amelia,* the married Booth's affair is
condoned because he is "a young fellow in the highest vigor of
life," and because the beauty of women leads inevitably to illicit
desire. Adultery is condemned by Fielding only when a husband's
rights are infringed. Amelia's rights weigh very lightly. On the
other hand, an attempt to seduce Amelia is vigorously condemned
because such adultery robs a man of valuable property. Fielding
does, however, condemn sexual adventures which harm the innocent, with Tom Jones persuading his friend Nightingale to honor
his commitment to the landlady's pregnant daughter.

Richardson, on the other hand, always condemns the double
standard. His ideal man, Sir Charles, protests against pardoning an
action by a man "which renders a woman infamous" and sets a
good example by combining masculine vigor with chastity. However, Richardson's most telling argument against the prevailing
codes of male sexual behavior is his portrait of Lovelace. As we
come to understand Lovelace, and through him the rake, we understand that such a man is pitiable rather than impressive. He persists
in destroying his own best chance for happiness through motives
of childish pride. Far from appearing powerful, Lovelace is like an
insecure adolescent worrying about the opinion of schoolmates.
This portrait of the rake, properly read, not only condemns him
but de-glamorizes him.

On balance, eighteenth-century novels probably reinforced the importance of beauty for women, since virtually all their heroines are beautiful, but many novelists stressed that intelligence was integral to beauty and that, in Lennox's words, "no woman could ever look well that did not think well." Novels also challenged the general view of women's intelligence and capability. The women novelists uniformly presented heroines who are intelligent, even though their intelligence is not always advantageous to them, and these heroines also display energy and initiative. Henry Fielding, as we will see, was derisive toward intellectual women, but his heroines, nevertheless, show considerable spirit and enterprise. Richardson insisted upon the intelligence of his heroines as a primary characteristic.

The most important way in which novels contradicted the image created by conduct books was by making women central to their own stories. All of the novelists considered in this study wrote novels in which a woman is the principal character. In most cases, when a man is the protagonist, women characters are still portrayed as worthy of attention and deserving of happiness in their own right rather than simply as the cause of joy or despair for males. The novel was an important voice for the aspirations of women because it took them seriously, refusing to see them as totally subsumed in roles which made them appendages to men. The concern demonstrated by most of these novels for the well-being of women as individuals encouraged real women to consider their own lives as worthy of serious consideration and themselves as deserving of real choices. The number of references to novels in letters and journals of the period does indeed show that women not only read them but discussed them as models for conduct. Poetry and drama are discussed far less often. Novels usually showed women that they could at least try to be the central character in their own lives.

CHAPTER 2

Daughters

NE EXPERIENCE that virtually all eighteenth-century women had in common was that of being a daughter. This chapter will discuss the education of women, normally the concern of parents, as well as the relationships between parents and daughters ranging from the outright rebellion of elopement to the more usual mutual fondness. The old saw that "a daughter's a daughter all of her life" was surely never more true than in the eighteenth century. One owed one's existence to one's parents, a debt that could never be repaid. Unquestioning love and, when appropriate, care were only partial returns for the gift of life, but they were obligations both normal and compelling.

In infancy and early childhood parents cared for their children; in the children's maturity they repaid this by their own service. Samuel Richardson stated the century's sentiments when he wrote to Frances Grainger that "a child never can make its parent amends for her pains in childbirth, in dentition, and for the anxiousness and sleepless nights throughout every stage of her infantile life—on to adolescency, etc., etc." (Carroll, 145–46). Before marriage the primary obligations of children to parents were obedience and love. After marriage a daughter transferred her first obedience to her husband who assumed a quasiparental role, and her relation to her parents became primarily one of love and gratitude. The rebellious declaration "I didn't ask to be born" seems almost never to have occurred to the children of the century.

While in theory filial obligations applied equally to sons and daughters, both the usual household structures and the virtues considered appropriate to women—meekness, obedience, compassion, piety—tended to make women more vulnerable to family pressures than men. When a family had daughters, they, rather than the son, often became the housekeepers or nurses for elderly parents. When the son fulfilled this role it was usually the daughter-in-law who bore the burden. An unmarried daughter would almost automatically succeed to the role because she would normally continue living at home.

The obligation of obedience also weighed more heavily on daughters for a number of reasons. Most importantly, it was grounded in the pervasive view of the nature of woman. All children were expected to bow to the better judgment of their elders and the authority of their parents, but men would eventually themselves assume authority while women would exchange the authority of parents for that of a husband. "A Father" (actually the Marquis of Halifax) in *The Lady's New-Year's Gift: or Advice to a Daughter* explains, "You must first lay it down for a foundation in general, that there is inequality in sexes, and that for the better economy of the world, the men who were to be the law-givers had the larger share of reason bestowed upon them; by which means your sex is the better prepared for the compliance that is necessary for the performance of those duties which seemed to be most properly assigned to it" (26). The upbringing of girls was usually designed, consciously or unconsciously, to produce a woman who would fit this role.

The pervasiveness of attitudes is often most evident not in arguments or discussions, which, in fact, indicate doubts or differences of opinion, but in assumptions. Elizabeth Amherst writes to her husband during her pregnancy, "For my part, I believe I shall like a girl best, for they stay at home." The emphasis in the education of girls was on competence in the skills necessary to run a household, and on mediocrity in a limited number of accomplishments thought suitable for women. Mary Evelyn, writing nostalgically in 1690 "of the days of our forefathers," describes how "the virgins and young ladies of that golden age put their hands to the spindle, nor distained they the needle, were obsequious and helpful to their parents, instructive in the managery of the family and gave presages of making excellent wives." She lauds the time when "young damsels were taught all these in the country, and in their parents houses." Decrying the reading of romances and the seeing of "plays and smutty farces" as well as visiting and "idle pass-time," she recommends instead retiring with "devout and religious books" and finding "recreations in the distillery, and in the knowledge of plants and their virtues for the comfort of their poor neighbours and the use of the family." Of a girl brought up in this fashion, she comments, "the portion they brought to marriage was more in virtue than in money, and she was a richer match than one who could have brought a million and nothing else to commend her."

A fairly typical view is presented in mid-century in *The Polite Lady: or, a Course of Female Education in a Series of Letters from a Mother to her Daughter*. The daughter, Sophia, writes her mother, Portia, "I am learning English, sewing, writing, cyphering and dancing: and Mrs. B— says I shall soon begin to learn French" (18). Later, drawing, music and geography are added to her curriculum. It is significant that both the names chosen for the letter writers and the daughter's attendance at a boarding school indicate an interest in women's education unusual for the period. Nevertheless, the "Polite Lady" apologizes for her authorship in the preface: "If, in this attempt, she escape censure, she does not aspire to fame. From the former, she hopes the indulgence which the good-natured part of the world have ever shown to the female sex, will, in some measure, protect her; and to the latter, she is not vain enough (though a woman) to think she has any just pretence" (viii). The attitude implicit in this self-denigration pervades the advice in the book.

The virtues "necessary to form the character of an accomplished woman" (172) are temperance, chastity, modesty, pity, and compassion—all primarily passive. Portia recommends knowing some history, but adds, "I don't pretend to say that we should be so thoroughly versed, or so deeply read in universal history, as the men are; far from it: I have already allowed that as our sphere of action is more narrow and confined, so our knowledge may be more slight and superficial" (139). And she cautions her daughter about music: "nor do I expect that you should arrive at the highest degree of perfection in this or any other accomplishment" (23, 24). Evidence of ability beyond the ordinary in a young lady is suspect and slightly vulgar "because, in that case, she must be supposed to have

ADVERTISEMENT.

AT the SCHOOL in *Kingston* upon *Thames*, in the County of *Surrey*, situate between *Richmond* and *Hampton-Court*, YOUNG LADIES are Boarded, and carefully taught all Sorts of Fine Works: As also the *English* and *French* Languages, Dancing, Writing, Musick, and all other Female Accomplishments,

By Mrs. BELLAMY.

The Rates of the said SCHOOL.

To Mrs. BELLAMY.

	l. s. d.
At first Admission, one Pair of Sheets, Six Napkins, Six Towels, and a Silver Spoon ; Or,	1 11 6
For Board, Washing, and Instruction in Fine Works, and the *English* Language,	3 15 0 *per* Quarter.

To the MASTERS.

	Entrances.			*per* Quarter.		
	l.	*s.*	*d.*	*l.*	*s.*	*d.*
For Dancing ——	00	10	6	00	12	6
For Musick ——	00	10	6	00	15	00
For Writing ——	00	05	0	00	5	00
For French ——	00	10	6	00	10	00
Total ——	1	16	6	2	2	6

Figure 4. This advertisement shows the curriculum of the average school for girls—"fine works" (e.g., embroidery and handcrafts), dancing, music, French, and other suitable "female accomplishments." By permission of the British Library.

employed more time in it, than is consistent with her learning all the other parts of a complete education. The business of a young lady is to acquire such a competent knowledge of all these polite accomplishments, as to be able, on particular occasions, to perform decently herself, and to judge with discernment of the performance of others" (24).

Arithmetic should be a part of every young lady's education because of its importance in household management. The higher reaches of mathematics are beyond her sphere, "for it is not necessary that she should understand it so perfectly as a man: as her sphere of action is more confined, so her knowledge, in this respect, should be more confined. You ought, however, I think, to be a complete mistress of the four simple rules of arithmetic, the rule of proportion, and a plain method of bookkeeping, together with some knowledge of fractions vulgar and decimal, which last will be of great use in rendering your accounts more short and expeditious" (15). The emphasis here is clearly limiting: arithmetic for usefulness, not mathematics for intellectual adventure. The same emphasis on the useful pervaded all aspects of a girl's education. This is obvious in such practical matters as sewing and "domestic economy." Even if a young girl could reasonably look forward to being surrounded by servants all her life she had to learn to understand their tasks so she would be able to direct them efficiently, while the middle-class housewife would be personally involved in many of the complex operations of the household— brewing, preserving, growing and harvesting produce, making clothing, and so on.

The orientation of other pursuits, such as reading, seems less obviously practical but it soon becomes evident that the difference is merely one of degree. The usual justifications for women cultivating a taste for reading, countering the assumption that any endeavor approaching the intellectual was unsuited to their capacities and role, ranged from the assertion that it was innocent entertainment which might keep them away from more dangerous activities to the hope that perusing proper works might improve their piety. Thus, *The Ladies Pocket Book* recommended, in an advertisement for *Theodora, a Novel,* "love of books" as "furnishing at once a harmless and varied entertainment." *The Ladies Defence,* a poem written by Lady Mary Chudleigh and published anonymously in answer to John Sprint's anti-feminist tract *The Bride-Woman Counsellor,* also recommends in the epistle dedicatory the reading of plays and romances as "very innocent, and very agreeable diversions." The writer goes on, however, to recommend even more highly sacred scripture and devotional discourses together with Seneca's *Morals* and the philosophy of Epictetus. In the body of the poem it is argued that education is desirable for women because it helps to make them reasonable and good. They thus become better companions for good husbands who can take more pleasure in their company and better equipped to bear patiently and philosophically with a bad husband. Reading will teach resignation and the hope of happiness in a future state: "We'll bear our Fate, and never once complain." This is in a work which regards itself as feminist.

The Ladies Magazine, or Polite Companion for the Fair Sex, while sufficiently feminist to condemn the double standard in morality and to advocate intellectual pursuits for women, sharply delimits its position: "The design of the present undertaking was not to make all her fair readers turn writers; nor much less to encourage their neglecting their more immediate duties for the vain pursuit of learning. All she means is to raise them from the languid indifference of ignorance by showing them that Heaven has made them capable of knowledge; and to promote that knowledge, by offering proper objects to its enquiries" (165). These proper objects have their own limits. "Though it is the duty of every rational being to search proper information, yet the abstruse and difficult parts of learning have always been looked upon as so peculiarly the pursuit of men, and the profession of them as his immediate and sole province, that a mere bookish woman is a phrase of as much contempt as a spinning soldier" (165). Finally, a rule of thumb is suggested. Women should "never think of taking a book, or pen, in their hands, while one domestic affair is unperformed. Adhering to such a maxim will obviate the difficulty, and oblige [men] to acknowledge that we are capable of being rational companions as well as pretty playthings" (249). Dr. Johnson's often quoted remark that Mrs. Carter could make a pudding as well as translate Epictetus implies a similar view.

Moral instruction, it went without saying, was fundamental to any scheme of education. In some cases it was education's chief purpose, especially when maternal care was deemed inadequate. Marthae Taylor writes in a sharply chiding letter to a friend that out of "compassion" for her daughter "as a motherless child" she should "prevent her ruin" by enrolling her immediately in "Mr. S—'s Boarding School where she will be not only out of harm's way but be taught to know the end for which she was born." That

46

end is not "to flirt about the world like a butterfly wholly governed by her inclinations, full of herself and fond admirers" who "may make a prey of her and her fortune e'er you're aware; abuse the first, consume the last, make her miserable and sting you to the heart." Taylor cautions, "It is easier to prevent mischief than repair it at any time, but in a case of this nature it is incurable. How necessary then is prevention."

She adds an estimate of costs: "I think the board is fourteen pounds a year besides entrances and wages to the teachers, for which a little cash should be lodged in Mr. P—'s hand; and also for her apparel for which I would not advise to allow above ten pounds a year, but leave room to make presents as the reward of merit. I guess the whole expence will be comprised in thirty pounds a year." A small enough sum to save a daughter from ruin. The small total allotted to "wages to the teachers" becomes important when one remembers that this was one of the few jobs open to women, and one of the still smaller number of paid occupations that a middle-class woman would consider acceptable. (Translating eighteenth-century sums into modern equivalents is very difficult. Once one goes beyond the bare necessities, the goods considered necessary for one's role in life differ from one century to another. The relationship of costs is also very different. Account books demonstrate, for example, that for eighteenth-century women fine fabric was very expensive but the labor of a seamstress very cheap. A recent estimate by Margaret Doody and Peter Sabor, the editors of Burney's *Cecilia,* suggests that "for very approximate modern equivalents, amounts should be multiplied by at least sixty" [951]. This seems a useful rule of thumb.)

Considering the usual attitudes towards the education of women, the life of a woman who sought to invade the realms of the abstruse and difficult parts of learning so peculiarly the province of men was not apt to be easy.[1] Elizabeth Elstob is a notable example. In a memoir of her life prepared at the request of George Ballard, she records the facts with stark simplicity: "From her childhood she was a great lover of books, which being observed by her Mother who was also a great admirer of learning, especially in her own sex, there was nothing wanting for her improvement, so long as her Mother lived. But being so unfortunate as to lose her when she was about eight years old, and when she had but just gone through her accidence and grammar, there was a stop put to her progress in learning for some years." She then explains that because her father was dead and her brother was underage, she became the ward of

Figure 5. Portrait of Elizabeth Elstob. Unknown artist. The portrait appears inside the letter *G*, which begins her translation of Aelfric's "An English-Saxon Homily on the Birth-day of St. Gregory." Reproduced by courtesy of the Trustees of the British Museum.

her uncle, Dr. Charles Elstob, canon of Canterbury, "who was no friend to women's learning." He would not permit her to pursue her studies despite repeated requests, but "always put [her] off with that common and vulgar saying that one tongue is enough for a woman." She nevertheless struggled to "improve her mind in the best manner she was able," succeeding in learning French and reading everything she could obtain in English and French, "not only because she had a natural inclination for books herself, but in obedience to her excellent mother's desire."

48

When she was nineteen her brother, who was ten years older, was given a parish, and she went to live with him. He "joyfully and readily assisted and encouraged her in her studies" and with him she "labored very hard as long as he lived." He died twelve years later, but during those years "she translated and published, *An Essay on Glory* written in French by the celebrated Mademoiselle de Scudery, and published an English-Saxon homily on the birthday of St. Gregory, with an English translation and notes etc. Also the Rudiments of Grammar for the English Saxon Tongue." The publications so briefly noted by Elizabeth Elstob are pioneering works in the modern study of Old English. She, in fact, designed for the Oxford University Press the type in which the Anglo-Saxon texts were set. After her brother's death her many plans for scholarly work, including a translation and a variorum edition of all Aelfrick's homilies, were "unhappily hindered by a necessity of getting bread, which with much difficulty, labour and ill health, she has endeavoured to do for many years with very indifferent success."

She was dependent on the bounty of friends, took up the exhausting task of being a schoolmistress, and finally was pathetically grateful to become the governess of the Duke and Duchess of Portland's children, aged four, three, and one. During her days as a school teacher she was asked to translate an Anglo-Saxon inscription for Lady Northampton. She apologetically declined, explaining that after seven years of trying to get a school she had obtained one, and had time for nothing else. Furthermore, she noted, "the unhappy circumstances I have labored under for several years deprived me of leisure to follow those studies which were my only delight and employment." Therefore, she confesses, "this long interruption gives me a just apprehension of my incapacity." Her work as a governess, while pleasanter than the school, was hardly less demanding on her time. In apologizing to a friend for a delay in writing she explains that is not due to neglect, but "my charming little ladies take up my time so entirely that I have not the least leisure to do anything. From the time they rise till they go to bed they are constantly with me." It is a sad comment on previous hardships when a day spent instructing a three- and four-year-old should cause this remarkable scholar to find herself "the happiest creature in the world."

Elizabeth Elstob's letters show little resentment of her difficulties, but we can surely agree with her when she sympathizes with George Ballard's difficulties with his book praising intellectual women (*Memoires of Several Ladies of Great Britain*): "This is not an age to hope for any encouragement to learning. . . . The honor of the females was the wrongest subject you could pitch upon, for you can come into no company of ladies or gentlemen where you shall not hear an open and vehement exclamation against learned women." Perhaps acceding at last to the expectations of her time, or perhaps deferring to the wishes of her employers, Elizabeth Elstob seems to have perpetuated the inequality of education between male and female within her own sphere. She writes of the young marquis, her former one-year-old charge now almost fifteen, "I can safely say without boasting or partiality he is an admirable scholar." His two older sisters are "sweet creatures" who are "continually employed about one ingenious work or other." The phrase is somewhat ambiguous, but in the vocabulary of the time it suggests shellwork or china painting rather than any scholarly endeavor.

While Elizabeth Elstob's accomplishments were unusual, many less learned women shared her dissatisfaction with the customary education given to girls. In 1701, Sarah Cowper, who was basically of a conservative temperament, shows ambivalence when she writes of a learned woman who "knows as much as any man can know but conceals her knowledge with all the discretion that a reserved woman ought to have. This I set down as a good pattern to be followed." The next month she records reading an account of "above three score eminently learned and otherwise brave women, beyond what I thought the sex to be capable of." This, she notes, "makes me regret the manner of my education since I feel in myself a natural thirst after knowledge," adding, "yet so it is, I have never been furnished with means nor opportunity for a right improvement."

Later in the century, Caroline Powys, also a woman basically contented with the status quo, shows flashes of dissatisfaction with the usual estimate of feminine intelligence. In her travel journal she apologizes for difficulty in describing a citadel because "the terms of fortification are quite out of female knowledge." Although "the men would perhaps say we should not endeavour to understand, yet I must own 'tis my opinion that women might be made acquainted with various subjects they're now ignorant of more for want of instruction than capacity." Seeing through the obfuscation that technical terminology can bring to simple matters, she suggests that "what at first may appear intricate after a quarter of an hour's converse might give entertainment, but is it anything surprising the sex should amuse themselves with trifles when those Lords of the Creation will not give themselves the trouble (in my conscience I believe 'tis for fear of being out shone) to enlarge our minds by making them capable to retain those of more importance." On a similar note, she remarks on seeing the manufacture of carpets at Axminster, "The weaving of it is extremely curious, and gave us ladies the more pleasure I believe as our own sex are here admitted to become artists, an uncommon privilege at this time of day when the men seem to engross every possible branch of business to themselves." In admiring a young friend, she describes her as "sweetly delicate in manners with every advantage in person," adding ironically, "and if any advantage to us females I might say learned as her Father instructed her in Greek and Latin from her earliest years."

The correspondence of the period supports the assumption that education for girls was usually synonymous in parents' minds with the acquisition of accomplishments together with a few practical skills. Mary Sneyd writes to a friend, "I shall fit up Maria this winter ready to go to school in the Spring, tho' I shall have a great loss of her—but it's necessary as she can learn nothing here but what I teach her myself and she is now big enough to learn to dance, write and cast accounts." And Catherine Pern, who plans to bring her daughter to stay with a relative in Worcester, can think of nothing that "would be so great an advantage to the child. She might go to day school, a very good school, to learn to dance, etc."

The voices raised against the usual education allotted to women were not only women's. Daniel Defoe and Jonathan Swift were two of the more noteworthy men who decried the disparity of the instruction given the two sexes. Sarah Talbot seems to yearn for the utopian ideal of ancient Lilliput when she writes, "Could reason be recovered and regarded as what our great creator intended it should be to us . . . our sex would early be taught to form their hearts by its dictates, and yours to regard and treat them as reasonable creatures. What the education of both commonly is among most people one would be glad should pass unobserved." Praising a plan to publish a book about learned women, she says she hopes it will "encourage and raise an emulation in others and convince the world women's minds are capable of equal improvements when the same care and cultivation is allowed to them."

Lack of education was the cause of whatever inferiority could be observed in women, according to a number of feminists. In *An Es-*

say in Defense of the Female Sex Judith Drake in 1697 writes that education for young boys and girls is "the same, for after children can talk, they are promiscuously taught to read and write by the same persons, and at the same time." After the rudiments are acquired the sexes "begin to be separated, and the boys are sent to the grammar school and the girls to boarding schools, or other places, to learn needlework, dancing, singing, music, drawing, painting and other accomplishments." The boys, meantime, are learning Latin and Greek.

The author, "a Lady," of *The Progress of a Female Mind,* published in 1764, proposes in her book "to condemn the custom of denying to women those means of information, the want of which is so conspicuous in the labours of her mind and so much lamented by her" (1). She continues, "I shall give my voice in behalf of the sex in general, that I think them unfairly dealt with in the usual methods of education which excludes them from the noblest pleasures, and is but transmitting ignorance and folly from one generation to another" (2).

The point is still more strongly phrased in *Letters from the Duchess de Crui:* "Women are educated in this age according to the idea of the Turks; as if the only intention of their existence was to appear lovely for the first few years of their lives, and afterwards to sink into total oblivion in this world, and unconsciousness in the next" (I, 80). The author states that she "has ever lamented her sex's being condemned to ignorance, or prevented from exercising their noblest mental faculties. She has, therefore, endeavoured to make them conscious of their capacity for attaining any knowledge to which they may aspire" (I, ii).

The duchess espouses a doctrine not merely of equal, but by implication, of better. "Now it is well known," she writes, "that the organs in our sex are of a finer texture than in men." This would make women better observers, more keenly perceptive, and "there would be no room to doubt but that they would be equal to them in the sciences and every branch of useful knowledge" (I, 77). This opinion is enthusiastically espoused in *The Woman as Good as the Man: or the Equallity of Both Sexes,* a strongly feminist text published in 1677, which is a translation of Poulain de la Barre, the French polemicist. He argues that women are fully capable of mastering sciences, of filling public offices, and of acting virtuously, and that "the difference which is observed between men and women . . . proceeds from the education which is given them."

Some positive suggestions were advanced to improve the educa-

Figure 6. Portrait of the Ladies Waldegrave. Reynolds. Engraving by Valentine Green. Three aristocratic young ladies engaged in embroidery exemplify "accomplished," well-brought-up daughters. The two on the left are winding floss, while the one on the right works on fabric held in an embroidery hoop. The worktable is a typical piece of eighteenth-century furniture. The elaborate hair styles and costly dress show the attention to feminine beauty so characteristic of the period. Reproduced by courtesy of the Trustees of the British Museum.

tion of women. One of the most ambitious plans was outlined in Mary Astell's *A Serious Proposal to the Ladies*.[2] Astell felt strongly about the deficiencies of the usual upbringing of girls. Writing in *Some Reflections Upon Marriage,* she complains that in women's education, "so much and no more of the world is shown them, as serves to weaken and corrupt their minds, to give them wrong notions, and busy them in mean pursuits; to disturb not regulate their passions, to make them timorous and dependent, and, in a word, fit for nothing else but to act a farce for the diversion of their governors" (65). Because "even men themselves improve no otherwise than according to the aim they take, and the end they propose," she observes, "perhaps the great secret of education lies in affecting the soul with a lively sense of what is truly its perfection and exciting the most ardent desires after it" (66). This quest for self-definition is denied to women, for "alas! what poor woman is ever taught that she should have a higher desire than to get her a husband?" Astell dismisses the common argument that there is an analogy between bodily and mental strength and therefore women's minds are weaker just as their bodies are frailer: "Strength of mind goes along with strength of body, and 'tis only for some odd accidents which philosophers have not yet thought worthwhile to enquire into, that the sturdiest porter is not the wisest man" (91).

In *A Serious Proposal* Astell suggests erecting a kind of monastery of "religious retirement" (to avoid terms reminiscent of popery) where women could dedicate themselves to piety and learning away from the frivolities of the world. It would be "so managed as not to exclude the good works of an active from the pleasure and serenity of a contemplative life, but by a due mixture of both, retain all the advantages, and avoid the inconveniences that attend either" (73). One of the chief works would be the education of girls, and it would "be a seminary to stock the kingdom with pious and prudent ladies. . . . One great end of this institution shall be to expel that cloud of ignorance which custom has involved us in, to furnish our minds with a stock of solid and useful knowledge [so] that the souls of women may no longer be the only unadorned and neglected things" (75). Of the prevailing mores, Astell writes, "Women are from their very infancy debarred those advantages with the want of which they are afterwards reproached, and nursed up in those vices which will hereafter be upbraided to them" (26). She issues a challenge to women: "If you allow [men] the preference in ingenuity it is not because you *must* but because you *will*. Can you be in love with servitude and folly? Can you dote on a mean, ignorant and ignoble life?" (4).

Despite the usual disparagement of women's intellect, most novels of the period presented intelligent heroines, although few were described as learned. Sarah Scott's protagonist in *Agreeable Ugliness* is typical. Because of her lack of beauty her father takes special pains with her education so that she will have charms "more valuable and lasting" but "he would often say he did not wish to make me learned" (14). It is the emotive power of her singing, one of the accomplishments deemed suitable for ladies, that attracts the regard of Dorigny, not her intellectual attainments. Scott takes a more positive view of women's learning in the depiction of Leonora, the heroine of the longest tale in *A Journey Through Every Stage of Life,* who manages to get a good education because, "having much emulation in her temper, and very quick parts" (I, 7), she insists on participating in the education given to her brothers. When she is forced to run away from home by a wicked stepmother this education serves her well by enabling her to function as clergyman and as schoolmaster. The narrator of *A Journey* insists that there is nothing ludicrous in the idea of a woman as teacher because "learning is of no sex, tho' it is chiefly arrogated to the one" (I, 119).

In *The Adventures of David Simple* by Sarah Fielding, Cynthia, the more intellectual of the two heroines, relates that as a child, "I loved reading, and had a great desire of attaining knowledge; but whenever I asked questions of any kind whatsoever, I was always told, such things are not proper for girls to know" (101). If she read "any book above the most silly story or romance, it was taken from" her with the caution that "Miss must not enquire too far into things, it would turn her brain; she had better mind her needlework, as such things were useful for women; reading and poring on books would never get [her] a husband" (101). While these voices are obviously not approved, the action of the novel tends to support their position. Cynthia's learning engenders envy in her sisters, depriving her of any support from them, and secures her only a miserable and humiliating job as a lady's companion.

Sarah Fielding's *The Governess, or The Little Female Academy* takes a still more conservative view of women's education. The work expresses its purpose in its subtitle, *Calculated for the Entertainment and Instruction of Young Ladies in their Education.* The work has as a frame a school run by Mrs. Teachum in which various incidents provide the occasion for the moral tales she uses to instruct the young charges "committed to her care in reading, writing, working and in all proper forms of behaviour" (2). Her principal aim "was to improve their minds in all useful knowledge, to render them obedient to their superiors, and gentle, kind, and affectionate to each other" (2).

One of the tales is "The Fable of the Birds," borrowed in large part from *Fables for the Female Sex,* a work (by the dramatist Edward Moore, author of *The Foundling*) published anonymously in 1744. The dove, in Fielding's version, is the exemplar of domestic bliss and is pronounced by the eagle "to be deservedly the happiest of the feathered kind" (140), despite the beauty of the peacock, the singing of the nightingale, the supposed (but suspect) wisdom of the owl, and the various claims of other birds. The exaltation by Fielding of quiet domesticity above any talent or achievement is even more striking when a comparison reveals that in the original work the dove is compared only to the sparrow, an example of promiscuity, contrasting the joys of a permanent union with the emptiness of a life of casual pleasure.

On another occasion, Jenny Peace, the most exemplary of Mrs. Teachum's pupils, tells how she has profited from the instruction of her mother. After she quarrels with her brother, her mother chides, "Jenny, I am ashamed at your folly as well as wickedness in thus contending with your brother" (17), and when her brother later helps her to jump over a stream, her mother presses the lesson home: "On this my good mamma bid me remember how much my brother's superior strength might assist me in his being my protector; and that I ought in return to use my utmost endeavours to oblige him" (18). Conciliation and decorous submissiveness are the lessons most consistently taught both by Mrs. Teachum and by Sarah Fielding's own narratives.

In *The Countess of Dellwyn* Fielding presents Mrs. Bilson as an exemplar of feminine virtues. In childhood her studies "had been judiciously directed by her father" and her "understanding improved by reading the best authors" (I, 192). Her intelligence benefits her when the wealthy Lady Dently finds her the most agreeable person she has ever met, "at once blessed with so lively a wit, so quick an imagination, and so sound a judgement" (I, 192), rescues her from financial distress, and makes her an heiress. Even then patience and faithfulness are portrayed as Mrs. Bilson's chief virtues. Earlier in the novel, when her profligate husband is imprisoned for debt, she cheerfully joins him in the Fleet and sets about making a living selling millinery and notions. His wandering affections now return to her and the couple is pictured as happy together with "Mr. Bilson turned schoolmaster to his sons, . . . to whose instruction he gave his utmost application" (I, 182–83), while the "girls assisted her much in her work, though the eldest was little more than nine" (I, 184–85). The intellectual advantages Mrs.

Bilson possesses are not going to be passed on to her daughters, although her sons are carefully taught.

Charlotte Lennox's novels each center on a notably intelligent woman who is usually also well educated. The heroine of *Henrietta,* for example, has been taught by her father "who had a very liberal education," and who "employed the greatest part of his time in the instruction of his children" (I, 77). Lennox's women all get their learning through males, either fathers, brothers, or (in the case of Sophia, the protagonist of her fourth novel) a family friend. This was, in fact, true of the century's best-educated women. Elizabeth Elstob was taught and encouraged first by her father and then by her brother, after being freed from the repressive custody of her uncle. Mrs. Carter, well known as a translator of Epictetus, was taught classical languages by her father. The only way a woman could learn the more scholarly disciplines was through private tutelage, almost always from a man. The mothers of Lennox's heroines, especially in the case of Harriot and Sophia, become the voice of convention, often discouraging learning and urging their daughters to study how to enhance their beauty and develop a fashionable style of dress and deportment. Such women are always depicted as foolish.

In Lennox's *Sophia,* the virtuous heroine is contrasted with her spoiled and shallow older sister. Sophia, largely through self-education, cultivates her mind while her sister cares only for beauty and fashion. Through reading, Sophia "derived the power and the habit of constant reflection, which at once enlarged her understanding and confirmed her in the principles of piety" (I, 6). The character of Sophia becomes an argument for all those, like Mary Astell, who believed that education for women would not only confirm and strengthen virtue, but act as a bulwark against the temptations of fashionable society. Her sister Harriot, on the other hand, who has been given "a polite education," is easily led astray by flattery, and, having been taught solely to value status and luxury, is all too willing to pay any price to obtain them.

Sophia also illustrates the practical value of intelligence and learning for women, for the heroine receives an advantageous offer of marriage from a highly eligible suitor, whereas her unlettered, frivolous sister is deemed suitable only to be a mistress. Sophia's intellectual attainments both add to her attractions and confirm her virtue, while the "fashionable education" given to Harriot makes her insipid and morally frail. Harriot enters a liaison with Lord L., but is all too soon discarded for another. She is then given a good dowry by her brother-in-law, but, characteristically, falls prey to a handsome young fortune hunter. After he has squandered her portion, she lives out a miserable existence in the colonies. In contrast, many years after Sophia's marriage "Sir Charles's tenderness for her seemed to increase every day." He explains that, had his passion for Sophia "been founded only on the charms of her person," he might have become "a mere fashionable husband; but her virtue and wit supply her with graces ever varied, and ever new" (II, 236–37).

In *The Two Mentors* and *The School for Widows* Clara Reeve presents intelligent and educated heroines. However, in *Destination: or, Memoires of a Private Family,* a novel concerned with proper modes of education, only the education of young men is discussed. In the work, Mr. Ashford, a benevolent bachelor, directs the education and careers of four youths, illustrating the principle that each should follow his natural bent and find a life which suits his own interests and abilities. The first hundred pages endlessly debate both the content (Latin or more practical subjects) and the manner (how much and what kind of discipline) best for the boys. On page 106 women are mentioned for the first time. A friend comforts a recently widowed man, noting that his "eldest daughter is grown . . . that is a fortunate circumstance" because she will be able to take over the household. The father is advised that although "she will one day make some honest man happy in a wife," that day must be postponed because he "cannot spare her until Patty is grown up and shall be qualified to succeed her." Even the phraseology of "make some man happy" indicates the bias that views women as primarily existing to ease the life of men—first fathers and then husbands.

The women in this novel are all stereotypes, either shrews or virtuous wives. One husband boasts that his wife is "what a woman should be, gentle, kind and affectionate, modest and unassuming" (II, 88). The exclusive focus on the education of young men suggests, of course, that the education of young women is of no importance, even for the only roles open to them, that of wives and mothers. If they are forward and argumentative, they will be laughingstocks and failures; if they are modest and unassuming, they will be admired. No intellectual attainments are needed therefore, but rather strict attention to deportment.

The heroines of Fanny Burney's novels are intelligent and lively, but not exceptionally learned. In the peface to *Evelina* Burney describes her heroine as having "a virtuous mind, a cultivated under-standing, and a feeling heart" (7), claims that could be made for Camilla and Cecilia as well. Mr. Tyrold, Camilla's father, tells his daughter, "the proper education of a female, either for use or hap-piness, is still to seek, still a problem beyond human solution" (357).

Camilla is, in part, a debate about the education of women. One extreme is represented by Indiana, a beautiful young woman who is encouraged by her foolish governess to believe that any cultiva-tion of the intellect is not only useless but harmful. Indiana's eccen-tric uncle and guardian, Sir Hugh Tyrold, decides to give her clas-sical learning, not because of any radical theories about women's education, but because, after both he and Camilla's brother Lionel prove hopelessly bad scholars, he does not wish to affront the tutor he has hired, Dr. Orkborne, by giving him nothing to do. Indiana, thoroughly spoiled, responds to these attempts with floods of tears which, ironically, are barely noticed by the self-centered pedant. She is rescued by her governess, Miss Margland, who convinces Sir Hugh that Indiana, "though beautiful and well brought up, could never cope with so great a disadvantage as the knowledge of Latin" (46). She asks, "What gentleman will you ever find that will bear a learned wife?" and insists that study will ruin her beauty.

Eugenia, Camilla's sister, is Sir Hugh's next experiment. She has been badly crippled from a fall and, on another occasion, greatly marred by smallpox, both through his own foolish actions. Out of contrition for destroying her beauty he makes her his heir, and now naively determines to fit her to be the wife of young Cler-mont, his ward, whom he mistakenly believes a "great scholar." Eugenia shows aptitude, becoming truly learned. Clermont, how-ever, returning from his grand tour abroad, proves to be a vain fop who emphatically rejects Eugenia, proclaiming that "her learning is worse than her ugliness" (579).

Eugenia's status as an heiress guarantees her some interested suit-ors, but even those not dismayed by her looks are discouraged by her learning: "This made Eugenia stared at still more than her pe-culiar appearance. The misses, in tittering, ran away from the learned lady; the beaux, contemptuously sneering, rejoiced she was too ugly to take in any poor fellow to marry her" (748). Miss Margland's fears are substantiated, and "some imagined her studies had stunted her growth; and all were convinced her education had made her such a fright." This attitude reflects the ignorance of the speakers, but, nevertheless, suggests that the young woman who wishes to attract eligible suitors had better follow Miss Margland's plan of education—"a little music, a little drawing, and a little dancing . . . but slightly pursued, to distinguish a lady of fashion from an artist" (46).

A more serious reservation about Eugenia's education concerns its emotional effect. Eugenia is imperceptive about nuances of feeling, even in those she loves, such as Camilla: "Early absorbed in the study of literature and languages, under the direction of a preceptor who had never mingled in the world, her capacity had been occupied in constant work for her memory; but her judgment and penetration had been wholly unexercised" (271). This defect can be seen as a flaw in her tutor, the pedantic Orkborne, but it also suggests the inadequacy of traditional training in the classics, with its reliance on rote memory, especially for women, who must be able to read emotions as well as texts. Eventually, however, Eugenia's education brings her tranquillity. When her first husband's death releases her from an odious marriage she is able to lead a secluded but contented life, "happily reaping from the fruits of her education and her virtues resources and reflections for retirement that robbed it of weariness" (912). When Melmond, her true love, finally realizes her worth and proposes, he finds in her "a companion delighting in all his favorite pursuits, and capable of joining even in his severer studies" (912).

Parenthetically, it should be noted that the education of young men is also portrayed as somewhat problematic in *Camilla*. Clermont, who turns out to be a cad and a fop, has been educated side by side with Henry Westwyn, the son of an old friend of Sir Hugh's, and the contrast between the two men is so marked as to "annul all hypotheses of education." They were "brought up under the same tutor, the same masters, and at the same university, with equal care, equal expense, equal opportunities of every kind," but "Clermont turned out conceited, voluptuous and shallow," while Henry is "modest, full of feeling, and stored with intelligence" (909). A contrast is also evident between the tutors, Dr. Marchmont, Edgar's tutor, and Dr. Orkborne, Eugenia's instructor. "Though the same university had finished their studies, and the same passion, pursuit, and success in respect to learning had raised and had spread their names and celebrity," Dr. Marchmont "with all his scholastic endowments, was a man of the world and a grace to society," while Dr. Orkborne, "though in erudition equally respected, was wholly lost to the general community and alive only with his pen and books" (749). The value of a classical education for a man is not deprecated, however. Sir Hugh's educa-

60

tional experiments begin because he sees that his brother, Camilla's father, is far happier in middle age with the resource of intellectual pursuits than he who has devoted his life to sport but is now crippled with gout. Camilla's brother, Lionel, refuses learning, and his heedless frivolity leads him into vice. While a scholarly education is not a guarantee of either moral virtues or social grace, it is some indicator of intelligence and discipline, and it brings contentment through the rational pastimes that learning makes possible.

Camilla's education is neither as rigorous as Eugenia's nor as frivolous as Indiana's. Mr. Tyrold, her father, sees the educating of women as especially problematic because they are "doubly appendant," passing from dependence on parents to dependence on a husband. Since both the station in life and the general character of the future husband are unknown, parents are in a quandary. If she has been "fashioned to shine in the great world, he may deem the metropolis all turbulence," whereas "if endowed for every resource for retirement, he may think the country distasteful" (357). In either case, not only has effort been wasted, but inclinations may have been formed which will be difficult to suppress. The Tyrolds have adopted a middle way, and Camilla, her father explains, "has been brought up . . . without any specific expectation." She has been educated "with as much simplicity as is compatible with instruction, as much docility for various life as may accord with invariable principles, and as much accommodation with the world at large, as may combine with a just distinction of selected society" (357). While Mr. Tyrold's phrasing may be somewhat more elegant, his philosophy of education is little different from that of Sarah Fielding's Mrs. Teachum. The theme is that women must be taught above all to be accommodating, docile, and submissive.

Conduct books often argued that some education was desirable for women because love of books furnished a harmless entertainment. This is true for Burney's heroines, whose intelligence protects them from growing as silly as an Indiana who cares only for admiration, eventually eloping with a worthless Scotsman. It is especially true of Cecilia, who even goes into debt to buy books. Both she and her future mother-in-law, Mrs. Delvile, distinguish themselves from the frivolous world of fashionable London by their preference for quiet retirement and intellectual activity. In contrast, the Harrels, one of Cecilia's trio of guardians, engage in a mad pursuit of social pleasure which plunges them into debt and leads to Mr. Harrel's suicide. Later, disappointed in her hopes of marriage and poorer because of the money she has given to the

Harrels, Cecilia retires to the country, where she fashions a happy and useful life for herself, a life made possible by her intellectual interests.

However, too much learning in a woman is usually looked upon with suspicion in Burney's works. Eugenia's learning has somewhat blunted her sensibility, although, on balance, it proves to be advantageous in her life. In *Evelina,* Mrs. Selwin is described as having paid a heavy price for her learning. "Her understanding, indeed, may be called *masculine,*" Evelina observes, "but, unfortunately, her manners deserve the same epithet," for "in studying to acquire the knowledge of the other sex, she has lost all the softness of her own" (269). Softness and gentleness are essential to true feminine appeal, but they must be tempered by other qualities. Miss Belafield, in *Cecilia,* is faulted by Mortimer because she cloys with her unvarying sweetness. "Simplicity uninformed becomes wearisome." A man seeks "spirit, intelligence and cultivation" (IV, 79). On the other hand, mere cleverness is equally tiresome. Lady Honoria has received "a fashionable education" in which "she sang a little, played the harpsichord a little, painted a little, worked a little, and danced a great deal" (III, 252). Although she has "quick parts and high spirits," her "mind was uncultivated and she was totally void of judgment or discretion," loving to "create wonder by her rattle." Burney's novels create the impression that the proper education of women is indeed a puzzle, treading a narrow line between foolishness and the danger of unfeminine rigor.

Henry Fielding's novels uniformly satirize learned women. Allworthy praises Sophia because she has "no pretense to wit" (882), showing always "the highest deferences to the understandings of men" (883). Amelia, the heroine of Fielding's last novel, confines her reading "to English plays and poetry" together with "the divinity of the learned Dr. Barrow, and with the histories of the excellent Bishop Burnet" (256), and Fanny is completely illiterate. Neither Mrs. Adams nor Mrs. Wilson professes any knowledge beyond how to care for a family.

Women who do make a pretense to learning or wisdom are not only guilty of affectation, but defective as moral examples. In *Tom Jones,* Bridget Allworthy, the unwed mother of Tom, "exercises [her] talents chiefly in the study of divinity" (104), and, in fact, it is a companion in scholarly pursuits who is Tom's father. Jenny Jones, who accepts a bribe to acknowledge Tom as her son, is another intellectual lady. She lives with Partridge, the schoolmaster, as a servant, and he, "discovering a great quickness of parts in the girl and an extraordinary desire for learning . . . had the good nature, or folly (just as the reader pleases to call it), to instruct her so far, that she obtained a competent skill in the Latin language, and was perhaps as good a scholar as most of the young men of quality of the age" (48). Her learning serves only to make her unsuited for the society of her equals and to engender jealousy, leading to the accusation that she is the mother of the unacknowledged bastard, Tom. Tom later meets her as the susceptible Mrs. Waters with whom he dallies in an inn at Upton, causing a rift between himself and Sophia.

Mrs. Western, Sophia's aunt, is also a learned lady: "She had lived about the court, and had seen the world," but "her erudition" did not stop with "manners, customs, ceremonies and fashions," for "she had considerably improved her mind by study" (272). The list of works she has read is, predictably, of dubious worth, and the narrator informs us that her knowledge of "the doctrine of amour" is entirely theoretical, "for her masculine person, which was near six foot high, added to her manner and learning, possibly prevented the other sex from regarding her, notwithstanding her petticoats, in the light of a woman" (273–74). Mrs. Western (whose title is a customary courtesy to older women, not an indication of marital status) is entirely confident of her judgment on virtually everything and is always wrong.

Mrs. Western is also a forthright advocate of women's rights. She tells her brother that the "fancied superiority" of men is only because their bodies, not their brains, are stronger than women's: "English women . . . are no slaves," she protests. "We are to be convinced by reason and persuasion only" (320). Vanity, however, is soon shown to be a more powerful force than reason in Mrs. Western's makeup when she is willing to send Honour to Bridewell for the reported offense of calling her ugly. At the same time she refuses to prosecute a thief who, while taking her jewels, had said, "Such handsome b—s as you don't want jewels to set them off" (357). Lady Bellaston, another defender of women's autonomy, gladly shelters Sophia, explaining that Squire Western "is one of those wretches who think they have a right to tyrannize over us, and from such I shall ever esteem it the cause of my sex to rescue any woman who is so unfortunate as to be under their power" (695). Lady Bellaston proves not only unchaste but foolish, trying vainly to capture the affections of the much younger Tom, and she is willing to act as pander, partly out of spite, making Sophia available to Lord Fellamar.

Another speaker for the independence of women is Mrs. Fitz-patrick, a cousin of Sophia's with whom Tom becomes entangled, fighting a duel with her husband which results in Tom's imprison-ment, and which, it appears at one time, may lead to his hanging. Mrs. Fitzpatrick tells Sophia that most women are more intelligent than men, and that "nature would not have allotted this superiority to the wife in so many instances, if she had intended we should all of us have surrendered it to the husband," adding that "men of sense never expect [this] of us" (595). Sophia's position is that she will "never marry a man in whose understanding" she sees "any defects before marriage" and that she "would rather give up" her own understanding "than see any [defects] afterwards." Mrs. Fitzpatrick is, not surprisingly, far from exemplary. One of the books she cites when boasting of her reading is *Atalantis,* a notori-ous scandal chronicle, and she is "so good an economist, that she spends three times the income of her fortune, without running into debt" (980).

Amelia, the heroine of Henry Fielding's last novel, makes no pretense to learning. In contrast, her friend Mrs. Bennet, who later becomes Mrs. Atkinson, knows both Greek and Latin. In the novel, learning is seen as essential for a man. Booth, Amelia's hus-band, who was destined to be a soldier, is "a pretty good master of the classics," because his father "did not think it necessary to breed him up a blockhead" (VIII, 5). When Dr. Harrison, a good clergy-man, is asked to support a candidate for Parliament who does not know Greek and Latin, he refuses, maintaining that "it is a very low civil capacity indeed for which an illiterate man can be quali-fied" (XI, 2). Learning in a woman, however, is quite different. Dr. Harrison asks Mrs. Bennet if she knows the passage from Homer where Hector tells Andromache, "Go home and mind your business. Follow your spinning and keep your maids to their work. Or how do you like the character of Hippodamia, who, by being the prettiest girl and best workman of her age, got one of the best husbands in all Troy?" (X, 4).

When Mrs. Bennet asks, "Where is the harm in a woman's having learning as well as a man?" the doctor counters with "Where is the harm in a man's being a fine performer with a needle as well as a woman?"—his point being, would she honestly "choose to marry a man with a thimble on his finger?" As Mrs. Bennet continues to contend that there is no reason that learning should make a woman unfeminine, Atkinson warns she "had better not dispute with the doctor; for . . . he will be too hard" for her. She immediately flares out, "Nay, I beg *you* will not interfere," adding, "I am sure *you* can be no judge in these matters." She has, of course, proved Harrison's point by not being properly deferential, especially to the man who is now her husband, and "the doctor and Booth burst into a loud laugh; and Amelia, though fearful of giving her friend offence, could not forbear a gentle smile" (X, 5).

On a previous occasion, when Mrs. Bennet spoke of the great pleasure her education has given her and commented on "that great absurdity (for so she termed it) of excluding women from learning" (VI, 7), the narrator tells us that "Though both Booth and Amelia outwardly concurred with her sentiments, it may be a question whether they did not assent rather out of complaisance than from their real judgement." Mrs. Bennet's character is an ambiguous mixture of virtues and failings. There is much to admire: she has suffered from a cruel stepmother and a jealous aunt, married a poor clergyman for love, been betrayed by a lecherous lord, lived an exemplary life as a needy widow until she marries Atkinson, and she now acts as a generous friend to the Booths, giving them aid when they need it. On the other hand, she keeps cherry brandy in her room "for comfort in all her afflictions" (IX, 6), on one occasion taking "a sip too much" (X, 8); she creates difficulties for Amelia when, disguised as Amelia, she solicits the favor of a commission for Atkinson; and she becomes a bit of a snob when her husband is commissioned. In their marriage, "Mr. Atkinson upon the whole hath led a very happy life with his wife, though he hath been sometimes obliged to pay proper homage to her superior understanding and knowledge. This, however, he cheerfully submits to, and she makes him proper returns of fondness" (XII, 9).

While the reader is perhaps left feeling that learning is only a minor detriment in Mrs. Bennet, her aunt is an object of outright ridicule. Like Sophia's aunt, Mrs. Western, she is very tall, together with being "very thin and very homely" (VII, 3). "Indeed," says Mrs. Bennet, discussing her aunt's failings, "I believe the first wish of our whole sex is to be handsome," at which she and Amelia "fixed their eyes on the glass, and both smiled." The chief product of learning for her aunt is "a hearty contempt for much the greater part of both sexes," while she herself "became . . . quite ridiculous, and ran into absurdities" (VII, 4). Her envy of Mrs. Bennet's beauty is aggravated by her envy of her niece's greater learning, leading to still more unkindness.

In contrast to Henry Fielding's heroines, Samuel Richardson's are all well educated, and learned women are never depreciated. In

Richardson's novels women are perfectly capable of mastering classical languages. Pamela is instructed in Latin by her husband, while Clarissa had begun the study of Latin and having "an admirable facility in learning languages . . . would soon have made herself an adept in it" (IV, 496). Pamela has been schooled in the usual feminine graces by her kind mistress, but her education is amplified by her husband who teaches her French and Latin and takes her on the grand tour. Pamela advocates this course for all couples when, as was usually the case, the husband's education is superior to the wife's: "What an intellectual kind of married life would such persons find theirs!" (II, 414). She comments bitterly on the usual education of women, who are "forced to struggle for knowledge" and, even then, "when a poor girl, in spite of her narrow education, breaks out into notice, her genius is immediately tamed by trifling employments, lest, perhaps, she should become the envy of one sex and the equal of the other" (II, 386). Noting that Locke advocates that mothers instruct their children, she asks who, "as our sex is generally educated, shall teach the *mothers?*" Furthermore, why "are not girls entitled to the same *first* education, though not to the same plays and diversions as boys?" She condemns the attitude of those men who relegate women to "common tea-table prattle, while they do all they can to make them fit for nothing else, and then upbraid them for it" (II, 413). Miss Goodwin, Mr. B.'s illegitimate daughter and Pamela's ward, is learning Latin, as well as French, Italian, and the usual accomplishments.

While there were, then, occasional voices of dissent, the century's daughters were being taught primarily to be dutiful, obedient, and submissive. The single most important issue on which parents and children were likely to come into serious opposition was marriage. The accepted position on marriage was fairly clear and constituted a standoff—a child must never marry without the consent of the parents; the parents must never force a child into an unwelcome marriage. While the first condition was held without reservation, the second was sometimes rather liberally interpreted. Since most young girls had a very limited experience of the world, concerned parents often quite sincerely felt that they knew what was best for their daughter and that prudent motives were more valid than romantic fancies. They were, after all, quite literally giving their daughter into the authority of her husband for the rest of her life. *The Lady's New-Year's Gift: or Advice to a Daughter* declared, it is "one of the Disadvantages belonging to your Sex that young women are seldom permitted to make their own choice;

their friends' care and experience are thought safer guides than their own fancies, and their modesty often forbiddeth them to refuse when their parents recommend, though their inward consent may not entirely go along with it" (25).

Most daughters acceded to parental guidance, and in most families the wishes of the daughter were genuinely regarded. It is ironic, however, that virtually the only self-assertive or rebellious action that was likely to succeed for a young woman was elopement. The opportunities for a young woman on her own to make a living, especially if she were estranged from her family, were so meager that any other way of casting off parental authority was usually doomed to failure. In eloping, the young woman by definition had masculine aid and protection; after eloping, her parents were forced to accept a fait accompli, because even if the legality of the marriage could be challenged their daughter was presumably no longer chaste and therefore ruined. *The Polite Lady* describes the condition of a young lady who loses her chastity: "She loses all inward peace and tranquillity of mind, she is forsaken and abandoned by her nearest friends and relatives, she is despised and contemned, hissed and hooted by all the world. Perhaps the humane and good-natured may pity her misfortunes, but seldom, or never, relieve her distresses; the rigidly virtuous and severe consign her over, without reluctance, to instant and irretrievable ruin." Even an undesirable marriage would be preferable.

The actual frequency of elopement is difficult to document, but runaway marriages were enough of a threat to prompt the Marriage Act of 1754 which made such unions illegal in England.[3] Lord Hardwicke's Marriage Act made only church weddings binding and provided that the marriage must be entered in the church register, signed by both parties. Furthermore, the marriage of anyone under twenty-one was not valid without the consent of parents or guardians. The enforcement of the law was transferred from the church to the civil courts, and substantial penalties could be imposed on clergymen who disobeyed. After 1754 eloping couples could only go to Scotland, where the law did not apply, and Gretna Green became the new destination for rebellious lovers, or, as the proponents of the act maintained, for venal fortune hunters preying on naive and impressionable heiresses.

The circumstances surrounding an elopement might range from actual complicity by one of the parents, to anger followed by acceptance and reconciliation, to unremitting bitterness and permanent estrangement. An example of the first is the marriage of Elizabeth

Horner and Stephen Fox. Elizabeth's mother, Susanna, evidently favored the match which was violently opposed by her husband, largely because he disapproved of Stephen Fox's politics. In March 1736, Susanna Horner writes to Mr. Fox, "Sir, I am very much concerned to acquaint you that Mr. Horner's answer to your proposal, which I thought would not be favorable, is more the contrary than I could have imagined." Mr. Horner's disapproval was evidently couched in strong language, since his wife adds, "I choose rather to let you know that it is such as will admit of no hope of alteration, than to repeat to you the terms of it." She asks him "to desist from any future thoughts of this kind," but indicates her own favorable leanings by implicitly disassociating herself from the refusal: "I dare say you will be so reasonable as to forgive my part in this." She assures him that once her daughter is settled she will be glad to renew an acquaintance that is "both an honour and a pleasure."

Stephen Fox evidently enlisted her as an ally. A brief note from Mrs. Horner reads, "I think this a good proper sort of a letter for you to send me about one o'clock the night of the enterprise. And if you don't keep your word with me, I will in earnest never pardon you. If you do, I am and shall be your most affectionate Mother." The enclosed "proper sort of letter" informs her that her daughter "is with me and I hope for my life time, for we are married." It goes on to say, "I hope in God you had no objection but Mr. Horner's not consenting," adding (and undoubtedly this was the information Mrs. Horner wanted very precisely conveyed), "I know you would not get over that, and therefore did not solicit yours after he had not only refused, but in so rough and uncivil a manner denied his consent," The letter continues, "I saw there were no great hopes of ever gaining him to alter his opinion of me," and goes on to promise exemplary behavior to her daughter, and to offer to make a suitable settlement of his estate.

The couple were, in fact, married twice, once on 15 March, in the presence of three witnesses, and a second time on 22 March with additional witnesses, the official document noting that the couple had been previously married "but not before so many witnesses." A later letter from Fox to Thomas Horner repeats the promises made to Mrs. Horner, saying his only excuse is that "I did and do love your daughter extremely and tried and found there was no way of gaining your consent." He gives assurances of his future conduct, promises "to come into whatever settlements you and Mrs. Horner think proper," and "as to my way of thinking in politics which the world says will be your chief objection to this match I am ready to give you any assurances that it shall give no disturbance nor appear in any shape in the county." Nor would "party quarrels" intrude into their private lives: "I will answer for it you shall not hear one word, nor see one effect of the difference that there is between our thought upon that matter." Pressure from all sides—Fox writes that his wife's only anxiety is for her father's and her mother's forgiveness—brought Horner to consent to a reconciliation, and his daughter seems to have been happy in her marriage. Fox managed to accumulate enormous gambling debts but his income was sufficient to pay them and still maintain the household comfortably.

An elopement in direct defiance of her mother's wishes was that of Anna, daughter of Letitia Barnston, with Charlton Leighton. Mrs. Barnston, a widow, writes to a friend, "She was firmly assured that I never would force her hand if her heart did not go with it, and but the morning before she left me gave me her word this affair was at an end and she would think no more of it, nor ever dispose of herself but with my consent." Love overcame duty and she "took that inglorious flight at six the same evening, drove with him in a hack to the Fleet immediately, and from thence to paltry lodgings. Nor could I by the most diligent search discover where they were till the next Thursday morning following." (The Fleet was one of the districts immune from superior ecclesiastical supervision where, before the marriage bill mentioned above, unscrupulous clergymen would marry anyone for a fee, with no questions asked.) A few weeks later, Mrs. Barnston writes to her steward, "On New Year's Day Mrs. Leighton received my blessing and (a Christian) forgiveness." The parenthesis seems to indicate duty rather than wholeheartedness, an inference borne out when she laments, "My mind is too much busied with my irremediable misfortunes to concern myself about loss or gain and what I ever did in the latter was with a view to (my once dear) Anna Maria's interest—but that is over now." Nevertheless, many instructions follow concerning the estate.

A few months later Mrs. Barnston cautions her steward that "Mrs. Leighton and her husband" may settle nearby but, "I charge you allow them no greater privileges at Condover [her estate] than as strangers—to walk in the gardens if they go there for an airing—for she has excluded herself from that place and whoever looks upon her in the same light as when she was my dear girl and heiress to all I had will but cruelly flatter her hopes." She adds, "As

Figure 7. A Fleet Wedding. J. June. This satirical print illustrates the problem of quick weddings available in the Fleet before the Marriage Act of 1754. A fawning parson hopes to preside at the marriage of the innocent sailor, who is being gulled into marrying the landlady's "daughter." Reproduced by courtesy of the Trustees of the British Museum.

she has carved she shall eat—for I detest the match and always shall." In a less vindictive mood she laments, "Indeed, since she left me so very ingloriously, all the world is a desert to me and all places alike."

Unfortunately, Charlton Leighton seems to have justified Mrs. Barnston's opposition to the match. In an undated letter, Anna thanks her mother for her "kind and affectionate letter" and confesses that she is virtually a prisoner. Mr. Leighton "is afraid anybody should acquaint me of his extravagancies which he has long with a great deal of art hid from me and as often protested that he was in good circumstances with asserverations that were now I find only used to blind me." She laments, "Every farthing is spent, God knows which way; I'm sure it has not been on my account." She adds bitterly, "He often tells me how great an opinion he has of me, and yet for all that will not take my advice in anything that regards the good of his family." She closes, noting that her husband is occupied for half an hour with the colonel: "So I shall finish this as soon as possible lest he should return. I know he dreads that I should write you word of anything, not considering that he is ruining me and his children—only he is afraid of being rebuked for it."

After Anna has been married for five years, mother and daughter are allies against a spendthrift husband and correspond clandestinely. Anna Leighton writes to her mother, "I am very apprehensive Mr. Leighton will not get the two thousand pounds without your consent by a letter I had from Mr. Coppingger, but I sincerely wish he may not; for if he does and with that can clear himself I fear he will be as bad again in a few years time." She goes on to give an example of her husband's idea of economy: "He is going, he says, to part with his fox hounds and get a pack of hare hounds. I told him the hounds were not so much as the horses." His reply to this sensible observation was that "If he had no hounds he would have the same number of horses and last week he bought Capt. Latham's so now he has seven." Evidently Mr. Leighton chose to exercise a husband's privilege of opening his wife's mail, for Anna writes, "I am glad Mama you have thought on Mr. Gwynn to receive your letters, for he is a good man and I am sure he will deliver them safe into my own hand." She adds that soon she will spend "a whole day" with Molly by herself "to be more at liberty to write" to her mother. Two months later, she confesses, "I hope, please God, Mama I have done for the best. This morning on Mr. Leighton's promise to live within bounds henceforward I consented to sign the deed to my uncle." Anna Maria did not live to learn the result of her action; two months later she died in childbirth. Her eldest daughter, also named Anna Maria, was adopted by her mother, who remained unreconciled to Charlton Leighton.

The elopement of Isabella Eccleston with John Everard is a more dramatic story. Isabella Eccleston was only fifteen when she married John Everard, the family's coachman. He swore on oath that both were over twenty-one and therefore free to marry. The couple concealed the marriage for more than a year, but then, either because they feared they would be discovered or because the situation had become intolerable to them, they ran away. Pregnancy was not the motive; Isabella did not become pregnant until some six months later. In its beginning the elopement seems much like that satirized in Jonathan Swift's "Phyllis, or the Progress of Love." John Everard writes to his ex-employer, now father-in-law, "Most honored Sir," and explains that he is now "lying under a necessity of leaving you by being lawfully married to your daughter." He asserts that it was "by a free consent of both sides though against your will . . . for which I beg ten thousand pardons." He promises to "use all lawful industry" to make Isabella "both easy and happy," and signs, with what is probably unconscious irony, "I remain your most obedient servant."

Isabella also wrote to her parents, in a touchingly childish hand, "the reason of my coming away in such a manner was by being married to John." She assures them it was her own desire, that she is well, and that "nothing more is wanting to complete my happiness but your forgiveness." She closes, again almost certainly with no conscious intention of irony, "My duty to you and my mama . . . I remain your dutiful daughter, Isabella Everard."

Neither of these letters did anything but increase parental wrath. Ann Eccleston, Isabella's sister, writes about her parents' plans to Richard How, a business partner of her father's who became a friend to the young couple: "The fellow took a false oath to get a license. They design he shall stand in the pillory." The purpose behind this was far more sinister than to subject him to the usual rigor of the pillory, for "some worse minded people than you or I intend to have him pelted to death by some vile wretch whom they think to bribe to commit the fact and that it will never be suggested who did it in the crowd." Ann pleads with Mr. How to stop this because "dreadful stings of conscience may follow when it cannot be undone." In a subsequent letter she writes, "I am almost mad for our two fools," adding that she is afraid her father will discover their hiding place through their letters. "Advise them to hide wherever they go for if my father should make them never so fair pretenses to them to appear, it will be all a bite [trick]." The couple hid under assumed names in a little village in Essex, but they became frightened when a traveller stopping at the inn regaled the company with the latest news from London, and "he told us of ourselves."

With Richard How's advice and assistance, both monetary and logistical, the couple went to Holland, where a business associate found them lodgings. Mr. How inquires closely from various intermediaries who encounter the couple about John Everard's behavior toward his wife. He is informed that he did "all that lay in his power to make her easy" and that a man who travelled with them in the boat to Holland noted that "he carried himself very affectionately to her." The observer was unknown to the couple, it is explained, and therefore this conduct could not be just pretense for a good effect.

Richard How was concerned because, aside from being above him in social position and potentially a substantial heiress, Isabella Eccleston was already entitled to a considerable fortune through legacies. John Everard might have been a venal fortune hunter, and one can well see why the Eccleston family would jump to this conclusion. However, Everard told Mr. How, "I hope you will find that I am not so much to be blamed as may be laid to my charge," because "there was something more than a full consent on both sides," which suggests that Isabella may have been an unusually mature fifteen. In any case, she did not regret her marriage. John Gurney, who encountered the couple in Amsterdam, writes to Richard How, "I cannot find any relenting in the young woman, who seems mistress of sufficient courage to support her at least for the present under consideration of her present condition." Regardless of the original motives for the match, romantic fantasy or fortune hunting, in contrast to Swift's ill-fated pair, true love and tenderness grew between the two. Despite an exile of some years in Holland living in penurious lodgings and suffering from the cold, despite Isabella's ill health and subsequent miscarriage, despite the continued refusal of her family to give her her fortune, the tone of loving concern one for the other continues in their letters. It is also remarkable that even in their letters to Mr. How, who was their partisan, no tone of bitterness or resentment creeps in about the intransigence of the Eccleston family. Both seemed to accept the judgment that their deed deserved prolonged resentment.

The Ecclestons, knowing that the couple had left England and foiled of their plan to murder Everard in the pillory, now made efforts to get a Letter of Privy Seal ordering John Everard to return to England. This was a very unusual procedure. Richard How sought advice of a lawyer friend about such a writ and was told that if the crown issues such a letter, and if the letter is personally served in the presence of witnesses, and if the person does not return within the stated time, he is then in contempt and may be subjected to forfeiture of estates. The writer doubts such a letter will be issued, since "it must be upon great interest or where the party absent hath been guilty of some very foul and enormous crime." The Ecclestons managed to bring "great interest" to bear, evidently, because the letter was issued. How felt that Isabella's father was less vindictive than her mother, as he writes to a Dutch associate: "My partner is obliged in complaisance to his wife and her brother, who is an elderly bachelor of great estate, to pursue with vigour his daughter and her husband. I believe it is entirely to satisfy them that he acts in the manner he doth, for I am much of the opinion his own inclination extends no farther than to obtain a reasonable settlement of her fortune, the man's inferior circumstances considered." Isabella's father retained complete control over the substantial estate which had been left her by her grandmother.

From the beginning, John Everard had made it clear that he would "readily join with any measures that should be proper to secure his wife's fortune to her and her heirs separate from any claim to be made thereon by himself and his heirs" asking "only that the interest may be applied for their joint support." In one letter to Mr. How thanking him for his continued financial support, Everard points out his dilemma: he can no longer earn a living in the only profession he knows, since his exile from England deprives him of the use of his language and his marriage makes him unemployable as a household servant. The Ecclestons' continued refusal to make any financial settlement and to give Isabella the inheritance to which she was entitled could only make their daughter's life miserable, and if it had not been for the friendship of Richard How she might not have survived the several severe illnesses she suffered in Holland.

Richard How continued to be a good friend to the young couple. One suspects that in her childhood he may have been a sort of adopted uncle to the young daughter of his business partner. He advised John Everard to take lessons in dancing, in language, and in writing to fit him for what will inevitably be a new position in society. He advises both of them to "by all means have a writing master to come home to you. The charge will not be equal to what the convenience hereafter may be." Since both can write adequately for legibility, this must be an indication that handwriting was an important social indicator. Finally, How writes to his confidant in Holland, John Gurney, that is it imperative to make up the quarrel. "I have reason to fear some people would take an opportunity of recommending themselves by doing what I dare not write." He suggests that "this is the best time to bring John Everard and wife to the utmost reasonable terms, and I am sure that is better than to have things carried to unreasonable extremes."

He suggests that Gurney write him a letter which he can show to Eccleston, in which Gurney reports receiving a letter from Everard who wishes to return to England for his wife's health and who expresses himself as being very ready to come to terms about his wife's fortune. How then dictates the following sentence to be added: "I have also been thinking as by John's letter his wife seems in no good state of health, should she happen to die while things are unsettled perhaps the fortune may all be left from the family. That would be a pity, especially to go to a man who has dealt so wickedly. And should she have a child first and the fortune come into her husband's hands. . . ." Whether this line of reasoning had effect or whether more humane motives won the day, after several years an agreement was reached. The couple returned to England and became hops farmers in Kent. A subsistence allowance was allotted to them from Isabella's fortune, and they led a happy life in modest comfort. Throughout her mother's life, Isabella continued to write to her in heartrending terms pleading for forgiveness. "Certainly it is one of the greatest of my sufferings to be banished from your presence," she writes. "All the desire I have of staying in this life is to see pardon offered to him who hath in all my afflictions been so kind and tender to me." Fearing death in childbirth, she concludes, "I write this in despair and as my last farewell so if you have any pity or tenderness towards your poor and unhappy daughter I beg and entreat you will find out means to return a favourable answer." Her mother died without ever seeing her again or offering any word of reconciliation.

The women novelists considered in this book depicted hardly any runaway daughters, despite the obvious dramatic possibilities of such a plot. In *The Adventures of David Simple* Sarah Fielding presents two heroines who are cast out of their homes, one by envious sisters after the death of their parents and the other by a wicked stepmother. In *Ophelia* the heroine is kidnapped. These plot devices enable Fielding to depict her women (who fare poorly) outside the usual protection of a loving family but without the stigma of daughterly disobedience. Similarly, Charlotte Lennox's heroine in *Harriot Stuart* is forced to act independently because the aunt who is supposed to be her guardian proves to be mad and paralyzed, while the protagonist of *Henrietta* is left an impoverished orphan. In Sarah Scott's *The History of Cornelia* the heroine, an orphan, is forced to run away to avoid the lecherous advances of her guardian, while a wicked stepmother is the cause of Leonora and Louisa's adventures in *A Journey Through Every Stage of Life*.

In contrast, these novelists uniformly present heroines who are exemplars of filial duty whenever parents are functioning in their roles. The protagonist of Scott's *Agreeable Ugliness* is a case in point. Despite her "ugliness," St. Furcy, a young aristocrat, falls in love with the heroine. Fearing to antagonize powerful neighbors, her father insists that she marry Mr. Dorigny, a kindly older man, to put her out of the reach of St. Furcy. She pledges complete filial obedience, yielding herself "entirely to your disposal," although, regarding Dorigny, she "can have no other sentiments for him than the esteem he deserves" (70). She consents to marriage, although she "resigned" herself to her "fate" with the "melancholy of a victim, not with the cheerful hopes of a bride" (94). In time, however, she does come to love her husband, thus confirming the views expressed in many conduct books that a young woman who followed her parents' wishes rather than her own perhaps frivolous or carnal desires would learn to love the husband chosen for her and would be rewarded with happiness. After Dorigny's death, when she is a widow with a considerable independent fortune, her father suggests another match which is repugnant to her. She declares, "I would die sooner than disobey or even displease you; but my obedience would kill me" (225). Fortunately, he does not insist, and eventually the heroine is united with the faithful St. Furcy who has remained single.

Agreeable Ugliness chiefly counsels daughterly obedience rather than the futility of empty-headed beauty. This is also the theme of Scott's *The Test of Filial Duty* in which two heroines, Emilia and Charlotte, are finally rewarded with marriage to their true loves after demonstrating that they are submissive and obedient daughters. In contrast, Emilia's half sister, oddly named Sophia, is unhappy after eloping with a romantic Scotsman. When Emilia's father tries to compel her to marry a man she feels she cannot love, she writes to her friend, "I would, without opposition, though with pain greater than at the separation of soul and body, obey my father" if only her conscience did not warn her that she could never make this man a good wife. She continues, "However, if my father will not relent . . . I am determined to sacrifice myself to my duty," adding that her unhappiness will undoubtedly shorten her life and she will have the comfort of not having offended her father, and so "will not carry guilt with me into eternity" (I, 240–41).

The suitor of each of the girls is not comparably obedient to his parents, each refusing marriage with another (as did St. Furcy, in contrast to the heroine of *Agreeable Ugliness*). The lover of Charlotte, in fact, finally defies his father and marries her against his wishes. The marriage of Emilia only becomes possible when her true love's father, who is competing with his son as a suitor, conveniently dies. The tale seems rather flawed as an exemplar on several counts. The happy resolution depends on the death of a parent in one case, and the defiance of a son in the other, not on any beneficial results of obedience itself. Perfect obedience would have had Emilia living out her life in lonely solitude and Charlotte dying of a broken heart. The plot supports a double standard, approving of disobedience for sons but not for daughters, even if obedience forces them to violate their moral consciences. The trite and perfunctory story of the eloping Sophia seems to provide the only fully acceptable example, and, ironically, Emilia's eventual happiness is in part dependent on her sister's downfall, since Leonard, her lover, was originally intended as a husband for Sophia.

In contrast to the strong messages of filial obedience projected by women novelists, all of Henry Fielding's heroines run away from home. Fanny impulsively leaves to find Joseph, while Amelia elopes with Booth. Amelia's act is sanctioned, however, by the good Dr. Harrison, a male authority figure, because he believes that her mother's reasons for forbidding the match to Booth are unworthy and materialistic. He gives the couple both his sanction and his aid. Sophia, threatened by her father, Squire Western, with an unwelcome marriage to the odious Blifil, nephew and heir of Squire Allworthy, also runs away. Her action makes her a rebel against patriarchal authority, but a qualified one. Sophia leaves because she realizes that she will not be steadfast enough to disobey a direct order from her father. "You know, Sir," she tells him, "I must not, nor can refuse to obey any absolute command of yours" (359). She has explained to Tom, "My own ruin is my least concern, I cannot bear the thoughts of being the cause of my Father's misery" (299). Sophia's devotion is completely uncritical since her father has been portrayed as a pig-headed boor, who, when she protests that she hates Blifil, replies, "If you detest un never so much, you shall ha'un," and when she says that the marriage will kill her, responds, "Then die and be d—ned" (297). Sophia, nevertheless, is about to yield to his wishes; she is saved only because she remembers that she has given her promise to Tom that she will never marry Blifil. Not trusting herself to resist her father's command, she runs away in order to keep faith with Tom. Sophia's own inclinations—her love for Tom and her detestation of Blifil—influence her decision, but the struggle is presented primarily as a conflict between her obligations to two men; her own integrity is hardly considered. Sophia's flight is possible because she has a refuge in London—Lady Bellaston, a champion of women's independence but dubious guardian who not only encourages Lord Fellamar to seduce Sophia but virtually permits her rape. Fortunately, she is rescued in time, but the dangers inherent in the position of an unprotected young woman are clear. (Fanny is also rescued in the nick of time, twice.)

In *Clarissa* Samuel Richardson gives a striking picture of the pressures that a conflict over marriage could bring to bear on a young woman. In this struggle Richardson dramatically embodies the plight of women under the normal code governing the conduct of respectable eighteenth-century society. Clarissa's plea "Only leave me *myself*" (I, 399) is a cry that illuminates the fundamental position of women in the age—having no independent, self-determined existence, but living all their lives in dependent relationships. The struggle here is between patriarchal authority—the Harlowes' determination "to triumph"—and Clarissa's concern for her moral life, for the integrity of her being. Against the actual conditions of life for women, Clarissa's ordeal was, fortunately, unusual, but it was also a natural outcome of the ideals of conduct proposed for women. Forced marriages were far from unknown—Mary Delany expressed great sympathy for *Clarissa* because she herself had been compelled into marriage—but in most cases family affection argued against forcing a loved daughter into an unwanted union. However, taken to its logical extreme, the belief that governed the treatment of women—their natural inferiority, based on a lack of rational intellect coupled with a dangerously emotional nature—not only demanded that they be placed under firm guidance but also dictated that they themselves were the least able to judge in what direction they should be guided.

James, Clarissa's brother, brings forth Roger Solmes as a match for Clarissa. The advantages for James are clear and may lead to a title. As Clarissa's mother explains to her, "Your brother, in short, has given in a plan that captivates us all," because "a family so rich in all its branches, and that has its views to honour, must be pleased to see a very great probability of taking rank one day among the principal in the kingdom" (I, 93). It is assumed that Clarissa will fall in with this scheme, because, as a model young woman, she is expected to be submissive and obedient. "My temper, I know, is depended on" (I, 93), Clarissa writes. Her struggle with her family then comes down to her asking "only to preserve to myself the liberty of *refusal,* which belongs to my sex" (I, 226–27). This is not permitted, on grounds which reveal the confusion of sexual attitudes beneath conventional courtship mores. On the one hand, Clarissa's declaration that Solmes is detestable to her is disallowed because nice young ladies are not supposed to have any inclinations toward sexuality and therefore any male judged acceptable by her family should be acceptable to her. On the other hand, women are known to be very susceptible to attractive males because of their innate weakness and therefore Clarissa's declaration that she will stay single rather than marry Solmes is simply not believed, but seen as a pretext which will eventually make her available to Lovelace.

Clarissa, whose real virtue blinds her to the pragmatic code that functions in her society, is constantly surprised that her most sweeping offers are refused. At one point she suggests giving over her grandfather's estate to her sister and brother and agreeing to live unmarried and dependent on her father's bounty the rest of her life. She sees this as a concession on her part which solves all problems, making Arabella now just as acceptable to Solmes and thereby bringing to fruition all the family's "darling schemes." The offer is refused, partly because the Harlowes fear that worldly opinion will accuse them of persecuting Clarissa to obtain her estate, but mostly because they simply cannot accept the idea that she is willing to live single. Since they see women only as they relate to men, the Harlowes can only understand her refusal of Solmes as a prepossession with Lovelace. They cannot grasp that Clarissa's aversion to Solmes is based on her concern for personal integrity and has nothing to do with a preference for another. And since women are seen as having power only when they are connected to men, they see

Lovelace as a continuing threat because as Clarissa's husband he would probably be successful in litigating to regain her estate.

The novel makes it clear that while the Harlowes may be somewhat intransigent, they are not atypical. Anna Howe's mother is depicted as being well-meaning if not too bright. Her judgment is somewhat slanted because she is being mildly courted by Uncle Antony, but her voice is that of good-natured society. She says of Clarissa that "it will be expected of a young lady of her unbounded generosity and greatness of mind, that she should *deny herself* when she can *oblige all her family*. . . . Will not Miss Clarissa Harlowe give up her *fancy* to her parents' *judgement?*" (I, 298). Anna summarizes her mother's reasoning: "Either, said she, the lady must be thought to have very violent inclinations (and what nice young creature would have that supposed?) which she *could* not give up; or a very stubborn will, which she *would* not; or, thirdly, have parents she was indifferent about obliging" (I, 293). Mrs. Howe, in her use of "stubborn," is employing the kind of rhetoric commented on by Sarah Chapone (see chapter 1), where fortitude and resolution in a woman become obstinacy and perverseness.

Mrs. Norton, Clarissa's beloved former governess, presents her arguments in the Christian context of gaining merit. After telling Clarissa, "It is your *duty* to comply," she continues, "But remember, that there would not be any merit in your compliance if it were *not* to be against your own liking." She adds, "Remember also what is expected from a character so extra-ordinary as yours: remember, it is in your power to unite or disunite your whole family for ever." She holds out some hope: "Your prudence . . . will enable you to get over all prejudices," and "the obligations you will lay all your family under will not only be meritorious in you with regard to *them,* but in a few months, very probably, highly satisfactory, as well as reputable, to yourself." Clarissa protests, "It is for my *life,*" but Mrs. Norton replies, "I consider everything," and points out that if Clarissa follows her own will and is unhappy, she has no one but herself to blame, whereas if she obeys her parents, then at least she will have "all that consolation which those have, who have been directed by their *parents,* though the event prove not answerable to their wishes" (I, 195).

In addition to these speciously reasoned arguments, Clarissa is subjected to the highly emotional pleas of her mother, the authoritarian directives of her father, and, finally, the threat of a forced marriage. Betty Barnes, her sister's maid, tells her, "They expect *fits* and *fetches* . . . without number: but everybody will be prepared for them: and when it's over, it's over" (I, 462), adding that she will "be easy and pacified" when there is no help for it. This theory is echoed by Lovelace later in the novel. Dr. Lewen, the parish clergyman, on hearing of Clarissa's dilemma, says that "for his part, he had ever made it a rule, to avoid interfering in the private concerns of families, unless desired to do so" (I, 364). (Pamela, in Richardson's first novel, also finds no help from the church. The local clergyman, Mr. Peters, declares that her persecution by Mr. B. "though it was a thing to be lamented . . . was too common and fashionable a case to be withstood by a private clergyman or two" [I, 116].)

Against these powerful forces of a family and custom, Clarissa insists, again and again, that she owes a duty to herself and to her own moral life. The nature and the seriousness of the marriage vows are clear to her. Her family maintains, she writes, that "PERSON in a man is nothing, because I am supposed to be prudent: so my eye is to be disgusted and my reason not convinced . . . and I am to be wedded to a *monster*" (I, 79). He is not only physically repulsive, but narrow-minded, coarse, and indelicate. Her difficulty, she explains to Anna, is not merely the sacrifice of "*inclination,*" but "an aversion so *very* sincere" (II, 166). She declares many times, "I cannot *honestly* be his" for "my heart is less concerned in this matter than my *soul;* my *temporary,* perhaps, than my *future* good" (I, 260). She envisions "a *duration of woe.* . . . Every day, it is likely, rising to witness some new breach of an altar-vowed duty" (I, 287). Even in the best of circumstances, marriage is "enough to make a young creature's heart ache," she declares, "to be given up to a strange man; to be ingrafted into a strange family; to give up her very name, as a mark of becoming his absolute and dependent property; to be obliged to prefer this strange man, to father, mother—to everybody: and his humours to all of her own." Surely, she concludes, one "ought not to be obliged to make these sacrifices but for such a man as she can love," and even then, "a thousand things may happen to make that state but barely tolerable" (I, 152–53).

The powerlessness of Clarissa and the modest nature of her demands are emphasized throughout the first part of the novel by the arrogance of her brother James. She asks him, "What right have *you* to dispose of my hand?", for even if "you govern everybody else, you shall not govern me" (I, 381). In spite of this defiance, it is clear that he is doing just that, and that the reverse could never be true. In contrast to James, who enjoys estates in his own right,

Clarissa has given the estate left to her by her grandfather over to the management of her father because of family pressures. When the terms of her grandfather's will are heard, James, of course, is furious, but "nobody indeed was pleased," and her "father himself," Clarissa writes, could not bear that she should be made "sole" and "independent" (I, 54). She, therefore, "to obviate every one's jealousy" gave to her father's management not only the estate but the money bequeathed her. When, on the other hand, James inherits property, Clarissa reports, it made them "all very happy, and he went down to take possession of it" (I, 55).

When Anna Howe urges her to take steps to resume her estate so that she can live independently, Clarissa is tempted. She quite sincerely feels that she would be content to live single the rest of her life, occupying herself with the round of small charities her income would permit. However, she decides not to make the attempt, partly because she is reluctant to bring suit against her own father, but, more importantly, because she realizes that she probably would not succeed. "My heart failed me," she reports, "when I recollected that I had not one friend to stand by or support me in my claim" (I, 264). (Clarissa is here almost certainly using "friend" in the common meaning of the time of "relation.") Her fear that her attempt "would but the more incense them without answering any good end," is undoubtedly correct. Her mother has warned her, "Take notice, that there are flaws in your grandfather's will," adding, "not a shilling of that estate will be yours if you do not yield." Isabella Eccleston's father succeeded in seizing the estate left to her by her grandmother, and Clarissa's family would also have succeeded. The law, an entirely male establishment, was most unlikely to support a rebellious daughter against a father, especially a father with wealth and influence.

Sarah Chapone, herself a mother, discussed with Richardson his depiction of Clarissa in the role of daughter. She admires his having shown "all the avoidable unhappiness of Clarissa" as "owing to mistakes in judgement" which combine with "feminine timidity" and a sense of duty "carried to some degree of weakness." These errors make Clarissa "amiable" and, because fallible, "more imitable." However, Clarissa is at fault in "too strict a sense of duty to her father." In this reading of Richardson's novel, Chapone revealed her own feelings rather than the author's intentions, as his reply to her letter indicates: "A relaxation in duty of the child's part is to be as little encouraged as possible" (Carroll, 201). Chapone also thought that Clarissa ought to have litigated with her father to force the return to her of her grandfather's estate. She reasons, "Wherever God lodges a power, there he exacts a performance. . . . It was therefore not a laudable action in Clarissa to make her Father her substitute as to the dispensing powers with which she was invested by her Grandfather." And furthermore, "Had she claimed that independence for herself she had never been a dependent upon the wicked Lovelace. That renunciation seems to me a defect in judgement."

Richardson offered a variety of defenses for Clarissa's original action—her youth, her desire to mitigate the jealousy of her brother and sister, and so on—and pointed out that after she was at odds with her family "she could not have done it with effect" (Carroll, 201) against the opposition of her father and uncle. Chapone concedes the first point, that her original action was "laudable and becoming," but contests the second: "My objection is to her determination afterwards, when she resolves not to litigate with her father on any account: that resolution is not represented (I think) as springing from her situation, but her principles, which principles I take to be indefensible." Sarah Chapone undoubtedly realized that a suit brought by an underage daughter against her father to gain financial independence, especially at a time when father and daughter were engaged in a bitter dispute about a suitable marriage, would have almost no chance of succeeding. She was adamant, however, in insisting that in principle litigation against her father was the only defensible course for Clarissa.

Although she fears a forced marriage with Solmes, Clarissa, like a dutiful daughter, has decided to risk a final confrontation with her family rather than to accept help from such a dubious source as Lovelace. When she meets Lovelace to tell him this decision, however, she is cleverly tricked away, and now she is in his power. In the eyes of the world she is already ruined once she goes off with a man, especially a man with a rakish reputation. Her intransigent family refuse any help and in the ensuing duel with Lovelace we learn how difficult it is for a woman to make her way without male assistance. As Clarissa declines toward death she sells her clothes to support herself.

Daughters who were rebellious enough to elope were rare. The encouragement of a suitor unwelcome to one's family in the hope that he would eventually be accepted was a less drastic form of self-assertion. Elizabeth Jeffreys writes to Charles Pratt, "I should be extremely glad to see you here but Mama won't approve it I'm certain, therefore I beg you would not come." Not easily thwarted, however, she adds, "I will see you tomorrow somewhere; I'll let you know in the morning where it is to be. I don't know whether they'll be at home or not." The signature is "Believe me to be yours and only yours." The letter was delivered by hand, and one can picture a sympathetic lady's maid right out of Restoration comedy aiding the romance.

The rage for playing at cards aided Elizabeth a few days later. The fashion of card playing is a satiric theme throughout the century from Mirabelle's "privisos" in *The Way of the World* and Belinda's ambiguous victory in *The Rape of the Lock* onwards. Anne Warde in Nottingham writes a friend, "Tomorrow I am engaged to another card party for such there is at every place I go to. So general are they now that the ladies cannot spend an afternoon agreeably without them." And Caroline Powys comments, "A London life now is every evening from card party to card party." Happily, Elizabeth Jeffreys was immune to the prevailing epidemic, and she writes her suitor, "I am set down with infinite pleasure to inform you I don't go to Mrs. Lock's this evening. Mama herself mentioned that she thought it would be very dull for me as I should be the only person that did not play at cards." She tells him, "You may be certain I am very happy upon the occasion, and what will greatly add to my happiness will be seeing you. I shall be at home ready to receive you."

Parental disapproval was apparently relatively minor, since Charles Pratt could be received at home, and eventually it was overcome. Elizabeth Jeffreys indicates, after all is well, how difficult it was for her to oppose her mother. "My spirits are infinitely higher than they have ever been since Mama's behaviour to me. I loved her too well to bear the least unkindness from her, and I've experienced much, but I hope 'tis all over. Her letter gave me great comfort." She tells Pratt, "Nothing but your love could have made me bear what I suffered as I did."

Mary Martin was another young woman involved in a courtship which was disapproved. In this case, however, it was the man's widowed mother who objected. Mary Martin writes to Isaac Rebow, referring to a gift of venison and produce from his country estate, "Pray, does Madam know of what you send me, and would you have me say anything to her next week about receiving them?" She realizes that a clandestine correspondence creates problems, for if his mother expects comment and thanks, her "silence on the occasion may create some suspicion of our corresponding." On another occasion, she approves his judgment about the secrecy of their letters: "I think you judge very right not to mention my writings," and again discusses the complications of an association partly known and partly hidden: "I intended to have wrote to Madam today, but shall now stay till I hear a better account of her, when I shall send a formal message to you, as I suppose she knows of your writing to me last Sunday." Her letters are addressed "in a disguised hand" and sent to an accommodation address where he can pick them up. The pair had other ingenious methods of conveying messages. On one occasion she asks him "to send me word in the *Weekly Intelligencer* (if you can) what day you think you shall be in town," adding, "for I count the precious hours till we meet, and (as you did not seem to disapprove of it when we last parted) will certainly be at Duke Street at the time I proposed." Both these courtships ended in happy marriages.

The attitudes of feminine assertiveness expressed or implied by these various rebels against the accepted order undoubtedly reflect the less defined or less acute feelings of many other women. In action, however, the century shows us many more dutiful daughters than rebellious ones. Ann Chaytor's devotion to her parents is characteristic of many of her contemporaries, even though her particular circumstances made the role of a loving daughter more burdensome than usual. She was the daughter of a very happy marriage. Her father, William Chaytor, created a baronet in 1671, married for love rather than for money, although he needed money. His sister, Anne, writes two years before his marriage, "Here is a report that you are to have my Lord Darcy's daughter but I can believe nothing of that kind. I fear she has not money enough." Subsequent letters inform her brother of eligible heiresses, but finally she congratulates him: "It is a great satisfaction to me to hear both from yourself and from everybody else of your happiness in your wife." William Chaytor was evidently in financial trouble from the start; his sister had difficulty in getting him to pay her promised dowry, ending up with only half of what she felt she was entitled to. In 1695, because of his debts, he was forced to alienate his estates. He could not settle with his creditors and he lived in the Fleet, a debtor in debtor's prison, for seventeen years, dying at the age of eighty-nine having outlived all his children. A nephew succeeded to the estate.

Financial troubles did not cause hard feelings between man and wife, however. His wife Peregrina writes him, "My dear, I give you thanks for your long and kind letters and must assure you they are more pleasing to me than any diversion." She goes on, "You write more like a lover than a husband, yet I must believe you well having had your affection for above these twenty years and not in the least lessened by the charms of those who endeavour to captivate your sex." And she assures him, "You may be confident of the like return from me which nothing but death can dissolve." Just before her death in 1704 she wrote her "last will," asking him not to sell Croft, the estate, and to be sure of a portion for Ann of 500 pounds. She writes, "My dear I have told you in this paper my desire and advice which I hope you will observe and not take amiss, they coming from a faithful wife who doth and will to her last breath most truly love you." This "is all the return I can make you for your great kindness to me which I beg you will continue to my dear children after my death and in particular to Nancy [Ann]." She has been in poor health for some time and ends with words of comfort: "Be not troubled at my death for you know my life has not been very easy for some time and if God think fit to take me out of my house to himself it will be a great happiness to me." Her last injunction is one of economy: "Neither would I have you make any great funeral for me."

Ann Chaytor, the only daughter, assumed a major share of responsibility for the household before her mother's death and total responsibility afterwards. She writes, apparently in reply to a somewhat testy letter from her father, "Dear Father you can't imagine might I choose but the first thing I should do should be to see my dear Father which is the greatest satisfaction I can ever propose to myself," and adds, "but 'tis never my fate to have my wish." She explains that her mother was doubtful about going to London because of the expense of keeping the family there, and therefore "all I said was to desire she would go up for both your ease and satisfaction." When her mother protested that she could not leave the younger children, "they would be so troubled," Ann answered, "Rather than that should be any hindrance I would deny myself the only thing I wished and stay with them." This was just one of many sacrifices Ann was to make. She nursed her mother through her last illness in London lodgings, later speaking bitterly of a cousin: "When my Mother laid dead by me and I not a farthing she never offered me anything to bury her with." She assumed the management of the estate, apparently quite competently if the many details of rents and improvements are an indication. She acted as tutor to the youngest brother, teaching him penmanship. Further, she reports, "I hear him both Latin and English every day, and though I can't pretend to improve him I hope he will lose nothing."

Meanwhile, she writes with gay bravado, "I doubt this will be a fatal year for losing my beaus, but if I must lose them I'm resolved not to take over sore on it but comfort myself with the hopes of getting new ones." In an exchange of letters concerning the possibility of a second marriage for her father (to a wealthy widow to repair his fortunes), she writes, "I agree that your circumstances have been the greatest lessening to me. I was sensible of that long since when Lady Millbank said she knew a gentleman with a great estate that was much in love with me, but would not tell me so because your circumstances were a lessening to him." She speaks of "several other instances I have had of that nature." "Yet I thank God I never repined at it," she tells her father, "I am content still to be lessened rather than see you uneasy with an ill natured, proud wife."

Later that year a new suitor, Mr. Mouleverer, appeared: "He is about my own age; he has the character of a very sober, good humored man; he has only a mother and two brothers at trade, and by what I hear all they desire is an agreeable woman of quality and breeding." She adds, "The mother is much in love with me. I have seen the beau twice and he seems very merry and civil." His mother "contrived all she could that her son might be in my company" and "we were pretty merry and free but I could not perceive that his thoughts were the same with his mother." He is a great lover of poetry, and he lends her "the Dispensery, an extraordinary poem done by Doctor Garth," scarcely a romantic choice. The matchmaking was unsuccessful.

Two years later Ann wrote her father about another suitor who was unwelcome to her. Her letter is lost, but it elicited an angry reply from him. She writes, "Dear Father I'm heartily sorry that anything I write should in the least make you uneasy when the chief desire of my life is your satisfaction," adding "I confess my error and beg pardon that I was not more cautious how I worded the letter." She had asked her father for advice about how to "handsomely put him off" since "the better his circumstances the more caution must be used." She explains with perhaps unconscious irony that she consulted him because he would understand "the pride and resentment of your own sex best." She rejects his intemperate advice, saying, "I can keep my state and when there's occasion show my resentment without a beating." She continues, "Of all things I care not how little I have to do with men, either in giving them hopes or provoking their malice. . . . I'm resolved to live as I do rather than do anything which does not become me."

As time went on, Ann Chaytor's dutiful life exacted its tolls. She writes, "This weather and so much business agrees very ill with me," explaining, "I can't ease myself as a great many can by talk but it works most on my spirits and either makes my head ache or else sick." She laments, "'Tis hard to be so plunged in business and nothing to divert for I may be from one week to another and scarce see the face of any but poor Nanny." And she worries that "if after all my brother should not consider me as he ought I may say what a sad fate is mine." Her brothers did not share her country isolation—one was abroad and one was in London. She answers her father's suggestion that she come to London: "As for my coming up I can't think out this winter money is so scarce," adding, "I heartily wish when Brother Harry comes over you would send him down to me." Not only would his company "be a great satisfaction to me" but it might "be better for his health and purse." On another occasion she cautions about her brother, "You must consider when he comes how to make him appear genteel and not too costly," adding, "I'm resolved to continue at Croft till you have got pretty clear at London of those trifling bills due at my Mother's death." When an advantageous match was proposed for her brother and refused by him she writes indignantly, "I think my Brother Chaytor should not be so nice in his Ladies. The Lady you mention is handsome enough for a widow." She adds, "I'm sorry he will neither consider his family or circumstances more for if he can have an agreeable woman and a good estate, 'tis sufficient." One can sense her resentment at the sacrifices she has made while her brothers circulated in the fashionable world, and she suggests, "Pray ask him if he marries not, which way he thinks to pay my five hundred pounds for since the estate is not sold I hope he will take care of me some other way." Ann Chaytor's concern proved to be needless. She died the next year at the age of thirty-one.

Vere Isham was another dutiful daughter. Her parents' marriage also had been exceptionally loving. After a long illness, her mother died on 22 August 1713 and her father was prostrated. In the middle of September she writes to her brother that her father "still keeps his bed, but he had promised me to rise tomorrow." The promise was kept, but at the end of the month she reports, "My Father rises but keeps his chamber and won't see any company." After another month passed she persuaded him to dine with an old friend: "My Father dined with him, but cried all the while and spoke not a word." She continued her difficult task of trying to cheer him but with little result: "'Tis the most melancholy thing in the world to see him; he takes notice of nothing and seems resolved never to admit of any comfort." The fact that all her best efforts were ineffectual was a bitter recompense for her love, and she writes, "I have the mortification to find 'tis not in my power to give any satisfaction." Writing to her brother in London, she notes somewhat bitterly, "I must tell you that if you passed the time as I do you would not think this life was stocked with pleasure." She continued to keep house for her father until he died seventeen years later. Then she became dependent upon her eldest brother, to whom the estate was left. She writes to a younger brother, "I can give you no account of my own affairs; they have not been mentioned since I writ to you, but I design in a little time to desire my brother to determine what he'll do." When her brother and his wife took over the estate she was transformed from that useful person, a dutiful daughter who cares for an aged parent, to the most troublesome of creatures—a spinster aunt. She writes, "When I parted with my brother Isham he promised me that he would let me have the annuity, and I believe I may depend on it." She adds, "To tell the truth I begin to wish I was settled somewhere and am almost tired of the moving way I am in." But "if my brother should not perform his promise it will be impossible for me." Fortunately, her brother did act justly, but it is evident from her letters that this outcome was by no means inevitable and that she is completely dependent upon her brother's generosity even after so many years of dedicated devotion.

While the role of the loving daughter was not always a happy one, the role of the unloved and unlovely daughter was unquestionably sad. Although relations with one's parents are an important factor in life in any era, for an unmarried woman in the eighteenth century they assumed special importance. She was dependent upon them for financial as well as emotional support, and she had virtually no opportunity to seek other roles or other settings which might bring her some measure of self-esteem. Gertrude Savile, in her journal kept from 1727 to 1731, ends each entry with a two-word summary of her subjective reaction to the day. Her days range from "not unhappy" to "most miserable" with "not happy" the commonest verdict. She often complains of her mother's treatment of her: "The best I had from my Mother was entire disregard which she has treated me with ever since I lived with her," adding, "She has always found somebody or other to take up all her care and thought and love instead of me." She speaks of her few diversions, and tries to comfort herself: "The providence of God in denying me the pleasures of youth has kept me from many temptations incident to it, which ought to make me satisfied, and I have good hope in the end will be better for me." Her life seemed so bleak to her that she could only take refuge in the prospect of a reward in heaven.

Daughters' problems with parents usually were much less heart-rending, ranging from Miss Lydia Lively's struggles to be good (described in *May Day* and "Intended to Improve and Amuse the Rising Generation"), through coaxing for new dresses or privileges (Elizabeth Deloval writes her parents that she is "most thankful" that they will allow her to learn Italian), to coping with intrusive grandmothers or crotchety elders. Mary Tinney speaks for many other women similarly burdened with the care of elderly parents when she describes her situation to a friend. Pleading for a letter and apologizing for her own erratic writing habits, she says, "Indulge me with a line and consider a mother of eight children and two old ladies besides a husband and house cannot have many moments to spare for her own amusement." She confides, "Indeed, my dear Mrs. Phripp, I confess I am almost worked to death." Declaring that she is the only one in the house that "can set a stitch," she comments, "My aunt you know of old can find full employ for her maid without work," and "my poor mother finds it very difficult to amuse herself. Her eyes are very sore and she is now almost totally deaf." To complicate the situation, the two old ladies quarrel constantly. Tinney relates that her mother blames her deafness on her aunt's "loud talking," adding, "I find it is very hard matter to keep them from a battle royal. You know they were never over fond of each other and the most improper people to live in one house surely that ever was." She concludes, "Since I am made so sensible of the many great infirmities attendant on old age I cannot but pray to be taken out of this world before that time of life in which the second childhood is more troublesome than the first."

Jane Papillon, writing to her husband, describes dealing with another common problem, the interfering grandmother. She says of their child, Anne Mary, the youngest of four, "Blessed be to God she thrives very well." She then tells how Anne Mary loved her "very fondly the first week or two" after his departure but then "discerned that her Grandmother was more fond of her." Because "her Grandmother often found fault that her humour was not more observed and took her part whenever I chid the child, she grew not to value me in the least but rather condemned me." She describes her strategy: "I was forced to say that if I might not have the government of my children alone, I would wholly give her over to her Grandmother's government." Then "for two or three days I never found the least fault in her nor seemed to instruct her in anything as I did the rest." The lesson strikes home and "Mother seeing the inconveniency of it desired it might not be so but that I would do by her as the rest." Her mother promises to leave Anne Mary to Papillon's discretion, "since which the child becomes very obliging and tractable." Papillon comments that Anne Mary "has great understanding and when she saw her Grandmother took her part against me she walked in defiance of me and scowled and turned her back on me when I came her way." Everything is settled, and "now bless God we have no wrinkle awry among us." She very wisely adds, to her husband, "You need take no notice of this."

The role of a daughter changed as one grew older, with the daughter, married or unmarried, usually assuming greater responsibility as parents aged. Ideally the fundamental relationship of obedience, gratitude, and unquestioning devotion remained constant, however, whatever the practical realities might be. Anne Chaytor would only go as far as making suggestions to her father about her brothers' extravagance, and Jane Papillon cleverly used overcompliance rather than remonstrance to cope with her mother's interference. Furthermore, the bond between parents and children usually remained close, with resulting emotional pressures as well as rewards. This was particularly true for women, who usually exchanged one relative self, "daughter," for another, "wife," without achieving an independent identity or any real control over their own lives.

If, as in the case of Gertrude Savile, the relationship with parents caused great unhappiness and marriage was not offered, a lifetime of misery could result. A young woman had no other opportunities to find fulfillment, not even the alternative of the convent (there being none in post-Reformation England until the nineteenth century). When misfortune, such as bankruptcy or the untimely death of a spouse, affected a family it was usually the daughters, not the sons, who suffered. Anne Chaytor became a lonely spinster, losing chances for marriage while directing the affairs of an estate she could never inherit, while her brothers frequented London society and married. Vere Isham devoted her life to the care of her emotionally devastated father, only to be dependent, after his death, upon the generosity of her happily married brother.

It was, of course, the lack of alternative opportunities which made the role of daughter potentially oppressive. Women were educated, or more accurately, refused a real education, with marriage as the exclusive goal in life. The debate about women's education focussed chiefly on equipping a woman to be a good wife. Proponents of a better education for women argued that learning would make her a more agreeable companion and give her virtuous ways to pass the time; opponents argued that women's chief duty was submissive obedience, and learning might lead to prideful assertion. Except for a few rebellious voices, women's education continued to be equated with practical housewifely skills and a few genteel accomplishments. The virtual absence of respectable and remunerative employment for women meant that the best way to rebel against parents was to enlist male assistance and elope. Ironically, this drastic step immediately put the woman under the authority of her husband without even the usual safeguards of marriage settlements.

The novelists of the period, Henry Fielding excepted, were reluctant to portray rebellious runaway daughters. The heroines are uniformly loving and obedient. When they are forced to function on their own it is usually because they are orphaned or the victims of cruel stepmothers or lecherous guardians. Young women who do elope in these novels, Amelia excepted, all find unhappiness in their marriages. The most vivid picture of the strains produced by both patriarchal family structures and the general view of women held in the century when there was a conflict between a daughter and parents appears in Samuel Richardson's *Clarissa*. Richardson makes clear that while the Harlowes are not necessarily typical, their fundamental views are characteristic of their society. Clarissa's plea, "Only leave me *myself,*" illuminates the paradoxical position of women. Their upbringing was based upon the idea that they were unfit to take charge of their own destinies. They were reared to be some man's wife and their presumed congenital lack of judgment made parents, especially fathers, better able to choose that man. The character of Clarissa, a woman clearly superior to the men who try to dominate her, is a powerful argument for women's right to live according to their own standards.

While novels generally counselled obedience for daughters, they did uniformly condemn forced marriages. They did also present women who are intelligent and capable, including some who succeed in living independent lives. Some novelists, notably Richardson, Charlotte Lennox, and Sarah Scott, also spoke for better education for women, showing heroines who make good use of the kind of learning usually reserved for men. Nevertheless, women novelists especially seemed to have been conscious of their obligations to social and moral norms when dealing with filial obedience. The dubious reputation of early fictions, which were seen as encouraging rash notions of romantic love, clung to the novel, and a respectable woman turned novelist might well be very careful to avoid such a charge. Henry Fielding, with the greater assurance of the educated male, felt free to ignore conventions, but dutiful daughters are the fictional norm, as indeed, they were in real life. While the novel condemned tyrannical parents, it held up loving obedience as a model for daughters.

C H A P T E R   3

Courtship

C OURTSHIP ASSUMED great importance for eighteenth-century women both because marriage was regarded as the only real route to happiness for a woman and because, somewhat paradoxically, the actual powers given by law and custom to the husband made the prospect of entering such a state of bondage, and for life, daunting. This chapter will discuss the many factors which entered into courtship—financial, personal, religious, social, even geographical—both from the point of view of the couple themselves and from that of their elders. It will also describe the attitudes towards courtship in eighteenth-century fiction and the progress, both successful and unsuccessful, of several typical courtships as they are documented in the words of the young women themselves.

It was generally agreed in the eighteenth century that marriage was a woman's natural vocation. It was, in fact, regarded as the best road to happiness for both sexes. Lady Dorothy Bradshaigh expresses the prevailing opinion when she writes of Samuel Richardson's heroine, "The perfectest happiness this world can give I would not (with my notions) give to Clarissa in a single state. Be-

94

cause the union of two hearts in a marriage cemented by pure love, upon good principles constitutes a friendship preferable to all others in which the greatest of our earthly joys consist."

The strongly Protestant spirit of the age viewed celibacy as a waste of human potential, not as an opportunity for spiritual improvement. Of a Roman Catholic friend who was planning to take the veil in Belgium, Arabella Clayfield writes, "I think every religious motive ought to inspire a love of social duties; one might as well be unborn as be useless to society." Of course, celibacy does not necessarily, or usually, imply being "useless to society," and Arabella Clayfield's disapproval was really based upon her friend's declining to marry: "She has refused the first offers, is possessed of every thing that can give a zest to life and therefore her conduct is the more unaccountable." And, she laments, "I am concerned that she should forsake the happiness arising from domestic connections, the dearest source of bliss, for the enthusiasm of visionary delights." While a Catholic culture gave at least intellectual assent to the judgment that marriage was the natural condition for most people but not the highest or the most desirable, Prostestant culture saw marriage as both the most natural and the most desirable, for both sexes. For a man marriage and domestic life formed only a part of a complex pattern woven of a variety of interests—estate management, trade, agriculture, politics, law, government, scholarship, science, and so on. For a woman domestic life and its attendant duties and pleasures usually formed the whole of her world. Marriage, then, was not only the natural destiny of every eighteenth-century daughter, but also the single most important determinant of her future happiness. Courtship was not to be treated in any casual fashion.

The degree to which courtship was an affair of the young couple themselves or was in the hands of their families varied considerably. In some cases marriages were arranged by the families of young people who had never mct; in others, parental approval was sought only as a last preliminary to marriage. Arranged marriages were far more common among the great families, where marriage was frequently the principal method of either increasing the family estates by matching with other landed families or of preserving the estates by matching with merchant wealth. As a general rule of thumb, the less property was involved the more freedom of choice was given to the young people, although such questions as similarity of religion were important in all matches. The concept of marriage as the concern primarily of the couple rather than of their families gained credence during the period, and by mid-century the ideal of married love as the highest form of friendship, the ideal articulated by Lady Bradshaigh, was commonly accepted if not always followed.[1]

At its worst, the system was close to the buying and selling of human beings, and satirists pointed out the dubious distinction between the prostitute who sold herself for a night and the fine lady who sold herself for life. However, in most cases negotiations about marriage, whether they were initiated by the families or followed the lead of the couple themselves, reflected a genuine and prudent concern of the parents for the welfare of their child. In any case, the child had the right of veto. *The Ladies Calling* states the traditional view: "But as a daughter is neither to anticipate nor contradict the will of her parent, so (to hang the balance even) I must say she is not obliged to force her own, by marrying where she cannot love; for a negative voice in the case is sure as much the child's right as the parents." The treatise tips the balance a bit, since the judgment of parents was considered more reliable than the romantic notions of the young, by adding, "It is true she ought well to examine the grounds of her aversion, and if they prove only childish and fanciful, should endeavor to correct them by reason and sober consideration," but "if after all she cannot leave to hate, I think she should not proceed to marry" (II, 20).

The novels of the period are unanimous in condemning forced marriages. *Clarissa* gives a moving picture of the dilemma of a dutiful daughter under constraint to marry a man she despises. The hero of *Sir Charles Grandison* declares himself opposed to any pressure on a woman to marry. While he advises his sister Charlotte to marry Lord G., he makes clear that the decision must be truly her own, just as while he hopes that his young ward Emily Jervois and his good friend Sir Harry Beauchamp will eventually marry, he asserts that Sir Harry must win her heart or he will not give consent. "There is hardly any-thing gives me more pain, than when I see a worthy woman very unequally yoked" (II, 45), he comments, and one of the charities he is "most intent upon promoting" (II, 11) is the giving of dowries to young women so that they will have a better chance of marrying someone of their choice. Clementina's family use emotional scenes to influence her to marry—"Shall a father kneel in vain? . . . Shall a mother in weeping silence in vain entreat?" (III, 391). Harriet Byron, when told "they will not *compel* her," replies, "Persuasion, Sir, in the circumstances this lady is in, is a compulsion" (III, 310–11). Despite both Harriet's and Sir

Charles's belief that the marriage is desirable, Sir Charles uses his influence to make the Porettas stop urging marriage for a period of one year.

Henry Fielding also condemns marriages not based on love. In *Tom Jones* Squire Allworthy declares, "I have always thought love the only foundation of happiness in a married state, as it can only produce that high and tender friendship, which should always be the cement of this union" (70). He considers it "a profanation, to convert this most sacred institution into a wicked sacrifice to lust or avarice," by marrying for "the consideration of a beautiful person or a great fortune" (71). Allworthy asserts that forcing a young woman into marriage is "such an act of injustice and oppression," he wishes "the laws of our country could restrain it" (883). The implication is that such marriages did indeed take place.

In *Tom Jones,* patriarchal authority is voiced by Sophia's father, Squire Western, who, despite her protestations that she will never marry without his consent, insists that she marry Blifil. He tells Sophia, "I am determined on this match, and have him you shall . . . though dost hang thyself the next morning" (840). Sophia's aunt, like Amelia's mother, sees marriage as a treaty for financial and social gain in which love is of little concern. "I have known many couples, who have entirely disliked each other, lead very comfortable, genteel lives" (334), she observes. While Blifil also regards economic advantage as primary—his love for Sophia "was of that violent kind which nothing but the loss of her fortune, or some such accident, could lessen" (858)—he finds that her evident aversion to him heightens her charms by adding the pleasures of "triumph to lust" (346). These attitudes are all portrayed as detestable perversions.

In Sarah Fielding's *The Adventures of David Simple,* Cynthia's father proposes a marriage for her with an arrogant, condescending dolt. She refuses: "I shall always call it prostitution for a woman who has sense, and has been tolerably educated, to marry a clown and a fool . . . only to know they have married a man who has an estate" (109–10). The protagonist of Fielding's *Countess of Dellwyn,* on the other hand, marries for money and ends up divorced and indigent, whereas Mrs. Bilson, in the same novel, marries for love and manages to surmount all obstacles and make her marriage a happy one.

Charlotte Lennox's heroines, with one exception, all insist on love matches, with Henrietta even running away to avoid an odious marriage. The exception is Euphemia, who marries Mr. Neville, her dying mother's choice, so that her mother will have the satisfaction of knowing that she is provided for. The marriage is bitterly unhappy. On the other hand, Sarah Scott rewards the heroine of *Agreeable Ugliness* with a happy marriage when she obeys her father and marries Mr. Dorigny. Although before the wedding she resigns herself to her fate "with the melancholy of a victim, not with the cheerful hopes of a bride" (94), she comes to love him, explaining that "his attentions, his regard" for her, "his indulgence and the sincere regard" he had for her all brought her heart "to make a grateful return" (158), until she finds she has "no other soul but love" (147).

Scott declares against truly forced marriages, however, with Leonora running away to escape a match with a destestable old miser in *A Journey Through Every Stage of Life.* Carinthia, the listener to these tales, expresses wonder that any woman would accept a "union with a brute" simply because he was wealthy and opines that "the world would scarcely blame a flight for such just reasons." Sabrina, the wise narrator, explains that most of the world looks upon marriage as "a union of fortunes, not a union of hearts." She believes "there is no divine ordinance more frequently disobeyed than that wherein God forbids human sacrifices, for in no other light can I see most marriages" (I, 16). In Scott's *Millenium Hall* Mrs. Morgan has been just such a victim of a forced marriage that is unhappy to the end, the disastrous union of an intelligent woman and a stupid boor.

In the preface to *The Test of Filial Duty,* Scott declares that, taking "advantage of the reigning taste for novels," she wants to show "youthful readers" that "filial obedience, more particularly in the important article of matrimony," is "one of the greatest duties of social life" (vi–vii). She also assures her young readers that she is "no less an enemy to the tyranny of parents, than to the disobedience of children" (viii). The parents in this novel nevertheless seem tyrannical, although none insists on a forced marriage. If the parents' wills had not been circumvented (without disobedience on the part of the daughters), both heroines would have led lives of celibate misery.

The legal ramifications surrounding the settlement of estates multiplied throughout the century, usually toward a constriction of the rights of the incumbent heir to insure the continuity of the estate. Marriage settlements also tended to grow more complicated to insure the rights of the woman both during marriage and in widowhood. The concept behind the dowry or portion for the bride was that because her husband would now be responsible for supporting her, it was both just and to the couple's advantage that she bring to the marriage something to increase their future prosperity. Depending on the circumstances dowries ranged from vast fortunes and estates—especially if the bride were the sole heir of the family—to a few hundred pounds (or less), enough to help the young couple stock a farm or set up as tradespeople. In return, especially if the values involved were substantial, the bride's family wanted some assurance that she would be maintained in a suitable manner and that she would be protected against any future coldness or profligacy on the part of her husband. The present possessions and income of the groom were an important consideration, and in the case where the heir of an estate could not hope to inherit before his father's death the woman's family would often insist that he be given a suitable allowance upon marriage so that the couple would not be dependent on the whim of his elders. Future prospects either in expected inheritances or in commercial ability were weighed, although they could not become the subject of legal agreements.

Furthermore, it was customary to stipulate a jointure or widow's portion to protect the wife from being dependent either on her husband's relatives, if she were childless at his death, or on an indifferent or venal son. Marthae Taylor voices her concern for future financial security in correspondence with a suitor. As an older, self-supporting woman whose parents were dead she was in the unusual situation of negotiating her own marriage settlement. Referring to an unsatisfactory proposal for a jointure, she writes, "To lay before you the probable consequence of my adherence to your late proposition, give me leave to suppose myself already married to a man with whom I've lived many years in good harmony, been the tender partner of his heart and kind sharer in all his joys and cares, the useful help-mate, the careful nurse and kind comforter in sickness, and cheerer of his health, the fast friend that never flinched though all besides forsook him." After "death (perhaps sudden and unexpected) snatches from me the darling of my heart," when still "o'erwhelmed with grief, while my heart is bleeding and my tears yet flowing, in comes the heir with 'Madam you have no further right or business here.' Or the same in substance though clothed in softer language." And "thus the little accommodations of life that might have administered to the consolation of my disconsolate widowhood and comfort of my old age are wrenched out of my hand." She concludes, "She that likes the picture may take it for I don't, and, in short, Sir, if you don't give me a speci- men for a more complete and better finished piece, I'll wear the crown of my virginity." The prospects for a widow were especially precarious when, as in this case, she was a second wife who would be dependent on the good will of a stepson.

The size of the jointure that could be demanded was propor- tional to the size of the dowry that was offered. The ideal was to guarantee the woman an income which would permit her to live independently in a manner suited to her station. A still more strin- gent stipulation for the security of the woman was to deny the husband any access to the capital of his wife's dowry, leaving the management of it with trustees and allotting only the income for current use. Usually, the capital sum would descend to the wife's children. Sometimes, if there were no children, it would revert to her family. All highly restrictive marriage settlements, contempo- raries lamented, tended to show an unbecoming mistrust of the husband to whom you were confiding your daughter, and this trustee arrangement certainly did. It was invoked only in unusual circumstances, such as those of Isabella Eccleston, who married the family's coachman (discussed in chapter 2).

Marthae Taylor gives voice to the woman's viewpoint about re- taining control over her fortune. She writes to her suitor, "A fool's cap would ill become her at this time of life and she's determined not to wear one." She declares that "she disdains the man that gives no better proof of his passion than the desire of being absolute master of her person and fortune. What? Shall I bribe high to en- slave myself? Resign all and then cringe to my master's purse for a pair of shoe strings?" She was also determined that her hard- won money should stay in her own family. She writes to a friend, "Have I been caring and scuffing in the world so many years for bread to eat, raiment to put on, and to improve an original small fortune . . . to give the said original from my ancestors into a strange family forever?" If she has children, she continues, "they should have the principal to them and their heirs forever, but for default of such issue to return into my own family." Whether be- cause Marthae Taylor's strictures reflected considerable hesitation on her part or because they finally discouraged her suitor, the mar- riage never took place.

As settlements tended to increase in complexity, there were sometimes such provisions as a personal allowance to be paid to the wife or a residence to be set aside for her use as a widow. The woman's family's ultimate goal was to insulate her from the all-powerful authority of a husband. These extensive legal arrangements were used only when the sums involved justified them. The vast majority of marriages were celebrated with nothing more than a verbal agreement, but where it was possible, even in modest circumstances, the bride's family would try to contribute something toward the new household. Counterpointed with these financial considerations was a vast range of intangibles. The social status, the physical appearance, the age, the reputation, the health, the geographic location, the religion (especially among dissenters), the occupation, and, of course, the affection of the candidates all came into consideration to a greater or lesser degree.

Mary Filmer writes to her son, John, thanking him for "a proposal from Mr. Drake of an offer of marriage to your sister Amy." She continues, "The character I have always heard of him inclines me to hearken to it," and adds that she believes "he is a man of too much honour and veracity to endeavour to represent his circumstances in a better light than they really are." She observes that to do so would not only be an act of deception but would also serve to bring "him into difficulties afterwards."

A discussion follows concerning Mr. Drake's financial position: "As to the farms, their value will be more or less according to what condition they are in." After suggesting that this be looked into, she turns to Amy's prospects: "As to your sister's fortune, she has 3,075 pounds in the three percent bonds annually consolidated which produces 92.5 pounds per annum." Her main concern is not so much that they are getting a fair exchange for Amy's dowry, but that the two will be able to manage: "It is to be considered whether this added to his will bring them in sufficient for a comfortable, decent maintenance suitable to their station in life." Such a sum was itself a variable, she recognizes, "and will depend a good deal upon his disposition, whether he is a man extremely inclined to expense or not." As to her daughter, she avers, "I think I can vouch for her good economy as far as will be consistent with decency and credit." However, "there will be a great difference in the expense between maintaining a family and each of them living single," and "I would have him think of this as well as we, before they engage their affections, being at present quite strangers." She concludes with a sentence which embodies much of the spirit of the century's marriage negotiations: "If after this is weighed they think upon acquaintance their tempers will be agreeable to each other, I shall be willing to part with her, though I shall greatly want her good service and company."

The match begins with prudent considerations of the man's good character and his fortune. Filmer considers both essential to her daughter's future happiness. "The character I have always heard of him" inclines her to the match, but it is also necessary to have a "comfortable, decent maintenance suitable to their station in life." In an age when the most ordinary household tasks involved labor that was hard, unremitting, and often unpleasant, the happiness of a wife would be enhanced by certain amenities.

Elizabeth Tomlinson puts the case well. Writing to her father-in-law to thank him for explaining his own financial affairs, she states that if her husband had been equally frank "most probably it would have made no difference in my sentiments," but she would have preferred to know the truth: "I am certain in my own mind that it is not riches that can make us happy, but still there must be a sufficiency," which "we generally estimate according to our bringing up." She concludes philosophically, "I hope I shall be content with whatever I may have. . . . I am certain that if your son is but as kind and affectionate to me as I have often heard him say you are to Mrs. Tomlinson, I think that I shall have little more to wish— for in my opinion no fortune in the world can compensate for want of happiness at home." Happiness at home was also a primary consideration for Mary Filmer; after all the prudent considerations are weighed, the couple themselves must discover "upon acquaintance" whether "their tempers will be agreeable to each other." This was, allowing for infinite variations in emphasis, the usual posture of parents regarding the marriage of a child.

More typical of the seventeenth century is the precisely calculating note which enters the correspondence of 1668 between Ann Massingberd and Henry Brondbeth concerning the marriage of her son and his daughter. She writes, "Since you have been informed of my son's estate in land, I shall tell you that for his wife's portion I shall expect £4000 at least." This, she continues, "may be laid out in land, or otherwise settled for them for present maintenance as shall be thought fit." She concludes, "If we meet such additional maintenance, such jointure shall be settled as I hope may be approved and thought reasonable of each party." Henry Brondbeth begins his reply, quite suitably, in a very businesslike manner: "Madam, in answer of yours of the second present. . . . I judge the common rule is whoever gives £4000 with his daughter will expect £1,200 per annum at least in present possession, out of which a jointure of £400 per annum is to be made." The only reason for "any considerable alteration to this rule," he adds, is "through some defect in nature or morals or that nature or morals hath something adorned the person above the ordinary line of woman." He concludes, "If you think meet to give way unto such reasonable proposals as are usual, I shall be ready to wait on you."

A canny negotiator, Ann Massingberd was not going to play by someone else's ground rules. "I have not heard of such a rule as you speak of," she bluntly begins her next letter. "Agreements made by some are no rule for all others." She suggests, "If you like not my proposals, do you propose what you would have or do," warning him that "what has been proposed in possession and reversion" will, she doubts not, entitle her son to "the like estate at least upon equal terms without defect of nature or morals." Evidently she found especially infuriating the implication that, in order to reap the financial benefits to which she aspired, her son would have to settle for damaged goods. Not surprisingly, the match was not made.

Two years later the beginning of another negotiation for her son reveals still another factor in the equation. "My son is free enough," she writes, "but if you refuse a Northamptonshire gentleman of £1100 per annum in possession because of the remoteness, though the next county to yours, you give me small hopes of accepting my poor son, though I could give him the revenue in possession which you mention." She then concedes, "The truth is I cannot promise to give him in possession and reversion above £600 per annum certainly." She adds that they should "consider the sobriety of [her] son, his pleasant and suitable employment," and holds out an additional carrot: "I name not his possibility of a very large estate, if the youth his cousin should chance to die." Again, personal and financial factors interweave, but here there seems to be a substantial emphasis on a monetary quid pro quo rather than simple concern for the welfare of the couple.

The correspondence of Thomas Papillon, dated 1666, concerning the marriage of his son to Dorothy Cartwright, the ward of Lord Townsend, is a good seventeenth-century illustration of some of the issues involved in the numerous marriages between country gentry and prosperous merchants. Such matches were common from the highest social levels down to the village tradesperson and farmer. Usually, the merchant family was seeking to ally with a landed family both because of the social prestige that land conveyed and because of the potentially greater stability of a fortune based both in commerce and in land. The landed family were usually seeking money either to improve the estate or to rescue them from debts. In this instance, lack of land on the part of the Papillon family was considered a grave disadvantage by the girl's parents, who felt that trade was unstable. Thomas Papillon writes, "As to my quality, I hope that will not be objected against at this day when persons of the greatest figure count it no dishonour to match into merchant's families." He then adds, "And I may say by descent I am a gentleman. My Grandfather was a person of great repute in the court of France." (The Papillons were a French Huguenot family who emigrated to escape religious persecution.) He goes on to specify that his ancestor "was Captain of the Guard, too, and employed in many public services by the great King Henry the fourth of France."

He then turns to finances: "And as to estate, I do not find, all circumstances considered, but that my proposals are every way answerable to the lady's portion." He promises, "She will live and enjoy as much or more plenty and content than any estate of £2500 per annum is capable to afford," and in the future, "besides what I settle in marriage, if God please to preserve me I intend a further blessing to my son in money, having no other to bear my name but him." (Unlike landed estates, which were usually entailed, merchant wealth was usually at the disposition of its possessor, so this assurance on the father's part would be an important consideration, although it would not be binding.) His son's character should be an important factor to consider, and he asserts, "I must say of him that he hath been always a dutiful child, . . . sober and free from all the vices and debauchery of the age." Furthermore, he is "of a very kind and loving nature so as to make a wife very happy," and finally, "if this affair succeeds the lady will be sure to have the virginity of his affections." The match did not succeed, and a little while later Thomas Papillon writes to a friend, "I have wholly conformed to your advice and have put a full end to that affair." He defends trade, adding, "I suppose all persons have not the like opinion of merchants and that some will count it advantageous to have two strings to the bow through land and trade. I am sure (and you know it) the latter affords more plenty and content though the other be a good stake in the hedge."

Meanwhile, the feelings of the young people whose fate was being decided by their elders can be perceived in an anguished letter from Phillip Papillon to "the Virtuous Lady Dorothy Cartwright." He writes, "Till I had the honour to see you, I did enjoy myself" through "pleasurable satisfaction . . . in the affection of my dear parents towards me, entirely depending on their care of and provision for me." All is changed and, he laments, "How it is now I cannot express." Yet "duty obliges me and interest engages me, and so both conscience and reason fix me in this resolution: to leave myself to their disposal." Nevertheless, he is in an agony of suspense, "while I hear nothing from them." He had hoped that all would be settled, and that he would by now "have had the liberty of making my addresses and opening my mind to your dear self." Meanwhile, he writes, "I find such workings and discomposure in my own spirit as makes me restless," and "after many turnings and tossings of my cogitations this way and that way," he wonders "what can all avail if there be not a reciprocation of affection."

He reounts some of his thoughts: "How can that be expected on so little knowledge?" But then, if he is in love, "Why may there not be a sympathy and the same workings in one as another?" The dilemma is, "How shall that be known since there is no freedom of access?" and, terrible thought, "What if my father proposes elsewhere and bar me here?" The result, he states, was that "this paper received a commission to attend you, dear Madam, and to supplicate that if a further prosecution be not unacceptable to yourself some intimation may be given me for encouragement." He also asks that "some way be found out for access." He hopes that "any obstacles on the part of your relations may be removed," and speedily, "lest my father otherwise do engage." He points out that her being an orphan has certain advantages: "God's providence having deprived you of your parents, you are more free and in a capacity of resolving." He urges her, "Dear Madam, let me receive a comfortable answer that I may not suffer, but ever have the felicity of being yours." The marriage never came to be. Thomas Papillon felt that he had been badly treated, and that Dorothy Cartwright's guardians were underhanded and greedy.

Even when the outcome was successful, lengthy negotiations could be a trial to the young couple. Susannah Isham writes to her brother about a prospective marriage in the family. After describing the consultations, she says, "I believe it will be a match but I'm afraid not for a good while. . . . The young folks seem to be much in haste and wonder at their dallying." She comments, "My Father raises so many scruples and difficulties and Mr. Lyne is so dilatory and incredulous that 'tis enough to distract anyone that has anything to do with them." And, in conclusion, she prays, "Heavens defend me from being engaged in such an affair and they to have a hand in it."

Edward Knatchbull's marriage was also delayed by the negotiations of his elders. On the fourth of May he writes happily to his parents, "Everything is settled with respect to Miss H. as far as I could settle it. I have spoke to her" and she "very readily consented to my proposals." Clearly, the young couple themselves are playing a far greater part in this courtship of 1780 than was permitted Phillip Papillon in 1684, a difference that reflects the contrast between the centuries. Knatchbull adds that he hopes that Mr. Filmer, Miss H.'s guardian, will "in the course of a day or two . . . wait upon" his parents. The young couple are accommodating to each other's wishes. His fiancée has agreed "to be settled as near Hatch [his family estate] as possible," he is happy to report, and, at her desire, he has declined a commission in the East Kent Regiment.

At the end of the month serious negotiations were under way. On returning from Kent to London with Mr. Filmer, Knatchbull writes, "Miss Hugessen is very happy that it is so settled that we are to live at Hatch," and assures his parents that "nothing will be wanting on the lady's side to make everything happy." On 1 June difficulties begin to appear. "I received my Mother's letter last night by which I find that Mr. Filmer's proposals about settlements were such that you did not quite approve of them." He goes immediately to Mr. Filmer and reports to his father that Mr. Filmer "says he shall be happy to give any of your friends a meeting in London" and that "he does not doubt but at a second meeting everything will be easily settled." A negotiator is sent to London and on 20 June Edward Knatchbull happily reports to his parents, "Everything was settled to my satisfaction and I hope you will approve the plan." He adds optimistically, "As things are now in such forwardness I thought I might now think of ordering carriages." Five days later, still hoping that they will "agree to everything," he writes, "Miss H. and myself have fixed upon the colour of our carriages. The coach is a Devonshire brown and the phaeton a green." He concludes his letter by declaring, "If you approve of it, it is my intention to bring matters to a conclusion as soon as possible."

However, on 18 July the parts in the settlement his parents had objected to were being clarified by Mr. Blake, a lawyer. Miss Hugessen's estate, his father has complained, does not produce "a neat thousand pounds a year." Mr. Filmer replies that "he imagines it will produce full that, real money, but cannot possibly be answerable for it." By a verbal agreement (Mr. Filmer does not insist on a formal covenant), Edward Knatchbull's father will allow him an annual allowance of £300 per year; the young couple, in turn,

106

will pay £600 toward the household expenses at Hatch. It was August before the agreements were finally signed and the couple could marry.

Not surprisingly, considering the great importance of marriage for determining one's future, matchmaking was a universal avocation. The eagerness of women to marry, especially if they were of a "certain age," was often remarked. Elizabeth Wheeler comments, "Cousin M. seems much satisfied with a change of her condition. I believe she did not want much courting, being resolved to embrace the first opportunity that was agreeable, she being almost in the number of old maids." And Elizabeth Rogers writes while visiting in London, "Cousin Nelly has not as yet got a Spark, but I tell you something. She and I were alone with a widower two hours and more. He has two sons but it won't be thought unproper for Nelly if we can bring it about."

Despite a general eagerness on the part of women to be married, custom demanded that they maintain an attitude of indifference or even of aversion. The lady who is the otherwise anonymous author of *The Whole Duty of a Woman: Or a Guide to the Female Sex from the Age of Sixteen to Sixty* cautions her readers that a young woman should only listen to proposals which are presented to her by her parents. "This course," she writes, "will repel no suitor but such as it is your interest not to admit," and, equally important, "it is most agreeable to virgin modesty which should make marriage rather an act of your obedience than your choice." Young women who actually encourage suitors "give cause to suspect they are spurred on by somewhat too warm desires" (57). Even in an approved courtship, she cautions, "as your love kindles . . . be sure to keep it from blazing outwardly" (58). Lady Bradshaigh, distressed by Olivia's conduct in Richardson's *Sir Charles Grandison,* comments, "There is something so monstrous in a woman's coming to court and make love in plain terms (be the man Sir Charles Grandison or an angel) that I can hardly suppose it possible." She then acknowledges, "Yet it is, I know it is. I have a lady, a proud lady, now in my thoughts who lowered herself in the like manner." Henry Fielding makes comic use of this convention that proper ladies were always supposed to seem sexually cold, needing the most ardent courtship by lovers to arouse them, in the opening portion of *Joseph Andrews.* The chaste Joseph is puzzled by the strange behavior of the amorous Lady Booby and her waiting-maid Mrs. Slipslop who try to seduce him while preserving the outward forms of decorum.

In *Camilla* Fanny Burney challenges courtship customs, showing in the courtship of Camilla and Edgar the difficulties that the usual protocol could create. Mr. Tyrold, Camilla's father, has cautioned her that while perhaps in equity women should be able to choose for themselves, in fact, since "where there are two parties, choice can belong only to one of them," propriety dictates that "Man must choose Woman" (358). She will, therefore, have only a negative vote, and it is in her best interest "to combat against a positive wish" and to exercise the utmost discretion so that she does not become an object of compassion by revealing "an unreturned female regard" (361). Such delicacy, he explains, will protect her reputation; if she should eventually marry another, she "will be shielded from the regret that a former attachment had been published," and, if she should not marry at all, she will be saved "from a blush that the world is acquainted it was not by your choice" (362).

Edgar, meanwhile, is being cautioned by his tutor, Dr. Marchmont, who has experienced two unhappy marriages. After his first wife's death he discovered from her private writings that she, still possessed by an earlier passion, has merely endured his affection; he therefore advises Edgar to be sure of Camilla's love before he makes any declaration of his own. When Edgar asks incredulously, "But . . . why did she accept you?" Marchmont replies, "Ask half the married women in the nation how they became wives." Citing the advice of relatives, the fear of remaining a spinster, and the need for financial security, he explains that "those who cannot solicit what they wish, must accommodate themselves to what offers." Marchmont's analysis points to the problem many young women faced and undoubtedly expresses the truth about many marriages of the period. His second marriage was to a "pleasing and innocent young creature, who gave me, unsought and unwished for, her heart." In this case, the marriage is unhappy for him because it is "unmarked by any consonance of taste, feeling, or understanding" (644). To avoid this error, Edgar must scrutinize Camilla's every word and action, pondering whether her behavior would bring happiness in future years, and whether it is entirely suitable as wifely conduct. The first command becomes an almost insuperable obstacle because her father's advice to Camilla precludes her showing any sign of affection, while the second leads Edgar to exaggerate minor faults and misinterpret youthful high spirits as symptoms of dangerous frivolity. He becomes, in fact, rather a prig.

With Camilla earnestly trying not only to conceal her preference for Edgar but actually to conquer it, while he waits for a spontaneous sign of affection lest she agree to marry him out of interest rather than love, the courtship is in trouble. The problem is exacerbated by Edgar's careful weighing of Camilla's every move from the hypothetical distance of their golden anniversary. The advice of both Mr. Tyrold and Dr. Marchmont is based upon social realities, however, and certainly echoes the wisdom proffered by conduct books. The difficulties encountered by Camilla and Edgar illustrate the difficulties inherent in the conventions of the age. At the end of the novel, Dr. Marchmont condemns his own advice, acknowledging "its injustice, its narrowness, and its arrogance" (913), but Mr. Tyrold's advice is never regretted or criticized. Through this novel, then, Burney seems to advocate greater openness and candor for men in courtship but draws back from recommending the same for women.

The courtship customs of the time are also questioned in Sarah Scott's *The History of Cornelia* when the heroine, in the course of one of her adventures, comes upon an Arcadian village where all the inhabitants have "a contented way of life" (96). Here the men all assist with women's tasks "when not employed in tillage," and a suitor courts his mistress not "by whispering tender things in her ear, and languishing and sighing"—such a man would be seen as lazy—but rather by vying in helpfulness, and "he who knit or spun most, or otherwise showed his industry in the most effectual manner, was looked upon as the truest lover" (97). Since the image of a man spinning was often used as a ridiculous example of reversed roles to denigrate women's desire for learning or other perceived masculine attributes, Scott is questioning not only courtship but the general pattern of relations between the sexes, suggesting that more androgyny is desirable. In the same vein, the women here are not coy, but "declare their sentiments as freely as the men," and while "their reserve gave no pain to the men," reciprocally, the men "never were so presuming as to give fears to the women." They are "like our first parents before the fall; their innocence as unblemished, their happiness as uninterrupted, and their tenderness as delicate" (98). Since no one is either poor or rich in this rural utopia, marrying for financial advantage is unheard of.

Given the fairly usual situation of a young woman eager to marry but restrained by rules of conduct from showing any interest lest she be thought to harbor unsuitable "warm desires," matchmaking was, on the whole, a helpful pastime. Lucy Aspin writes to Miss Rogers that "a cousin, Ralph Hawtrey, is come from Ireland."

She reports him to be "a very agreeable young gentleman and in very good circumstances." At dinner they drink Miss Rogers's health and Lucy Aspin assures her friend, "I told him what a great fortune and what a charming pretty lady you was. He seemed mighty attentive." There is no record that a match was successfully completed. The two attractions mentioned here, money ("great fortune") and attractiveness ("charming pretty lady") are, as one would expect, the principal factors in matchmaking. It was often remarked that the latter was useless without the former.

Marthae Taylor writes of an acquaintance, "She's about sixteen, tall and slender . . . sweet countenance, a genteel symmetry runs through her whole form." She continues, "She's rather grave in her deportment, humble, modest and very good natured." After a further listing of admirable qualities, she concludes, "But after all this there is a great fault, or to speak more properly, a great misfortune. . . . She has no fortune." Anne Warde writes, gossiping about the marriage of Captain Wrightson and Miss Bland, "She is extremely young, not at all handsome, but she has a fortune to outweigh everything else. It is very large at present, but is to be £5,000 a year more at the death of her mother. Very convenient I dare say to Mr. W." Anne Chaytor writes on two occasions urging her brother to marry a rich bride. In April she informs him that Lady Lee "has found out a wife for you. She has six or seven thousand pounds for fortune and at her own disposal. She is a pretty well-bred woman under twenty and she had kept her father's house for some years before he died." This came to naught, and in December she writes much more cynically about her brother's marriage prospects: "I am sorry you could not like there; it would have been very convenient in many respects. If she be old Ned Burdett says she may die of her first child and then you may get another."

Concern with a wealthy match touched most rungs of the social ladder. The Countess of Banbury writes to her son, "I could recommend an agreeable acquaintance at Hammersmith Mills, a gentleman, his wife, and one sweet amiable daughter, £45,000, ten on the day of marriage. Just twenty-one." She adds, undoubtedly to stir competitive instincts, "Mrs. Barker wishes her son could have her." And Anne Warde reports, "Mr. Wright the barber married his fifth daughter to a Mr. Edwards, an Irish gentleman. The lady is only eighteen, but as it is an advantageous match in point of fortune the impediment of her youth which was at first an objection is overcome."

In the eyes of some, however, money could not compensate for other defects. Mary Trenchard writes a friend about Mr. Turner, whom she describes as "a very queer mortal, a perfect citizen. Neither you nor I could spend an hour in his company without being sick of him." She continues, "I don't know whether he comes into the country to buy an estate or a wife, but according to my judgement the lady that marries him should be obliged to eat gold like Midas by way of having enough of what she sells herself for." And Caroline Powys comments, "I believe you've heard Miss Gatahier is going to be what is called well married, but 'tis never my sentiments that a fine girl exceedingly clever can at eighteen really esteem a man above fifty." She adds, "But if the man will think so he must take the consequence. At present he's in the South of France for his *health*."

Social position was another factor in matchmaking. Anne Foley writes angrily of her brother's prospective bride, "If you please you may call a tinker's daughter a tradesman's daughter. Was not her Uncle John your grandfather's man; was not her Aunt Eals your Aunt Master's maid? Was not John Oliver your father's butcher many years?" Furthermore, "I am sure I have more reason to know her than you and I always took her for as simple a creature as ever I conversed with in life and you are not the first man that has took simplicity for modesty." She warns him, "If you marry her I don't care what her behaviour is to me, for I don't desire to have any correspondence or to keep company with her when I can avoid it." Vere Isham comments on another match, "What furnishes the discourse chiefly here at present is Sir John Danver's match who was married last week to a daughter of Mrs. Hutchins. Most people think the young woman ventures a great deal for a ladyship."

Still other factors could outweigh both fortune and social position. Margaret Blanchard urges her nephew, "Marry in some reasonable time, for I should be sorry you should let the estate go out of the family for want of heirs." She urges him to come down to the country so that she can give him her best advice "as to the choice of a wife. I don't much like your London ladies." She advises, "You ought to consult a good woman and one likely to bring you heirs and not mind the largeness of her fortune, for sometimes for that reason people marry women not capable of bringing children into the world."

The courtship of Anne Woodgate and Edmund Mapletoft foundered because of his fears for her health. Upon being presented with a living in Hertfordshire of £300 a year, the clergyman felt able to propose marriage. He writes to Mr. Woodgate, explaining that he has an additional private fortune of £90 a year, that he is forty-two years old, and that he gives as a reference Mr. Manesby, who "is perfectly acquainted with my circumstances and connections and will very readily answer any inquiries you may do me the honour to make." He also writes to Anne Woodgate herself, that "since it is two full years since he had the pleasure of meeting her with Mr. and Mrs. Humfry at Mr. Manesby's, she probably will not be able to recollect him," but asking permission "to wait upon her." Her reply was favorable, and he writes, "It affords me great consolation to find your affections are not engaged, and should it be my good fortune to be the object of them I will envy no man's happiness." His courting evidently went well, but some months later he writes to Mr. Woodgate, "I request the favour of you to give me your opinion of your dear daughter Anne's health." He explains, "When I had the pleasure of seeing her in the Summer I flattered myself she had gained ground of her disorder, but the relapses she has had since have almost led me to despair." He continues, "I suppose you will agree with me that with such a state of health as she has unfortunately had these two years, matrimony could be productive of no happiness." He concludes, "Under this idea I have sometimes thought we might as well put an end to that proposed connection," adding somewhat disingenuously that he "should be extremely unwilling to give Miss Anne the least concern."

Her father evidently turned this letter over to Anne for reply. She writes, "Your letter to my father, dear sir, I must own surprised me and very much affected me." She explains, "You may be assured that if my affection had not been very great (and I still flattered myself with returning health) I should before this have declined the correspondence. But believe me my dear sir I am far from accusing you of any impropriety and my health has been so indifferent this winter that I have often had thoughts of writing to you on the same subject." She wishes him "that first and most invaluable of all earthly blessings, health." She concludes, "You have my sincere and best wishes that whenever you change your situation your happiness may be answerable to your merit," and pledges, "Though it has pleased the almighty to prevent a nearer connection I shall ever remain your faithful friend." The exact nature of Anne Woodgate's illness is a matter of speculation, but she mentions trouble in breathing, which, coupled with seasonal variations in her symptoms, suggests asthma. She lived to a good age, unmarried despite subsequent proposals, and was the favorite aunt of her many nieces and nephews.

The most important characteristic of all for a future spouse, it was agreed, in theory if not always in fact, was a good character. This was understood to include both moral virtues and a pleasant disposition. The obligations and duties of marriage were serious and the relationship itself virtually permanent. A wise man or woman thought seriously about undertaking such a grave responsibility. Marthae Taylor responded to a friend's urging her to marry by explaining, "I'm conscious that the duties of a wife and mother are two of the most important in life, and consequently, according to the idea I conceive of them, there lies more difficulty in the discharge of them than there can be in any incumbent on a single capacity." A woman must wait to be chosen, and "a man of worth sufficient to deserve what I think all wives should be may be too wise to make a choice of me." She adds, "I, on the other hand, am too nice to dispense with less." She continues, referring to the suggested suitor, "Those superficial qualifications your friend boasts are no more to me than a good picture or fine music which gives a pleasing entertainment but steals not my heart longer than when I attend to them." She adds, "While myself possessed of some stock of beauty, I resolved to discountenance the man that should be attracted by it." Some, she states, "have discerning enough not to prefer the husk or shell to the kernel." She concludes, "You'll perceive I like to run no risks in matters of such great moment. . . . Alas, I've cracked many a fair nut and found only a worm it it." However, if anyone could give her "an infallible rule to choose by" she would bid good-bye to her maiden state.

Sarah Fox strikes the same note of primary emphasis on character in commenting on her sister's fiancé: "The present candidate for her affections is of a disposition truly desirable—steady in his religious duties, and in the possession of more simplicity of mind than is usually to be met with in one so conversant in life. To all these advantages are added a good understanding and a person uncommonly pleasing." A similar emphasis appears in Anne Warde's report of a recent engagement: "Your lively acquaintance Miss Ibbetson is soon to take upon her the important character of a wife." She then reports that in a letter Miss Ibbetson gave "a very pleasing description of the gentleman," and, from every other person that knows him she has "received a favourable account." She adds, "I am told his fortune is large and what is still more material his disposition and character unexceptional."

An acquaintance of Mary Sturge was less wise in her choice of a husband. "She appears to be a very serious, prudent young woman," Sturge writes. "It seems very strange to me how anyone possessing the thoughtfulness and sobriety that she apparently does, durst venture to form a connection for life with such a wild young man." An optimistic note concludes the letter: "I find by her that his conduct has been a good deal better of late." She adds her sincere wish "for both their sakes" that "a thorough change and reformation may be wrought in him."

Sarah Fox recounts a rather charming romance in which the woman quite unwittingly gained an eligible suitor through her letters. "Her brother," Fox reports, "had a clerk's place in the counting house of a Turkey merchant who was in very affluent circumstances, bore an excellent character and was a seeker after religious truths. Often did this partial brother read him parts of his beloved sister's letters. The piety and sensibility which appeared in them pleased him so much that he thought if her person was as agreeable she would make him such a companion as he wished for." Evidently not trusting the partial brother, "to settle this point he came to Bristol, though he did not disclose the purpose of his visit." The young lady passed inspection, and "on his return he made proposals to her father and mother whose consent he easily obtained." They were very happy to see "their daughter raised from a state of dependence which she had striven to bear with fortitude." It is not clear just what her position was, probably upper servant or governess, but, as in the Cinderella story, the poor heroine possesses both virtue and beauty.

Marthae Taylor summarizes the factors involved in the choice of a spouse when congratulating a friend. "Your affairs are at last brought to so happy a conclusion," she writes. "A competency of fortune, a fair character, a healthy and amiable person adorned with all the virtues and valuable qualities of her sex are blessings that want no addition."

Novels of the period all stressed qualities of mind and character over wealth or social position. In Burney's *Cecilia,* for example, Mortimer Delvile has declared that he sought in Cecilia neither "an heiress . . . nor yet the light trifler of a spring or two" (IV, 56), but "a companion forever" (IV, 57). Sincerity and mutual esteem, he tells her, are just as important as love because they are the foundation for a relationship that will endure "through every period of life." His mother, Mrs. Delvile, stresses that she admires Cecilia for "that wise and uniform command, so feminine, yet so dignified," she maintains over her "passions" (IV, 304).

Mrs. Delvile is also a woman of intelligence and strength of mind. In her youth "she had been married to Mr. Delvile by her relations, without any consultation of her heart or will" (III, 247). Through determined effort she has attained calm but not happiness, since it is impossible to love her husband. "Proud without merit, and imperious without capacity, she saw with bitterness the inferiority of his faculties" and "found in his temper no qualities to endear or attract" (III, 248). She makes the best of it, always acting with strictest propriety and finding some pleasure in her son and her books. Mortimer "loved his mother not merely with filial affection, but with the purest esteem and highest reverence," finding this love a strong motive for good actions because her love for him, while originating in "maternal indulgence," is "no effusion of weak partiality," but dependent upon his rectitude for its continuance. In contrast, "duty and gratitude were the only ties that bound him to his father" (III, 249).

Mrs. Delvile, scorning an opposition founded principally on sordid interest, becomes convinced that her son should marry Cecilia. She feels that even though Cecilia will be disinherited she "offers in herself the noblest reparation" (V, 184). Failing to convince her husband, who remains completely opposed to the match, she nevertheless gives her personal consent. Cecilia is amazed. "Good heaven!" she exclaims, "this from Mrs. Delville!—a separate consent!" (V, 186). The exclamation emphasizes how extraordinary, in the eyes of contemporaries, it would be for a wife flatly to contradict her husband in a matter of such importance as the marriage of an only son. That a woman known as a model of virtue and propriety would do so is almost unthinkable. Mortimer, however, is not at all surprised. "She has always maintained an independent mind, always judged for herself," he explains, adding that she is "no sooner convinced than ingenuous in acknowledging it" (V, 187). Mrs. Delvile's consent is sufficient for both Mortimer and Cecilia, and they marry against his father's wishes.

Despite a general predisposition in women toward marriage as both desirable and natural, an eager lover could find his offer rejected. Teresa Charlton writes to her brother, "As for your Tom, he is quite low spirited and lover-like, quite despairing since his last refusal at Tanfield." She explains, "I understand he is never to go there as a courtier, for the young lady is determined not to have him." The firm but polite letter of refusal is found in many variations. Susan Hanmer's letter to John Williamson is a good example of the genre: "Since your last visit I have given your proposal the utmost consideration the circumstances of the case will admit of and as you could not fail to observe an indifference or rather a reluctance in me to change my condition, you will, of course, be less surprised when I tell you I cannot accept of your obliging offer." She then offers a rather dubious consolation: "Permit me further ingenuously to confess that unless there was a greater probability of your engaging my affections than I have hitherto experienced, you have no reason to repine at my resolutions." She tries to prevent future importunities by adding, "I have now only to entreat that I may be no more solicited on this subject and that I may occasion you no additional trouble. For this reason, I waive the impropriety of writing when I have never received that favour from you and at the same time assure you of my very sincere wishes (perhaps with a better grace than I could speak them) of success and happiness in all your future undertakings."

In a similar vein, Marthae Taylor tries to convince an unwelcome suitor that her refusal is actually a favor to him. She writes, "I thought I had convinced you in our last conversation that I am altogether an improper person to make you a wife, being not only quite the reverse of you in matters of highest consequence, but in those of a lower nature which regard civil life." She continues, "The first is an essential, the latter a necessary to happiness, and I would as soon sell myself to Algiers as marry a man whose sentiments are so opposite to my own, similitude being absolutely necessary to harmony in a married life. This I've learned from my studies on human nature, and that that which is not good for both cannot be good for either." Her letter concludes, "Hence, believe me, I can't do you a greater favour than that of refusing you; so according to the proverbial saying, as we met friends so let us part." The same Marthae Taylor again stresses "similitude" in refusing a younger suitor. She writes that he "can ask nothing modest, quiet, and prudent" that she'll refuse, "but take notice the last is a bar to marrying a man that came into the world some years after her." She will only marry "if a proper occasion offers in a person suited to me in years and every other respect, similitude not being more necessary in anything than marriage." Her letter concludes, "Those who would be happy must match as well as marry, and till I do that I shall subscribe myself M. Taylor."

Apparently financial difficulties were the chief motive for a letter of refusal written by a Dorset lady. (Her signature has been torn off the letter.) "According to your desire I have perused your last but one and consulted my own breast and find there is no possibility of acquiescing to what you propose, for were you really possessed of what you say you have a right to, and what from the good opinions I have of you I believe you deserve, yet even then there would be some points to be settled before I could resign my liberty, for once that is done it is done forever." She prudently observes, "And since it is not in my power to help you out of your present difficulties I will not add to them by plunging with you in an ocean of troubles." Offering doubtful consolation, she suggests, "Perhaps you may find some person of less experience who will not be so cautious with whom you may be perfectly happy, for I have not the vanity to think myself so much mistress of your heart but that another may soon take my place." She concludes on a more gracious note, assuring him that "as you have always said and done everything consistent with a man of honour in relation to myself so I hope you'll believe in gratitude I would not do anything should lessen your merit."

In making such an important decision, it was natural for the devout to turn to prayer for guidance. Sarah Fox records in her journal, "On a subject so important to my happiness, I was fully sensible nothing short of the aid of unerring wisdom would insure a right determination; and I ardently desired that no prospect of worldly ease on the one hand nor timidity on the other might influence any decision." She accepted the proposal.

The same tone of sincere devoutness and piety informs the courtship correspondence of Joshua Wheeler and Elizabeth Tuke, both Quakers. He writes, "And now beloved Friend, though I must acknowledge that poverty, my usual attendant, is my present companion, yet my mind is and has been often since our parting—on reviewing my movements in this weighty affair—attended with a quiet calm." He continues, "A favour I hope will be permitted to continue with me in my future movements. . . . I hope the same may accompany thine. . . . I think we may without presumption entertain a well-grounded hope that our own steppings along are in and under the orderings of unerring wisdom in which we both desire to move." Finally, "may we be so united as to be true help-meets to each other—endeavouring according to ability given to adjust and bear each other's burden so as to be truly one another's joy in the Lord."

Elizabeth Tuke describes the agitation which fills her mind when she thinks of the "momentous change" in her future; then she writes, "After all these cogitations and more was I to give way thereto, I have had to wonder nearly to astonishment at the almost perfect quietude which is the result thereof."

Wheeler responds, "It was (and is) truly comfortable to find by thine of the 26th that a precious quietude was the companion of thy mind respecting the matter between us." He notes that this is true for him in his "most favoured moments" and reaffirms that he "is willing to look upon it as a seal that [they] have hitherto moved in this matter under best guidance." He adds, "May it continue with us to the end." Early in the correspondence he speaks of the openness of his letter. "Trusting thou will expect an unreserved freedom on my part, I am careful not to make an excuse for it," he writes. "I hope that freedom may be maintained though perhaps it may only more and more expose my weaknesses," but since after "we be united I well know they will be found out, therefore perhaps it may be well for thee to discover some of them beforehand." Just before the wedding day he writes, "It is a day for which I look forward with increasing hope that it may be blest to me, believing that my motives (however selfish) have been lawfully so." He affirms that he looks forward to joy and that he has "faith to believe it will be permitted to be the case." They did indeed have a happy marriage.

There was considerable jesting about courtship manners during the period. The preening beau and the languishing belle are often the butt of satirists. Marthae Taylor writes jokingly about a journey on which she shared the carriage with "three ladies from York and an old bachelor with whom we did not fail to divert ourselves all the way." Evidently, they considered the "old bachelor" fair game for she reports they "all courted him by turns." Describing her own performance, she states, "For my part I did not scruple to mimic all the arts of his sex." The catalogue that follows is evidence of her idea of the various styles of courtship. "Today I addressed him in the languishing vein, tomorrow in the heroic; now I speak my passion with a certain plainness and simplicity of style, by and by I adorn it with all the flowers of rhetoric and garnish of gesture that my sportive fancy could suggest, nor were sonnets, gentle airs or soft poetry omitted." She continues, "Not yet discouraged, and considering the various tastes of men I next assumed the north country lass and became a downright Miss Hoyden," but, she complains with mock regret, "I succeeded no better. The gentleman had discernment enough to see that all I meant was to pass a few cheerful hours at no other expense than a ridicule of the extravagancies of mankind in love." Mankind in love has been a tempting subject for humor in every period, but the evidence is that actual courtships were far less extravagant than Marthae Taylor implies.

Betty Fothergill's journal gives an account both of the progress of her courtship and of the reactions of a lively young woman to a visit to London. Fothergill was already engaged to Alexander Chorley, the "AC" of her journal, whom she had known from childhood, when she came to stay in 1769 with her uncle, Dr. John Fothergill, the well-known London Quaker physician, and her aunt, his sister. Her comments on various visitors provide insights into her views on men, manners, and marriage. Affectation in all its forms, Betty Fothergill concludes, is the worst of the social vices. She praises Katherine Barclay for "an ease and gentility of behaviour that is very pleasing" and that she thinks "can scarce be acquired but must proceed from a native complacency and a mind free from affectation—that grand foe to beauty and everything that's agreeable." She adds, "I think our sex ought to avoid [affectation] out of mere policy . . . it's a greater enemy to a fine face than the small pox." Henry Beaufoy, on the other hand, provokes her censure: "In entered H. Beaufoy in full dress. He bowed to the company with a most superb air." She laments, "Harry has certainly lost part of that manly sense which once so much distinguished him." Now, "his conversation is adorned with well chosen phrases, but is rather superficial. A certain degree of care about dress is necessary and becoming in every man, but to make it a study is below his dignity."

Another caller gains approval for his lack of ostentation. "Cornelius Rhodes came to pay my uncle a visit after his journey to Switzerland," Fothergill reports. "Most young men return from these foreign tours with more conceit than knowledge and if nature has given them a sensible feeling heart it is exchanged for, at the best, modish affectation." Rhodes, however, "retains his native simplicity." She concludes her estimate of his character in hoping that, "though he is not formed to make a brilliant figure in the theatre of life, he will shine perhaps in its private domestic scenes." Polly Barnes, on the other hand, while "a genteel agreeable looking woman," also "seems to affect a mighty delicate languishing air." Fothergill notes, "They made a very short visit which I did not at all regret."

Boring conversation is the second most grievous social vice in Fothergill's calendar. She recounts, "J. H. was obliging enough to accompany us home in a coach," and "the excellence of horses and the pleasures of the chase engrossed a considerable part of his conversation." She declares, "I have esteem enough for this young man, were I intimately enough acquainted with him, to take the freedom of endeavouring to lessen his propensity and fondness for horses so that at least it would not continually intrude in his conversation. However useful these creatures may be in their station, they are by no means worthy of the principal attention of a man whose pursuits ought to be directed to something more rational and becoming the dignity of his nature." She concludes, with perhaps a bit of smugness, "How miserable should I be with a man of this turn, to think that a beast rivaled me in his affection."

Other bores who come under Fothergill's censure are those who affect speaking in foreign languages and a young man whose sole interest in life seems to be navigation. She feels, in fact, that the company of women was good for a young man because "it gives a polish and delicacy which he would never acquire with his own sex." Women, however, could be equally boring when they talked endlessly about housewifery and child rearing. She remarks approvingly of an acquaintance, Mrs. Hoar, that she "is an agreeable woman and a remarkable good manager of her family, but she does not make that parade with it others do whose whole knowledge is centered in domestic concerns." These women make household management "their constant theme in all companies who are unfortunate to fall in their way." Mrs. Hoar avoids this because her "understanding enables her to make proper distinctions."

Fothergill takes ironic notice of the two chief attractions women have for men—beauty and money. She writes of Jack Hanbury, "He is a great admirer of our sex, and more particularly, like all other men, the beautiful part of it." On the other hand, she reports, "Prissy seems to be good natured and obliging, though no ways else particularly agreeable," and then notes cynically, "but she possesses a power of attraction which few men pretend to resist—that is a fortune of eight or nine thousand pounds." She adds, approvingly, "But this circumstance does not give her that self importance which it is too apt to do to many others." In discussing marriage, Fothergill herself decries both physical attraction and financial security as proper motives. Of a recent match she writes, "I never had an opinion of love at first sight which it seems was the case here as he had never been but once in her company or heard her speak." She comments, "A capricious prepossession indeed and what I should not choose much to depend on, for is not the mind the chief object that constitutes happiness, and does not it require time to discover these internal beauties? Certainly, or I have formed a very erroneous opinion about love."

In another journal entry, Fothergill describes a rustic and rather dull young man who is courting Cousin Elsy. She comments that "with a woman of suitable capacity whose knowledge would not extend much further than his own he would undoubtedly be as happy as he is capable of being and render her the same." Clearly, she feels that her cousin is made of better stuff, however: "If Cousin Elsy accepts of him I shall always attribute her motives to interest and convenience. The idea of raising herself into ease and affluence may for the present have charms but these will soon grow familiar and tasteless." She concludes on an idealistic note, "Without a union of minds that most exhalted station may become wretched and with it the lowest station may in part become happy. It is not external circumstances on which our satisfaction depends; the mind is the source of both happiness and misery."

Union of minds, then, was the proper ground for marriage. On one occasion Fothergill's uncle, who, she reports, "delights in making young people cheerful which is the reason he is so generally beloved and respected by them," started a conversation which drew them "into a dispute upon the prerogatives of husbands and wives." Dr. Fothergill "insisted on blind obedience of the latter to the former," while the young people "as strenuously opposed him." Then, "after he diverted us a little he placed the affair upon a proper footing: that there should be no obligation on one side more than another, but a mutual endeavour to promote each other's happiness." She concludes, "We all concurred in this sentiment and so the affair was amicably adjusted."

Alexander Chorley is, we assume, in Fothergill's eyes a young man capable of participating in a "union of minds" and in this "mutual endeavour"; nevertheless, their courtship did not always run smoothly. "How ungrateful is Man," she writes, soon after coming to London: "I imagined that I had got a Phoenix that would always love me, always be grateful, always be complaisant and in short always be everything, but his letter convinced me he was like the rest." She explains, "In my last letter I ventured to give him some advice upon a few things I had observed with respect to himself—they were slight errors which I knew he could easily correct. Acting the part of a real friend I thought it my place to remark them."

She continues, "I did this in the manner my real regard suggested, and not with the acrimony of a severe critic. Judging of his heart by my own I thought this instance of my friendship would have given him pleasure." For "where is the advantage, where the happiness of this connection but in an unreserved communication of sentiments," since "it is the basis of friendship and its support too." Neither her letter nor his seems to have survived, so the "slight errors" must remain a matter of speculation. The tone of the quarrel, however, is evident from her journal: "But how was I mistaken in my conjectures when instead of tender acknowledgments I received a few cool thanks and several accusations of want of affection and in short an air of coldness and dissatisfaction ran through the whole. It shocked me to see such a spirit of mistaken pride which I plainly saw was the source." And all this "in a man whom I had flattered myself, without mentioning the influence of affection, had candour and good sense enough at least to acknowledge the kindness of the intention." She concludes on a philosophical note: "But it seems none of these Lords of the Creation will bear remonstrances from the lips of poor Contemptible Women." The next day she notes that she answered his letter "in a proper manner." She supposes that he will be expecting a letter of apology, "but I was too conscious in this point of the rectitude of my own conduct to submit to any such meanness." Gratifyingly, the apology comes from Mr. Chorley, who writes to Fothergill's sister "in the most penitential terms" begging her "to intercede with me for his forgiveness." She observes, "This proof of AC's flexibility gave me pleasure. I thought it was not in his nature to persist in an error that might be and was the effect of hasty warmth."

Despite this reassurance, a few days later she records: "December 21st. This day I shall remember from taking the first solemn step toward matrimonial preparations: I may well sigh at the name." She continues, "These men—how came I to be entangled with one of them, though really and impartially my better judgement pleads for a single life? Yet I cannot help proceeding from one step to another, for when any of my former objections occur this AC by one means or another persuades me to think differently." This, she supposes, is "the case with other poor women who are cajoled by degrees to lose their liberty." She speculates about her married acquaintances: "What have they gained by sacrificing themselves to care and confinement? Perhaps a sullen husband, and to increase their joy several children whom they have brought into the world at the expense of their health, perhaps forever." And then "what anxiety, what solicitude does their education certainly inflict, and the more in proportion as the parent is careful to dis-

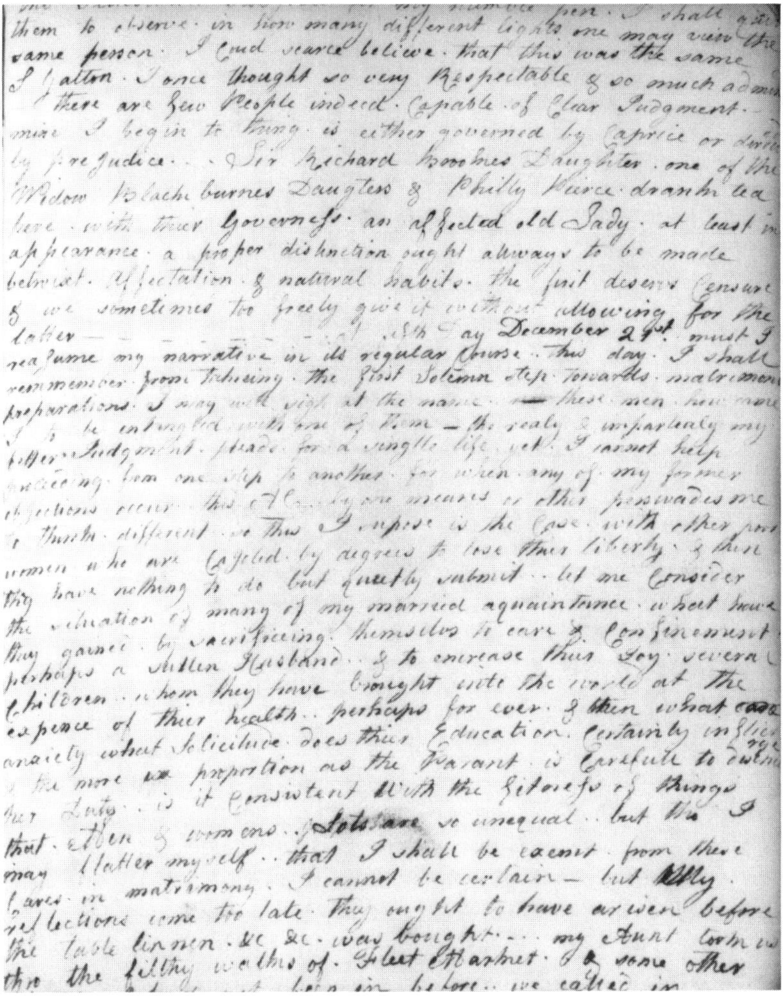

Figure 8. A page from the journal of Betty Fothergill. Vol. 1, December 21, 1769. Reproduced by courtesy of the Library of the Society of Friends, London.

charge her duty." She laments, "Is it consistent with the fitness of things that men's and women's lots are so unequal. Though I may flatter myself that I shall be exempt from these cares in matrimony, I cannot be certain." The entry concludes on a note of amusing, if realistic, anticlimax: "But my reflections come too late. They ought to have arisen before the table linen etc. etc. was bought." Doubts again assail her when visiting an old school friend. "We found her engaged in making a frock for her little Belle: How different did the grave mother appear from the sprightly girl she was at school. Two children and a third near coming are solemn circumstances."

The next day Fothergill receives a letter from her fiancé that, far from being reassuring, is infuriating. "What has he done with his art of pleasing? Perhaps he thinks it's unnecessary to exert it to a person whom he thinks himself sure of," she writes. "The dry inanimate style of this and some other of his letters shows he is either incapable of a lively, animated affection, or that it is already sunk into the insipid regard of a husband." She grows dramatic: "In spite of myself my heart recoils at the thought of such a lover, and how much more at the thought of a more intimate connection." Perhaps some of her dissatisfaction with Alexander Chorley rubbed off on the day's caller: "G. Wheeler paid us a morning visit. He is a good sort of a young man, which in this degenerate age is a great deal, and he has much complacency and good nature. But, yet, wants a manly ease, etc. etc." She concludes, regretfully, "I begin to think I have formed a creature in imagination too perfect to be found."

Fothergill's dissatisfaction with her fiancé continues. "AC in his letter informed me of his intention of being at Lane's quarter meeting that week and requested me to write him there, not considering how little his short letter deserved an immediate answer," she writes. "He shall find himself mistaken in thinking that further solicitude or attention is unnecessary." His next letter does nothing to mend matters. "I received a letter from AC which not a little astonished me." It is in answer to her letter which criticized "his short insipid letters," but makes no mention of her complaint, "which argues so much indifference for me." Furthermore, his letter is couched "in expressions I once thought he could never have made use of." She questions, "Does he renounce all pretensions to a further connection? Unworthy and ungrateful as he is does he think this conduct more eligible than endeavouring to remove the cause of complaint? I shall soon entertain a contemptible opinion of the man who acts in such a manner and can relinquish him without one sigh. This letter gave me not the pain it would have done had it proceeded from any other source," and "it shall serve as a future lesson how I place so unbounded a confidence in a man, let his attachment to me be ever so sincere." Then she admits, "A few tears would force my way in spite of my efforts to prevent them."

Fothergill's sister Molly has received a letter at the same time from Chorley, "who had appealed to her judgement which he un-

124

doubtedly thought would approve his." Sisterly solidarity prevails, however. Molly "too well understood what was due to the character of her sister." They agree that Fothergill herself should preserve silence since his letter to her "deserved not an answer," but Molly writes a letter of reproof. The result was satisfactory. The journal reports in swift narrative, "My sister Molly received a letter from AC. I confess my curiosity was great to know its contents. We retired together into the little parlor and there read it. Oh, Man, you are indeed fluctuating as the wind. What a contrast was this letter to the last, what a change has one single week produced in the language of the writer." Excuses are pleaded—"hasty warmth and a wrong construction of my letter"—but, she declares, "nothing will excuse this action." She then softens. "But as we are all so liable to imperfection, I must pardon this and hope to see more firmness and command of temper for the future in AC."

He decides to come to London to "better compromise this affair in person" and she deliberates her proper stance. "It is not to be treated as a trifling quarrel," she begins, but then thinks that perhaps she will "resolve to entirely overlook it, which will strike him more than any resentment I can express." As an opening strategy she asks her sister "to write a few lines to desire him not to be in haste to come up." One has the feeling that this lover's quarrel is at least in part inspired by a desire to inject a bit of drama and tension into what was in essence the serene and happy culmination of a childhood friendship, but Fothergill may also have been a genuine victim of nervous doubts produced by the seriousness of the step she was about to take and by separation from her fiancé. He writes that he will be in London the following Wednesday, and she records that the letter "threw my heart into no small palpitation, so strange did the thought of an interview appear with a person I seemed to have been so long separated from." When he does arrive she reports, "My ideas the whole of this evening seemed confused: Absence gives a certain strange air and one can scarce think it is the same person one last saw." They had been separated a little more than three months. The strangeness soon wore off and she writes, "We spent the forenoon happily, sister Molly, AC and myself together. We had so many things to say that time seemed to fly much too fast for our purposes." In the afternoon, she continues, "We took a walk in Gray's Inn Gardens and were as happy as unrestrained friendship and something beyond could make us." The reconciliation is complete and she observes in a subsequent entry that absence "could not disjoint the union of minds which is the seat of intellectual love," for "friendship and esteem from a real knowledge of each other's worth is its basis and these absence cannot lessen. They will grow spontaneously when once the root is firmly fixed in the heart."

Their "union of minds" does grow. Fothergill notes, "AC had promised to write a few lines from Coventry which was to have reached me today." The letter does not arrive, but she does not react with anger: "On the whole I was not sorry I did not receive any for I knew he must arrive there very late and be much fatigued with his journey and it would have given me great pain to think he had sacrificed his rest to my satisfaction." The letter is only delayed, however; it arrives the next day, and the "few lines" gave her "great pleasure." Rather than complaining about short letters, she "immediately went into my Aunt's parlour and wrote a few lines to thank him for this proof of attention."

Fothergill's high spirits militated against so submissive a posture lasting long, however, and a few weeks later she writes, "I stole a considerable part of this afternoon to write to A. Chorley, for these unreasonable Men think the duties of civility, relationship, etc., etc., should all be sacrificed to them—and they would think any of these a very insufficient plea for neglecting their Lordships." The couple were married a few months after Fothergill's journal stops. She writes of her journal, "Although the subjects of it may be trifling and the animadversions trite, it will if I should live, some years hence afford me pleasure and perhaps profit to trace back past scenes and to see my own sentiments at that time upon them." Then, she hopes, "I shall perceive the difference a few years has produced and learn from thence not to depend too strongly upon my own present judgement." Journal keeping "must be beneficial in a future retrospection and be an undeniable proof of many foibles self-partiality would persuade us we had never strayed into." Perhaps during the more than thirty years of their married life they did "trace back past scenes" and enjoy sharing this record of one part of their courtship. Fothergill's journal provides insight into the goal of intellectual companionship and mutual respect that had become the ideal, if not in all cases the reality, for courtship and marriage by mid-century.

Nevertheless, the age demanded a certain amount of role playing on the part of the lovers. Demure reticence was the proper posture for young women, lest they be thought the victims of warm desires unsuited to modest maidens. Men were expected to exhibit both adoring deference and evident eagerness. Some of Betty

Fothergill's dissatisfaction at not being courted with sufficient as-siduousness no doubt arose from this general view of the roles proper to the two sexes, in spite of her general preference for open-ness and a true union of minds. In some cases, however, the young woman was quite willing to defy convention and express her whole-hearted attachment in unambiguous terms. The match be-tween Mary Martin and Isaac Rebow was opposed by his mother, apparently chiefly on financial grounds, since Martin writes of "the vexation and inconvenience my want of proper fortune occasions to you." They corresponded in secret, resorting to such subter-fuges as disguised handwriting and newspaper advertisements. The correspondence was begun at Martin's insistence, an unusual breach of propriety since a young woman was never supposed to initiate letter writing. She writes Rebow, "I beg you will recollect how long I solicited for your correspondence before you would in-dulge me with it, and in order to make up for the many years I was deprived of that satisfaction you ought to send me a letter every week, especially when I tell you it is the only comfort I can possi-bly receive when absent from you."

On another occasion she again teases him about his reluctance: "I am very glad you laid the saddle upon the right horse in regard to the delay of our correspondence, for to be sure I solicited for it many years and (strange to tell) should not, I believe, have suc-ceeded at last if I had not in a manner forced you into it. However, I am firmly persuaded the comfort we now derive from it is recip-rocal and that we shall never repent it." In one of Rebow's letters he evidently campaigned that she should write two letters for every one of his, on the grounds that she was less occupied by the press of worldly affairs. She points out "that in strict propriety it ought to be directly contrary." Furthermore, she writes, "I have often told you there is much more reason for my having two for one than you, as the hearing from you is the only pleasure I can possi-bly enjoy when absent from you, whereas you must meet with many things to divert and draw your attention." Despite this sound reasoning, she accedes, admitting, "I live but to comply with every the least of your wishes."

Far from pretending to aloofness, Martin is forthright in expres-sing her feelings: "To say, my dear Mr. Rebow, that I did not think you took a long time to answer my last would be telling you an untruth, for I must honestly confess I had watched the post very anxiously for many days. However, I did attribute it to the right cause." On another occasion she regrets, "I wish I could tell you I had acquired so much philosophy since our last conversation on that subject that I bore the account of your being obliged to defer your expedition to town with all the nonchalance imaginable," but "indeed I thought myself so certain of having you with me *this day* that the disappointment was too great and I could not help being very much vexed. However, from your kind assurances I am confident you will not make me suffer the pangs of absence a day longer than you can help."

As their courtship stretched to eight years, absence grew even harder to tolerate. Martin writes, "It appears to me much more like three years since we parted than three weeks and I can hardly believe it possible that it is only three days since I heard from you. However I flatter myself many hours will not elapse before I shall have the comfort of another letter from you." Apparently he was trying to make arrangements for her to stay near Colchester where his family seat was located, for she writes, "[I hope] that you will tell me what you have done in the lodging way, for I do think if I have only something like a prospect of being with you things will not appear so dreary and tedious."

Martin's disregard for the accepted standards of maidenly propriety surfaces in a lighter vein also. Many of her letters evidently refer to private jokes between herself and Rebow, and where the exact significance of certain passages is not altogether clear, the tone and the subject matter indicate a less than solemn approach to disingenuous modesty: "I am amazed at your fancying it a new fashion for Misses to walk in the park in a high wind, but I have a notion I shall amaze you still more with telling you a certain gentleman's modesty is grown so very great, that because he had looked at a lady's legs, he could not look at her face for fear she would abuse him." In a still more obscure exchange, she reports that "the nights are hotter than ever" and that because she has been sleeping so badly her hostess wants her to change to a cooler room, but "I don't believe it will be of any consequence to change for in my opinion it is entirely owing to the want of my *usual method of going to sleep*. What do you think?" It is probably an error to read anything very improper into this reference, but Martin was not loathe, at any rate, to raise the topic of sleeping habits. On another occasion, she asks, "I likewise beg you will remember to remind my Aunt of the two hens she promised to send me, for I am sure you would laugh to hear the continual complaints I have of the poor cock." She adds, gleefully, "Mrs. Davenport assured me with a very grave face the other day that it was quite a *Sin* and *Shame* to keep him so."

In a letter written early in the courtship, Martin expresses her ideal for marriage: "I sometimes fear you flatter me, but soon recollect you have assured me 'Our hearts are one' and then, of course, your words must be sincere." She hopes that "our sentiments exactly correspond" and that "they may ever do and that we may experience every felicity this world can afford"—which, "according to a maxim of Lady M. W. Montagu's I think we stand a tolerable chance of doing, for she says, 'True felicity consists alone in friendship, founded on mutual esteem, fixed by gratitude, supported by inclination, and animated by the tender solicitude of love.'" Mutual esteem is indeed evident in the letters, and Martin frequently deals with practical problems for Rebow—hiring servants for his London house and taking care of financial transactions—but "the tender solicitudes of love" are also proclaimed without reservation. "What would I give, my dear Mr. Rebow, that I could express half what I felt on hearing your kind assurances of perpetual regard," she writes. "I find it is vain to attempt it, therefore must content myself with begging you will accept the warmest gratitude that a heart entirely your own is capable of bestowing, I never yet uttered a thought to you that was not perfectly sincere, and can solemnly assert in you consists my all and only happiness." And on another occasion she declares, "I only wish you would believe me sincere in what I have so often told you, (viz) 'that in possessing your heart, I shall have everything desirable to me in this world.'" She tells him that except for any inconvenience it might cause him, she would never "desire a sixpence more" of fortune, "for as my favorite Aura says, 'We have health and ease— Is Heaven scant? Here take my hand—We have all we want!'" Martin remained remarkably good-humored through what must have seemed an endless courtship—the letters begin in 1767 and she and Rebow were married in 1776. The result was a deservedly happy marriage.

The courtship correspondence of Elizabeth Jeffreys and Charles Pratt, continued for nearly four years, also gives insight into the tensions as well as the joys that even a loving couple could experience during this often trying time. Although the match was originally opposed by their families, her family did become reconciled, much to Jeffreys' pleasure. The exact cause of the initial difficulty is not clear, although financial inequalities may have played a part since Jeffreys was an heiress, whereas Pratt, although well educated (Eton, King's College Cambridge, Middle Temple), was an impecunious third son. Frances Jeffreys, Elizabeth's mother, writes of the past, "The case was indeed extremely particular and from wrong proceedings on all sides great misunderstanding ensued." She is now very pleased with Pratt as a prospective son-in-law, but lack of money still stands as a barrier. Pratt is energetically riding the court circuit and building up his practice as a lawyer, and the young couple look forward to their eventual marriage.

Pratt writes, "In reality, my dear girl, I have but one cause for complaint in the world which, however, is hard to be cured, and that is present poverty, nor should I complain even of that, but that it is mischievously interposed to delay and protract our union." Three years later, the young lawyer is beginning to make his way: "As to money, if you are half the philosopher that I am, we can be happy together in spite of scanty circumstances. I will not be unhappy while I am possessed of you. Do but resolve the same on your side and we'll both defy the world." A few months later Jeffreys replies to another letter, "You tell me your business succeeds as you could wish and that if I can be content with competency and a moderate station, you may hope to place me far above the lowest, though short of the highest rank. You ask my answer and if I can be satisfied with this. It is as follows, and is the sincere thoughts of my heart—that whatever state I'm destined to with you, I shall be happy. But that you have assigned me is just what I have ever wished to be placed in, a middle station between the two extremes. By the little observation I have made in life I think it much the happiest and am sure it will be so to me. Grandeur I've ever thought brought much more trouble than pleasure to the possessor and were I to choose, I really had rather struggle with Fortune, than be too much favoured by her."

As the actual marriage approaches, further discussions of money ensue. Pratt writes, "Your Mama, to be sure, has a right to apply her own present, if she pleases, and may perhaps expect you should lay out the whole in clothes. If that should be done she will deliver you into my hands very elegantly dressed but in debt, which will not suit so well with our circumstances as if I was to receive you out of debt and but neatly dressed." He says that he really needs to know more about the extent of her debts and the cost of clothes: "For if after your debts are deducted, there should not remain sufficient for that other purpose [clothes] I would rather distress myself than suffer you to make a mean appearance." He leaves it up to her: "If you understand my intention, you are the fittest judge of what should be done so as to steer between sordidness and ostentatious show. I have an entire confidence in your discretion and would rather leave this to your choice, for if I had not been assured of your prudence and regard to me I should never have married you." He concludes, "But indeed, this as will everything else that concerns either of us will concern both equally."

His letter elicited an apologetic reply from her, and he writes, "You give yourself a great deal of unnecessary pains in your last to apologise for I know not what extravagance." He reassures her, "I shall only say that, as long as I have a good opinion of your prudence, I shall always be pleased with your contempt of money. If you have spent something more than usual within these last two years, I shall ascribe it to a desire of pleasing me by being a little more lavish in your dress. You say you have been a great expense to me. For God's sake how can my money be so well employed, as when it is bestowed upon my second self, for all that I have or ever shall get is and shall be as much yours as mine. I should think it as unnatural to reproach myself as you with spending my money. Therefore, if you love me, never say one word more upon this affair, for I never loved you for necessary ends."

Pratt disdained the fashionable affectations of the age. Of a capricious friend who affected the role of a belle, he states, "Hessey is a fool and does not know either the virtue or the happiness of love. None but foolish and worthless people ever change or quarrel. What can this hoydenish coquette mean by having a forest of favourites and loving none? Either she conceals some very serious love under this mask of indifference, or else she loves a carnal unplatonic variety." He directs, "Tell her I won't be imposed upon, and she may as well deny the appetites of hunger or thirst as her inclination for the angelic race of animals called man."

Pratt's and Jeffreys' love, in contrast, is founded on mutual esteem. He reassures her when she apologizes for the lack of literary quality in her letters, telling her they have given him more pleasure than the finest authors: "Yet I do not mean to intimate they owe all their merit to that blind love I have conceived for you. No. They are to unprejudiced persons the letters of a sensible woman." He concedes, "To me they are infinitely higher, as they are animated with that tenderness and affection that make me the happiest of men. Notwithstanding, however, the exceeding love I bear you, I courted you as a sensible woman and as such intend to marry you, for I could never be happy with a silly one, though nature had

Figure 9. A Perspective View of the Grand Walk in Vauxhall Gardens and the Orchestra. Unknown artist. Vauxhall was one of the great pleasure gardens of the eighteenth century, where patrons strolled, flirted, displayed their finery, listened to the orchestra, and partook of refreshments in private boxes (far left). The suicide of Mr. Harrel in the novel *Cecilia* takes place at Vauxhall. Reproduced by courtesy of the Trustees of the British Museum.

formed her the wonder of the world for beauty." He also recognizes that a sensible woman will make many aspects of marriage go more smoothly. When Jeffreys reports favorably on a visit to his family, he writes, "If you are pleased at Kingston, I am happy, for to make a match prosperous the families should marry as well as the couple." His letters adhere to his principles and they are different from the stereotyped lover's in being entertaining as well as passionate. Jeffreys records that they have received high praise when she reads portions of them to her friends, one of whom "is turned half a convert to love on finding a man may be a reasonable creature under these circumstances."

In the same vein, Pratt worries about excesses of romantic emotion on her part. He chides her for a tearful farewell, and she writes, "I could not command my eyes from disclosing the trouble of my heart. They are, as you have told me often, very tell tale things." She adds, "My happiness is wholly centered on you; therefore parting from you to one of my temper is hard to bear." He replies, "Though I can never consent you should love me less, yet I could wish you had more resolution and a better flow of spirits, and therefore I would advise you to get rid of that gravity you seem to indulge as soon as you can. Our love has been a great deal too grave already and should now begin to change its countenance. Upon the whole we have more cause to be happy than wretched. We love one another, are engaged, and all our friends consent to our meeting and hear no other obstruction of all we can wish but our own prudence. . . . I see no reason why you should not be as gay as ever you were, except for this short separation which however will pay us at our next meeting with interest of pleasure. Take my advice, then, my dearest girl, and divert yourself any way you can contrive." He concludes, "For my own part, since I have gained you I am determined not to be sad, but thank providence for this happiness, and trust it for the rest."

Early in the courtship Pratt tells Jeffreys that he no longer goes to many balls and concerts, not because he is "graver" but because his taste in pleasures has changed: "As the great charm that draws young people to these places is the hopes of pleasing each other and making mutual conquests, I look upon them as so many fairs where the men and women expose themselves for sale and therefore are obliged to attend regularly till some opportunity offers of buying or being bought. When this end is obtained there is no occasion to go again to fair till you want to make a new purchase. For my own part I have contracted for a very pretty girl and have done my business, and I shall have no inclination to look out for another." He then notes, "However, I can bear well enough to go some time to enquire how the market goes out of curiosity though I have no business there myself, in which I would have you imitate me, and not mope alone by yourself when I am absent."

On another occasion Pratt writes, "I hope your health improves and I shall find you plumped up when I return, not for the sake of your person which can never endear you more to me if it was the perfection of all beauty, but because health will of course be affected with your natural cheerfulness and gaiety which has been somewhat overcast this last year. But I am apt to think those gloomy days are past." She assures him, "I'm in hopes to meet you rather fatter than we parted; every body tells me my looks are much mended. I think my stays are not quite so big for me as they were."

She also explains her worries about him during his arduous travels: "I, like most fearful women (ready to create uneasiness upon an uncertainty) frequently can't help having a strong suspicion that your good nature has inclined you to deceive me in regard to your health." Speaking of her sadness, she writes, "If you are inclined to chide me for this softness of temper, think of my present situation and only remember our contention of which loves most, and seriously reflect (barring the difference of sexes) how you should be affected in the like case and then if I don't deceive myself I think I am secure from your resentment."

Pratt's letters often speak of his impatience both with the absence necessitated by his following the circuit and with the long wait for marriage. He writes that the circuit will soon end: "This is the extent of my absence which I believe is more irksome to me than you, because I fancy I love the best," a claim that engendered the "contention" mentioned above. He writes ruefully that he is going to visit a married friend: "I shall be enjoying his happiness and wishing for my own. I am quite weary of waiting, and would not spend such another year as the last for the world. I hope you are as tired as myself though I am afraid your modesty won't let you own it."

Letters, they both declare, are their chief comfort, and they carefully mark a variety of anniversaries. "It is now near twelve months since I have been your declared lover," he writes, and on another occasion notes, "I expect to hear from you tomorrow night and to receive as good news as I did by the same post last year when I first heard that you were not disinclined to accept my love, and if I find by the next that your inclination is not altered I am satisfied, for I desire no better news." He demands of her, "Do me justice to own my affection has never flagged since it first began, notwithstanding I have been so long sure of you. So it shall always remain or I will live no longer."

She also notes various milestones. "Yesterday being August the first, it brought to our remembrance how merry we were three years ago." She records, "We endeavoured to recount over the three weeks of our first acquaintance but found ourselves very deficient in many particulars." And on her birthday she writes, "I'm perfectly well in health and I look upon this day as the happiest I ever experienced in the whole four and twenty, as it tells me I was born to be yours."

The letters, naturally, contain exchanges of loving sentiments. Jeffreys writes, "You tell me I have taken total possession of your mind. I must return you your own words, as I can think of nothing which will express my own situation in regard to you so well. You are indeed, Mr. Pratt, ever in my thoughts." And a few months later she writes, "Every letter of yours brings fresh instances of your affections, and you express all your thoughts so naturally that I will not look upon them as flattery but as the real sentiments of your heart." She then adds in modest depreciation, "However give me leave to assure you, I have not the vanity to imagine I deserve all those encomiums you bestow so thick upon me." Cupid has blinded him, and "[I am] conscious to myself you'll not find me that perfect creature you now represent me," for "I even this moment experience how deficient I am, a mind too full of the tender love and esteem I bear you, but at the same time so unfurnished a head that I am sensible it is not in my power to pen my sentiments."

She writes of his letters, "Believe me when I tell you they are my chief happiness at present." Evidently an older friend of the family has commented that in his day it was considered improper for an unmarried woman to correspond with a man, for she continues, "Nor would I be debarred the pleasure I receive in hearing from you and writing to you were this age like that Mr. R. lived in where it would be thought improper." She concludes, "I'm of the opinion that where the world is so very unreasonable in their notions, they are not to be complied with." Pratt replies, tongue-in-cheek, "How the girls in Mr. R.'s days came to be so much more reserved than ours I don't know, but I should be apt to suspect he had taken to prevail with them to do *bolder* things than write letters to their lovers. And yet I have got no further in a year and a half's courtship, so if you are to be the example of modern boldness, I will match the coyness of our age with any other."

Despite his scorn of many of the more extreme affectations of lovers, Pratt did adhere to the convention that while the man was expected to evidence sexual desire, the woman was presumed to be immune if not actually averse to "warm thoughts." He must have known, however, that his fiancée was far from prudish—in one letter she writes, "If kisses will pay the obligation I lay under to you for refusing the brief from Dorchester my lips shall be entirely at your service till you are fairly tired of them"—and he often jokes delicately about future pleasures. He writes, "I am now writing about seven o'clock in the morning when I suppose you are fast asleep and I hope dreaming of me, for this is a time when dreams are the pleasantest." He continues, "If I were to frame a wish for my own delight it would be to be suddenly transported to Bedford Row and to steal a kiss just at this instant before you waked." Her reply was apparently not indignant, for his next letter begins, "I have received yours. I thank you and can't help wishing again to be in that happy situation I longed for in my last, especially since you seem to doubt whether you could be very angry. I am sure you would not, for I should make no improper attempt. Yet, I would have you make good use of your time and be angry now you may, for I hope it will not be very long before this power of being angry will be taken away from you and I may be where I please without incurring the least spark of your ladyship's displeasure."

During the July preceding their marriage he jokingly admonishes her, "I hope you grow fat and are cheerful and learn to bear hot weather better or else I must order the worked bed to be made as big again." Throwing aside the conventions of maidenly modesty, Jeffreys writes to him later that summer, "You tell me 'You're happy in thinking our affair, which has hung so long, begins to draw towards a conclusion.' Judge of my love by your own as I'm not ashamed to own to you what you merit in so great degree, and you will know my happiness is not inferior to yours on this occasion. Be assured there is nothing I wish so ardently for as to be wholly yours and yours only." He replies, "I can't help thanking you for confessing your own joy at my approaching happiness. This gives me infinite pleasure and makes me love you, if possible, ten times the better."

A relative of the couple, Maria Jeffreys, commented on the match, saying, "In such a union I foresee a viable probability of a happy state, for when a man of character with good sense and a knowledge of the world and a woman of a sweet temper and complying disposition and no strangers to each other make it their choice to be companions for life, I am led to believe from their prudence there may arise such an established friendship to render a married life the most happy situation that can be experienced." Her prophecy was correct. Pratt gained renown as a lawyer, was attorney general under William Pitt, sat in Parliament, and became lord chief justice of the Common Pleas, acclaimed a popular hero when he acquitted the outspoken rebel John Wilkes on legal grounds. He later served as lord chancellor. He was knighted, created baron of Camden, and finally the first earl Camden. The couple had four daughters and one son and lived together most happily for thirty years, until Elizabeth Pratt's death.

In a more general sense, however, Maria Jeffreys' statement illuminates the ideal of courtship of the age. The man and woman each bring certain qualities to the union, although usually it would be argued that these qualities should be different. The man should have "character with good sense and a knowledge of the world" whereas the woman should be "of a sweet temper and complying disposition." They should be "no strangers to each other" and it should be freely "their choice to be companions for life." From their prudence, Maria Jeffreys continues, "may arise such an established friendship" as will "render a married life the most happy situation." The idea that friendship is a more desirable basis for marriage than are the transports of love recurs often, and indicates, perhaps, a realistic acknowledgment of marriage as a mutual enterprise dependent upon partnership rather than dominion, best grounded in esteem as well as physical attraction.

The novels of the period strongly supported this view of courtship and marriage. They uniformly decried forced marriages, although they also usually supported filial obedience. However, when the reasons for parental refusal are portrayed as unworthy, as in Henry Fielding's *Amelia* or Fanny Burney's *Cecilia,* the couple are justified in their disobedience. (In each novel, it should be noted, approval is given by one authority figure—the quasi-parental Dr. Harrison in *Amelia* and Mrs. Delvile in *Cecilia.*) Novels also called for greater openness in courtship, criticizing the mores which demanded excessive modesty and shyness in women and excessive gallantry in men. Instead, they showed their idealized couples as seeking a rational companionship which would endure. Women who encourage conventional romantic rhetoric in courtship instead of sounding out their suitors through intelligent conversation are apt, Pamela declares, to find "a strange and shocking difference" when "fond lovers, prostrate at their feet" are changed into "surly husbands trampling on their necks" (438).

While most novels strongly endorsed the first part of the compact understood to govern marriage in the century—that children must not marry against their parents' wishes—they even more dramatically supported the second part of this compact—that no daughter should be forced into a marriage against her will. With their emphasis on mutual esteem between the couple and their condemnation of sordid motives for marriage, novels encouraged the tendency toward companionate marriages based on love rather than on family alliances. The courtship correspondences also suggest that there was indeed a movement during this period toward a courtship which involved the young principals rather than just their families. The letters of Phillip Papillon to Lady Dorothy Cartwright, written in 1684, show a marked contrast to the letters of Edward Knatchbull to Miss Hugessen, written in 1780. This shift toward familiarity and mutual affection as the basis of a happy marriage was fostered by all the novels considered here. The women writers as well as Richardson and Henry Fielding insisted that marriage should be a "high and tender friendship," and that courtship should be an opportunity to explore those qualities of mind and character that would be the basis of an enduring and loving relationship.

CHAPTER 4

Wives

❧❧❧❧ O R   M O S T eighteenth-century women, the role of wife ❧ F ❧ defined their lives once girlhood was past. Marriage, ❧❧❧❧ both in theory and in practice, was seen to be the natural and desirable state for women. In theory it was a condition ordained by God that provided them the widest opportunities for practicing and promoting virtue. In practice marriage was usually the only way that women could achieve some measure of economic security. Forces both positive and negative impelled young women to seek a husband. However, considering the prevailing moral attitudes and legal codes, marrying was, as one young woman declared, "a most courageous act."[1] In this chapter the conduct book expectations of marriage will be described, together with comments on marriage by a variety of women and a picture of some actual marriages, both happy and unhappy, in the words of the wives themselves. Depictions of marriage in fiction will be considered against the background of these real marriages.

Mary Astell, in *Some Reflections Upon Marriage,* writes that "a woman has been taught to think marriage her only preferment, the sum-total of her endeavours, the completion of all her hopes, that which will settle and make her happy in this world." Furthermore, during courtship she "has seen a lover dying at her feet, and can't therefore imagine that he who professes to receive all his happiness from her can have any other design or desire than to please her." At the same time, her "eyes have been dazzled with all the glitter and pomp of a wedding." She "hears nothing but joy and congratulation" and she "is transported with the pleasure of being out of pupilage and mistress not only of herself but of a family too" (56). Unfortunately, "she who is either so simple or so vain as to take her lover at his word either as to the praises he gave her, or the promises he made for himself: In sum, she whose expectation has been raised by courtship . . . will find a terrible disappointment" (57).

The eighteenth-century wife in her marriage vows solemnly pledged obedience and was obliged by these vows regardless of the conduct of her husband. The woman might reign supreme during courtship, but in marriage the roles were reversed. Mary Astell comments, "Let the business be carried out as prudently as it can be on the woman's side, a reasonable man can't deny that she has much the harder bargain, because she puts herself entirely into her husband's power, and if the matrimonial yoke be grievous, neither law nor customs affords her that redress which a man obtains" (28). Lady Bradshaigh describes the relationship in a letter: "The power you [husbands] give up is no more than a cat allows the poor mouse in its claws, giving it hopes of power yet never out of reach, and ready to assert prerogative upon the first effort it makes towards liberty."

In 1699, a conservative clergyman, John Sprint, preached a wedding sermon, later published with the title *The Bride-Woman Counsellor,* which expressed the extreme patriarchal view of a wife's obligations. "'Tis a duty incumbent on all married women to be extraordinarily careful to content and please their husbands" (5). He supports his statement with biblical authority: "Because the woman was made for the comfort and benefit of man (Cor. 11.9, Gen. 2.18) . . . she should be careful and diligent to content and please him, otherwise, she doth wickedly pervert the end of her creation." Furthermore, "because of the woman's occasion the man was ruined and undone (I Tim. 2.14)" and, therefore, "God imposed this task upon her, as a punishment for seducing her husband (Gen. 3.16)."

All difficulties are the woman's responsibility, Sprint instructs, and "therefore it is not the woman's pleading that her husband is hard to be pleased that will excuse her negligence herein." Indeed, "this may be a momento to her of her original sin," since "man in his innocency had nothing of morosity and sourness in his temper." It was after the fall that "the nature of man was sadly changed, his temper grew harsh and severe, and humours became troublesome and tedious." Sprint concedes that "the pleasing of him is now become a business that requires a great deal of art and skill, of diligence and industry." Still, woman has been at fault from the start: "You may thank your mother Eve for it" (16). In addition to biblical reasoning, he cites at much less length a practical reason: "Because upon the doing or neglecting of this, the happiness or misery of a married life doth depend" (7).

The way in which married women were to please their husbands was, according to Sprint, "to love, to honour and to obey them" (9). In each case internal disposition must be reflected in external observances, and regarding honor he chides, "It is a custom more common than comely for women to call their husbands by their christian names, as if they esteemed them at no higher a rate than their very servants" (12). It is obedience which receives the strongest emphasis, however. "I know not of any duty belonging to men or women in the whole Book of God that is urged with more vehemency or pressed with stronger or more cogent reasons than this is. Obedience to their husbands is required from wives as absolutely and peremptorily as unto Christ himself (Ephes. 5.22)." He exempts only sinful or impossible commands (13).

In a section directed to men John Sprint comments, "You may from this doctrine learn how great a friend religion is to the comfort and happiness of man in this life. God hath given such laws for your wife to observe as will, if duly regarded, make her a helpmeet for you" (15). He urged husbands, "Though it is true they are in subjection, yet still remember they are part of yourselves, and therefore let your authority be united with love." His rules for husbands are evidence of the traditional attitude that the proper relationship of the husband to the wife was not one of equality and companionship but rather of parental care and discipline. He gives four rules: "first, By bearing with and pardoning her weaknesses; secondly, By being willing to submit to many inconveniences for her sake; thirdly, By interposing yourself betwixt her and dangers; fourthly, By endeavouring to promote her spiritual good and welfare" (15).

John Sprint's sermon occasioned a certain amount of discussion but surprisingly little real opposition, telling evidence of the power of his use of biblical texts as his chief authority. There was objection to his contention that the wife's obligation to love, honor, and obey must be fully carried out in her every thought as well as in external form.

The author of *The Female Advocate,* for example, suggests, "Methinks it should suffice that the women don't contradict their Lords and Masters, that they tamely submit, and bear with patience what is imposed on them: No, unless they are enamoured of their miseries, and the very desires of their hearts brought under, and in subjection, they are threatened in our author's preface with judgment and damnation" (28). Commenting on Sprint's dictum that a wife must comply with all her husband's commands unless sinful or impossible, she satirically supposes, "She may be obliged to go barefoot twenty or thirty miles to some eminent wood, and thence cut and lug home a bundle of sticks, each of which may be made use of as a pastoral staff to discipline her bones withall" (47). Nevertheless, she agrees " 'Tis granted the Woman was created for the man," and declares that "a woman who . . . put[s] on breeches does certainly pervert the end of her creation" (22). Her modestly argued point is that a wife should be "a social help not a servile one" (21).

The anonymous female author (actually Lady Mary Chudleigh) of *The Ladies Defence: or The Bride-Woman's Counsellor Answer'd* contends, "It would be very difficult for a rational, ingenious woman, were she mistress of never so much virtue and blest with the greatest strength of resolution, if it were her ill fortune to be married to a foolish, passionate, stingy, sottish husband, to have as high an esteem for him as if he were possessed of all those good qualities which she sees and cannot but like in others. I think she may be allowed secretly to wish that he were as wise, as generous, as temperate as such a man, as much a master of his passions, as obliging and sincere as another."

Other important objections to John Sprint's position concerned the inequality in obligations that he proposed and the lack of any forceful plea for moderation on the part of husbands. Lady Mary observes, "And did our husbands treat us with that kindness, that sincerity, I will not say with that respect, for fear that should be thought too much for a wife, but only with that common civility which is due to strangers, they would meet with a grateful return, and have much less reason to complain." However, the writer also declares that she wishes all women were faultless, "and if it is their hard fortune to be married to men of brutish, unsociable tempers, to monsters in human shape, to persons who are at open defiance

142

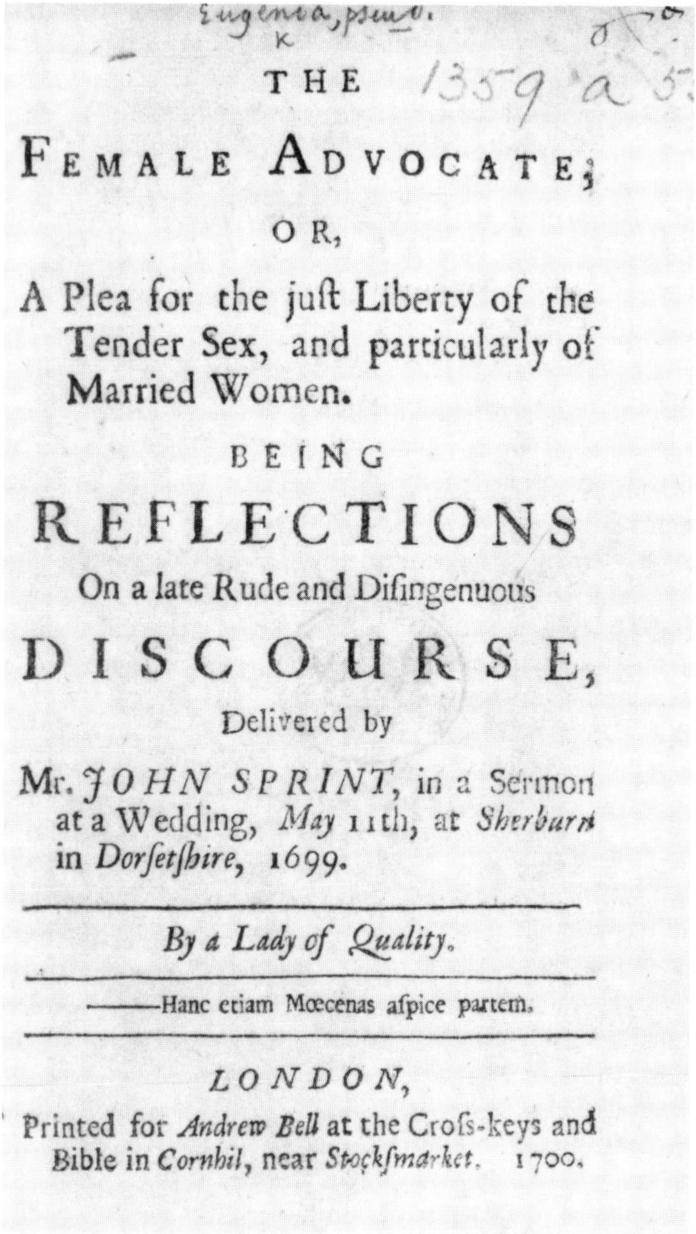

THE *1359 a 5*

FEMALE ADVOCATE;

OR,

A Plea for the juſt Liberty of the
Tender Sex, and particularly of
Married Women.

BEING

REFLECTIONS

On a late Rude and Diſingenuous

DISCOURSE,

Delivered by

Mr. *JOHN SPRINT*, in a Sermon
at a Wedding, *May* 11th, at *Sherburn*
in *Dorſetſhire*, 1699.

By a Lady of Quality.

———Hanc etiam Mœcenas afpice partem.

LONDON,

Printed for *Andrew Bell* at the Croſs-keys and
Bible in *Cornhil*, near *Stockſmarket*. 1700.

Figure 10. Title page from *The Female Advocate*. This illustration is
typical of an eighteenth-century title page, with its long subtitle,
Latin motto, and use of the long *s*. By permission of the British
Library.

with their reason and fond of nothing but their folly, and under no government but that of their irregular passions," even then, she declares, "I would persuade them to struggle with their affections and never leave contending till they have gained an absolute victory over every repining thought, every uneasy reflection."

Her final position is essentially the same as Sprint's: "Though it is extremely difficult, yet I would advise [these wives] to pay [their husbands] as much respect, and to obey their commands with as much readiness as if they were the best and most endearing husbands in the world." This course, she assures, "will not only put a stop to the invidious censures of their spiteful enemies, but give them the possession of that inward joy, that unspeakable satisfaction which naturally arises from the apprehension of having done good and laudable actions."

The Ladies Calling also describes the proper role of a wife. "The first debt to [her husband] is Love, which we find set as the prime article in the marriage vow. It should be the study of wives to preserve this flame . . . and to that end carefully to guard it from all those things which are naturally apt to extinguish it, of which kind are all forwardness and little perversenesses of humour, all sullen and morose behaviour, but of all, I know nothing more dangerous than that unhappy passion of jealousy." Wives "must be nicely careful to give their husbands no color, no least umbrage for it," and at the same time "be as resolute to resist all that occurs to themselves." They are to be "far from that busy curiosity" and always "put the most candid construction upon any doubtful action" (II, 23).

If the husband should make this course of action impossible by boasting of his infidelities, then "a patient submission [is] the one catholicon in all distresses. They are therefore far in the wrong who in case of this injury pursue their husbands with virulencies and reproaches." While "obedience" is "a word of a very harsh sound in the ears of some wives," nevertheless, it "is certainly the duty of all." This comes "not only by their promise of it, though that were sufficient, but from an original of much older date," for it was "the mulct that was laid upon the first woman's disobedience to God, that she (and all derived from her) should be subject to the husband." Therefore, "contending for superiority is an attempt to reverse that fundamental law which is almost as ancient as the world." God "will not make acts of repeal to satisfy the petulancy of a few masterless women," and this statute, if it "cannot awe them into an observance, will not fail to consign them to punishment" (II, 33). It is not clear whether the punishment will be in this world, the next, or both.

In his depiction of the Harlowe marriage in *Clarissa* Samuel Richardson criticizes the concept of unthinking submission on the part of a wife. Clarissa's mother is completely subservient to her husband, always yielding her will and judgment to his to keep the peace. The Harlowe marriage is the very model proposed by the conduct books, where the husband's and father's word is law. In fact, it is just this model that is used to justify the Harlowes' tyrannical stance toward Clarissa, and that also serves to exacerbate the conflict. Clarissa's father sees the question of her marriage to Solmes not in terms of his child's welfare or happiness, but as a test of his power. "Be assured of this," he declares, "we will not be baffled by her. We will not appear like fools in this matter, and as if we had no authority over our own daughter" (I, 192). Mr. Harlowe's attachment to "the prerogative of manhood" which makes him "so *positive,* so unpersuadable" (I, 61), has been fostered by a wife who is always willing to "give up her own will, her own likings, to oblige a husband" (I, 133). Anna Howe condemns a "mother that puts it out of her power to show maternal love and humanity, in order to patch up for herself a precarious and sorry quiet" (II, 287).

Clarissa is loath to criticize her parents, but she does come to agree that her mother's meekness has been morally wrong and self-defeating. "In my mother's case," she writes to Anna, "your observation, I must own is verified, that those who will bear much, have much to bear" (I, 93). She notes that, rather than securing peace, her mother's weakness has encouraged "encroaching," whereas "*steadiness of mind* . . . when we are absolutely convinced of being in the right . . . brings great credit." While she loves her mother, Clarissa comes to see her as a warning rather than an exemplar. When Mrs. Harlowe, trying to persuade Clarissa into compliance, points out, "*I* am forced to put up with many humours," Clarissa replies, "That you *are,* my ever-honoured mama, is my grief. And can it be thought that this very consideration, and the apprehension of what may result from a much *worse*-tempered man (a man who has not half the sense of my father) has not made an impression on me to the disadvantage of married life?" (I, 102).

In *Some Reflections Upon Marriage* Mary Astell gives a vivid portrait of the miseries for a woman of an unhappy marriage. "To be yoked for life to a disagreeable person and temper, to have folly and ignorance tyrannize over wit and sense, to be contradicted in everything one does and says and borne down not by reason but authority, to be denied one's most innocent desires for no other cause but the will and pleasure of an absolute lord and master, whose follies a woman with all her prudence cannot hide and whose commands she cannot but despise at the same time she obeys them, is a misery none can have a just idea of but those who have felt it" (4). At the least, women "ought to be treated with civility, for since a little ceremony and outside respect is all their guard, all the privilege that is allowed them, it were barbarous to deprive them of it" (24). She then cautions against believing the protestations of courtship: "She must be a fool who can believe a man, proud and vain as he is, will lay his boasted authority, the dignity and prerogative of his sex, one moment at her feet but in prospect of taking it up again to more advantage. He may call himself her slave a few days, but it is only to make her his all the rest of his life" (25).

Even legal settlements were not necessarily a protection for the wife, Astell believes: "There have been but too many instances of husbands that by wheedling or threatening their wives, by seeming kindness or cruel usage, have persuaded or forced them out of what has been settled on them." This is possible because "covenants between husband and wife, like laws in an arbitrary government are of little force; the will of the sovereign is all in all" (39). The wife has only one course in marital disputes, for "he who has sovereign power does not value the provocations of a rebellious subject." The husband can subdue with ease and will make himself obeyed. The wife must turn to "patience and submission" as her only comforts. "Not Milton himself would cry up liberty to poor *female slaves,* or plead for the lawfulness of resisting a private tyranny" (29). For patience and submission, "woman must be endowed with a wisdom and goodness much above what we suppose the sex capable of, I fear much greater than ever a man can pretend to, who can so constantly conquer her passions and divest herself even of innocent self-love." And for what purpose? "To give up her cause when she is in the right and to submit her enlightened reason to the imperious dictates of a blind will and wild imagination even when she clearly perceives the ill consequences of it, the imprudence, nay folly and madness of such a conduct" (35).

Astell observes that the institution of marriage can only be justified by the prospect of heavenly rewards. "Hereafter may make amends for what [a wife] must be prepared to suffer here, then will be her reward, this is her time of trial, the season of exercizing and improving her virtues" (57). The reality is that "a woman that is not mistress of her passions, that cannot patiently submit even when reason suffers with her, who does not practice passive obedience to the utmost, will never be acceptable to such an absolute sovereign as a husband. But how can a woman scruple entire subjection, how can she forebear to admire the worth and excellency of the superior sex?" Men's "vast minds lay kingdoms waste, no bounds or measures can be prescribed to their desires. They make worlds and ruin them, form systems of universal nature and dispute eternally about them, their pen gives worth to the most trifling controversy, nor can a fray be inconsiderable if they have drawn their swords in it." Therefore, "it is a woman's happiness to hear, admire and praise them, especially if a little ill-nature keeps them at any time from bestowing due applause on each other." This is the role society has given to woman, "and if she aspires no further she is thought to be in her proper sphere of action; she is as wise and good as can be expected from her" (59). Despite the rebellious tone of much of her tract, Astell does, in fact, subscribe to the position that a wife's responsibility to her vows remains constant no matter what provocations are offered. "An ill husband may deprive a wife of the comfort and quiet of her life, may give her occasion of exercizing her virtue, may try her patience and fortitude to the utmost, but that's all he can do; it is herself only can accomplish her ruin" (6).

The universal advice in conduct books was to cultivate patient submissiveness and to try to win favor by wheedling charm. The anonymous female author of *The Whole Duty of a Woman* advises, "If a husband prove not what you expected in relation to temper and good humor, yet by a wise use of everything he may, by degrees, be turned to be very supportable, which prudence neglected might in time beget an aversion." She suggests, "Consider then, since the greater share of reason is bestowed on man as the lawgiver; our sex is the better prepared for the compliance that is necessary for the better performance of those duties that seem to be most properly assigned to it." While conceding that "this may seem something unpleasing at first," she asserts "that Nature is so far from being unjust to us that she is partial to our side" and "it is in our power not only to free ourselves but to subdue our masters." She explains, "Our looks have more strength than their laws; there is more power in our tears than in their arguments" (69).

In *Pamela II,* the continuation of *Pamela,* Richardson shows a situation in which adherence to this customary advice actually worsens the situation. Mr. B. becomes involved with a widowed countess. They meet at a masquerade, and begin a platonic friendship which is widely reported to be a love affair. Pamela, informed of the affair by "a well-wisher," at first suffers in silence, following the marriage manuals' advice to ignore a husband's transgressions and to strive to keep up a cheerful demeanor so that his home will seem attractive. She even, at her husband's request, entertains the countess at tea. Finally, however, Pamela asks for a separation, explaining that she cannot share his love with a rival. "I will therefore, Sir, dear as you are to me . . . give up your person, [asking only] that you will be so good as to permit me to go down to Kent, to my dear parents," taking their child with her. She promises, "I will there pray for you every hour of my life" (II, 312). When he asks, "Can you so easily part with me?" she replies, "I can Sir, and I will!—rather than divide my interest in you knowingly, with any lady on earth."

Fortunately, Pamela learns that she is mistaken. Mr. B. and the countess are still only friends, despite appearances. Pamela also learns that she should have met the problem head-on from the beginning, rather than trying to hide her distress. In striving to ignore Mr. B.'s conduct she has only aggravated him. Mr. B. explains that her "unwonted reception" of him, with red eyes and watery smiles, when, in his own eyes his conduct was innocent, gave him "great disgusts," while, on the other hand, "the Countess [was] ever cheerful and lively" (II, 423). He was rapidly coming to believe that Pamela's temperament had been irretrievably changed for the worse by motherhood, and, not surprisingly, his platonic friendship with the Countess was beginning to change into something warmer.

The anonymous "Father" who is the author of *The Lady's New-Year's Gift: or Advice to a Daughter,* actually the Marquis of Halifax, writes in much the usual vein of conciliation. Giving advice on how to deal with a choleric or ill-tempered husband, he warns, "There must be an art in it and a skillful hand, else the least bungling maketh it mortal. You are dexterously to yield to everything till he begins to cool, and then by slow degrees you may rise and gain on him" (46–47). Most faults and especially sexual promiscuity should be simply ignored by a wife. "You live in a time which hath rendered some kinds of frailties so habitual, that they lay claim to large grains of allowance." He admits that "the world in this is somewhat unequal, and our sex seems to play the tyrant in distinguishing for ourselves by making that in the utmost degree criminal in the woman which in a man passes under a much gentler censure" (34). However, "the root and excuse of this injustice is the preservation of families from any mixture that may bring a blemish on them" (34). He continues his prescriptions, cautioning, "Next to the danger of committing the fault yourself, the greatest is that of seeing it in your husband" (35). He reasons that a sensible man will reform himself and the others are probably hopeless, adding a final warning, "Besides it is so coarse a reason which will be assigned for a lady's too great warmth upon such an occasion, that modesty no less than prudence ought to restrain her" (36).

Marthae Taylor refused a number of proposals and never married. However, while declaring, "In matters of love, never fear me making a fools-bargain," she also proclaimed herself no enemy to marriage, stating, "The institution itself is sufficiently recommended by its being the ordinance of God." The present state of the institution, however, left much to be desired and, "it is the general, I had almost said the universal, depravity of manners that makes mortals so miserable in marriage." Therefore, "it may be said of [marriage], as of all other excellent things, that by corruption and abuse they become the very worst." On two occasions she offered advice to unhappy wives, one married to a drunkard, the other to a spendthrift. Despite the marked independence characteristic of her own refusals of marriage offers, her advice to married women is not very different from John Sprint's.

Taylor opens her letter to a friend married to a drunkard bluntly: "Pardon me if I should tell you you may in a great degree contribute to the misfortune you complain of by unamiableness of behaviour either sullen or sour, perhaps clamourous, which no man will bear from his mate that's vowed obedience and to love and to cherish." This obligation, she reminds, binds the wife "in such sort that be he better or be he worse she can't be exempt from duty on her side." Perhaps, she speculates, "he had recourse to his bottle and companions to drown the remembrance of domestic feuds." Then, "loath to return to what's so painful to him, he stays to an unreasonable hour, for which his health, his purse, his sobriety and your quiet pays dear." Finally, "this by repetition becomes habitual and thence too often unalterable." She advises, "Drinking is a disease a woman can never purpose to cure in her husband by anything but a little art and a great deal of good humour. The art consists in making herself, his own house and business more agreeable to him than any other by studying his taste and suiting it." The wife should observe his disposition and then provide "neatness, cheerfulness, plenty, economy, company or retiredness, or whatever your judge-

ment . . . may suggest." She continues, "And be sure ever to receive him with a cheerful countenance if not open arms, a civil and
obliging salutation, if not a kind and tender one." This conduct
"will be no slight advance towards preserving your empire in his
heart" and "by degrees you'll gain an ascendant over his foibles."
She asserts, "A woman should have the wisdom of Abigail, the patience of Griselda, the good humour of Harmonia and a heart full
fraught with amity and candour," and "her admonitions, if ever
she presumes to give any, must appear as friendly advices tendered
in the softest and most obliging terms."

Even this conduct may not succeed, Taylor admits, and "if a
man's inflexible, as they often are even to the soundest reasoning of
their wives from misjudging that she encroaches on his prerogative
(a tender point of honour indeed)," her friend "may as well attempt to stem the course of the sea." She then relates how "when
mariners see a whale they neither essay to fly him nor yet oppose
him, but artfully throw out a plaything to divert him," adding,
"the application is easy." Returning to her original point, she urges
her unhappy friend to "consider, when a man transgresses, if the
wife grows sour upon it she hurts herself and him and does good to
none." She details the many evil consequences—"she lets it gnaw
her own heart, embitter her life and injure her health; she sets an ill
example to her children; she incurs the guilt of murmuring discon-
tent and rebellion with all its train of ill consequences; she enrages
him and provokes him to double the crime, yea perhaps tenfold."
Taylor again counsels "the virtue of patience with all its collateral
attendants, peace, tranquillity, a cheerful heart, a contented mind
and a continued disposition to please and be pleased." She concedes, undoubtedly with justice, that her doctrine is "hard to practice," but declares it "practicable" and adds that the only way to
get through life is "by an absolute dominion over our passions."

The real distress of Taylor's friend, whose letter has not survived, can be inferred by her next strictures: "Your reflection that a
little time will put an end to all is but a melancholy comfort," since
the friend is in the "prime of youth and health." Taylor turns to
religion for what seems a very dubious encouragement: "You that
have more afflictions have a larger field to raise virtues in," and
"You married people have a double advantage for even the duties
of nature to your husband and children are accepted as religious
acts of piety." This, she exhorts, "ought to encourage you to exert
yourself."

Taylor's tone is a bit more sympathetic toward her second correspondent: "I confess a narrowness of fortune occasioned by ill conduct offers many motives to wrangling betwixt a man and his wife." She observes that if they both "encourage a disposition to be sour, peevish or forward" there will be no end to it, but if the wife "has a good understanding she will correct her own passions and pity rather than be angry with his." She counsels, "All reproaches and upbraidings are industriously to be avoided, as you would the setting fire to your house," for "few men, bad as they are, are such monsters as not to be worked upon by a continued series of good natured and obliging behaviour." She declares, "I never saw happiness in a married state where the wife was not very circumspect in her whole conduct," and for this reason a homely woman is often a happier wife because she does not depend on mere beauty but "has been studious to recommend herself by all the excellencies of her understanding and other faculties." By gaining a husband's esteem, such a wife has also "cemented a lasting passion in his heart, and gained such an ascendant over him as to influence him in every action of his life," and thus she "insensibly engages him never to thwart or disoblige her, even in a trifle." The consequence of this is a happy marriage where there is "a mutual disposition to please and be pleased, accompanied with a cheerful tranquillity of mind." Then, for a wife, "instead of a task, her duty becomes her delight, and while others are complaining of the miseries of a married life, she exults in its joys!" This desirable result is not dependent on the husband, who is often "far from being a man of a finished character for a good husband," but on the efforts of the wife, because "with a woman of another turn, he would have been one of a miserable pair."

While the vast majority in the century felt that marital harmony was overwhelmingly the responsibility of the wife, Catherine Talbot suggests a mutual responsibility. She writes, in her meditations, "Next to the bonds of nature are those of choice. Married persons are bound to the observance of very sacred vows and ought therefore often to recollect them and examine their conduct by them." She especially notes that "they should carefully consider whether they have so strict a guard upon their temper as they ought, now the happiness of another person is made so greatly to depend on their easy good humor and cheerfulness." They also should "assist and improve one another," being "ready to receive assistance and advice as kindly as to give it" and preserving "delicacy of behaviour, a neatness of appearance, a gentleness of manner, a mildness of speech." They should take care that "they enter kindly and affectionately into one another's interests and concerns."

Richardson gives two extensive pictures of model marriages which embody this ideal of mutual respect. One, in *Pamela* and its sequel, *Pamela II,* might be called the progress of a marriage, since the relationship of Pamela and Mr. B. changes as Mr. B. himself changes, influenced by her virtue. In *Sir Charles Grandison* we see the ideal marriage of an ideal couple, together with a gallery of less perfect but workable matches. *Clarissa,* on the other hand, gives a picture of a faulty marriage through the Harlowes. In all cases, the degree of authority demanded by the husband is in inverse relationship to his wisdom and goodness. Richardson deliberately challenges the normative view of the century on marriage.

At first, the marriage of Pamela and Mr. B. follows an authoritarian pattern. Mr. B., spoiled by an indulgent mother, is accustomed to having his own way, and his sister says of him that "he is too lordly a creature by much" (I, 399). Mr. B. recognizes his own faults: "In my conscience, I think I should hardly have made a tolerable [husband] to any but Pamela" (I, 399), and the assembled company agree that a happy marriage "must be owing to [Pamela's] meekness, more than his complaisance." When he gives Pamela a list of rules to follow so that arguments will be avoided, Lady Davers, his sister, comments, "Why, what a wretch has thou got," adding, "Everybody will *admire* you, but no one will have reason to *envy* you" (II, 58).

In fact, Mr. B. is not as intransigent as all this suggests. He assures Pamela, "I always intend, my dear, you shall judge for yourself: If you have anything on your mind to say, let's have it" (II, 168). On another occasion he insists that she speak "without reserve, for many times I may ask your opinion as a corrective or confirmation of my own judgement" (II, 227). While he approves of a wife who soothes a husband rather than causing anger by "*scornful* looks" and "words of *defiance,*" he objects to the discreet manipulation often suggested by the conduct books. Once, when Pamela succeeds in wheedling a favorable decision out of him, he chides her: "This looks so artful, that I won't love you . . . your talent is nature and you should keep to that" (II, 279).

Only two major disagreements are recorded in the marriage. The first concerns Pamela's desire to nurse her child, which Mr. B. vehemently opposes. When she argues that she considers it "the *natural* duty of a mother" and therefore "a *divine* duty," he responds "that if a wife thinks a thing her duty to do, which her husband does not approve, he can dispense with her performing it, and no sin shall lie at her door" (II, 203). Pamela is incredulous at Mr. B.'s version of the principle of coverture, turning to her parents as arbiters. Her parents respond that, while they think her in the right, when he "thinks so highly of his prerogative" she should "give up the point and acquiesce," citing "the laws of the realm" which "excuse a wife, when she is faulty by the command of the husband" (II, 235). Mr. B. admits that he takes pleasure in Pamela's "easy, genteel form," but he principally values her companionship, not wanting "even a son and heir" as a rival for her time. He declares, "My chief delight in you is for the beauties of your mind," and he does not wish his wife to be engrossed by those "baby offices which will better befit weaker minds" (II, 229). Reluctantly, Pamela gives in to his wishes.

The second crisis in the novel is Mr. B.'s liaison with the countess, discussed above. After Pamela speaks out, the couple are more firmly united than ever, with Mr. B. realizing that virtue based only upon "*moral* foundations" and "the proud word *honour*" (II, 422) can never be secure. He declares, "And now, my Pamela, from this instant you shall be my guide. . . . I will leave it to you to direct as you please." Mr. B. is converted to religion, convinced "that nothing but RELIGIOUS CONSIDERATIONS . . . can be of sufficient weight to keep steady to his purpose, a vain young man" (II, 423), and with his conversion gives over the direction of his life to Pamela. He even gives her Locke to read so that she can direct the education of their children. The narrative becomes a series of scenes in which we see the couple as exemplars of wedded bliss, bringing happiness to relatives, friends, and, indeed, the whole neighborhood.

Sir Charles Grandison does not have to overcome the faults of Mr. B., and his marriage therefore starts off on a footing of equality. During courtship, when Sir Charles is pleading with Harriet to set an early date for their wedding, he complains that it is hard "to be thus prescribed to," and Harriet replies, "What, Sir, in my day?" (III, 129). She is jokingly referring to the convention (discussed in chapter 3) that courtship was the one time when the woman reigned, if only briefly. Sir Charles replies, "That was what I was going to urge, because *mine* will never come. Every day, to the end of my life, will be yours." He tells her that he expects her to make him more worthy of her by "her sweet conversation, *uncoupled* with fear" (III, 124), and that when they are mar-

Figure 11. Illustration from *Pamela II*. Gravelot. This illustration to
the second part of the novel *Pamela* shows Pamela surrounded by
her children, telling them instructive tales, while in the background
nursemaids and other servants listen. This charming depiction of
motherhood indicates Pamela's eventual position in her marriage as
educator and standard setter. By permission of the British Library.

ried "you will then be more than ever your own mistress. Your will, Madam, will ever comprehend mine" (III, 103). After their marriage, he declares, "You must advise me. I will not take any important step, whether relative to myself or friends, but by your advice" (III, 346). On another occasion he tells Harriet, "In everything . . . shall your wishes determine mine. I will have your whole heart in the grant of every request I make to you, or you shall have the cheerful acquiescence of mine with your will" (III, 175). Sir Charles is, in fact, turning the conventions upside down. It was generally agreed that the obligation of obedience became easy in a loving marriage because the will of the wife was in accord with her husband's; when any difference arose, however, it was the husband who made the decision and the wife who gave "cheerful acquiescence."

The ideal marriage of Sir Charles and Harriet is prefigured by the happy union of Lady Caroline, Sir Charles's sister, and Lord L. As an example of the cooperation which characterizes their marriage, they each have access to the money drawer and Lady L. explains, "When I want money, I have recourse to my key; I minute down the sum, as he himself does" (II, 249). Their life is one of mutual respect and harmony, Harriet notes, and "one sees their love for each other in their eyes" (I, 210). In contrast, the very foolish cousin of Sir Charles, Everard Grandison, maintains that marriage is, for women, a state "of servitude, if they know their duty" and that women should "stand in awe" (I, 299). Lady L. jokingly asks her husband why he does not think it worth his while "to *over-awe*" her, and Charlotte, Sir Charles's other sister, replies, "Lord L. is a good man, a virtuous man: None but rakes hold these *over-awing* doctrines." The cousin eventually marries a wealthy merchant's widow, chiefly to ameliorate his fortune, and it is reported that his wife is duly impressed with her aristocratic mate. Sir Charles remarks that "she has a greater opinion of his understanding, than she has of her own," and, while the reader knows the assembled company would agree that it is highly unlikely that this could in fact be true, given the unfailing stupidity of Everard, Sir Charles indicates that it is just as well that she grants him a superiority because "this seems to be necessary to the happiness of common minds in wedlock" (III, 348).

Henry Fielding, on the other hand, presents a picture of marriage which is very different from the ideal of Richardson. Marriage, in Fielding's novels, is depicted as desirable for both men and women as, indeed, it is in the work of all of these novelists. Fielding's good men are all said to be uxorious, enjoying the company of their wives and the happiness of the hearth, but the relationship of husband and wife is not that of equals. Both *Joseph Andrews* and *Tom Jones* end with the marriage of their heroes and a promise of wedded bliss to follow, but in *Amelia* Fielding gives a much more detailed picture of the workings of an actual marriage. Whereas Pamela is seen most often in the parlor, Amelia is characteristically seen doing domestic chores. The narrator doubts "whether it be possible to view this fine creature in a more amiable light than while she was dressing her husband's supper, with her little children playing about her" (488).

Despite Booth's failings, Amelia is the embodiment of the conduct book's precepts for a wife—never suspicious, never reproachful, always cheerfully submissive and loving. Far from finding her role difficult, she glories in it, and, in the midst of their difficulties, while allowing that "our circumstances, it is true, might have been a little more fortunate," she declares that she would not "exchange that lot with any queen in the universe" (239).

On one occasion, "Amelia, having waited above an hour for her husband, concluded . . . that he had met with some engagement abroad" (212). She therefore eats with the children and, when he returns, never asks the reason for his absence. Discovering he has not dined, she "bestirred herself as nimbly to provide him with a repast as the most industrious hostess in the kingdom doth when some unexpected guest of extraordinary quality arrives at her house." On another occasion, she again waits an hour for him and then sits down to supper alone, denying herself wine to save sixpence. At the same time, Booth is gambling away all they own and more, but the next day she cheerfully dismisses his action, declaring, "Let it give you no further vexation" (435). He calls her "thou heavenly angel," then says, "Oh, no, thou art my dearest woman, my best, my beloved wife!" In still another episode, Amelia, "eating nothing but a slice of bread and butter" for her own dinner, prepares his favorite dishes for his supper but, when he arrives, learns that he cannot stay because he is engaged to sup abroad. "My dear," says Amelia, "I say no more," and "when he was gone the poor disappointed Amelia sat down to supper" but "preserved entire for her husband" the wine she has bought. On this occasion, he is dining with her rival, Miss Matthews.

Booth is always free to seek entertainment or company outside his home. Amelia declares that even to express regret at the loss of his company is unreasonable, for she ought always to rejoice in the thoughts of his being well entertained. As for herself, she asks Booth, "Do you believe that I am capable of any sensation worthy the name of pleasure when neither you nor my children are present or bear any part of it?" (187). When Amelia is invited to go on an excursion to Ranelagh, the famous pleasure garden, an invitation Booth cannot share because the bailiffs are pursuing him for debt, he exclaims, "May I be damned . . . if my wife shall go" (247). Astonished, Mrs. Ellison suggests that Amelia speak for herself, and Amelia dutifully replies, "I hope, madam, I shall never desire to go any place contrary to Mr. Booth's inclinations." When Mrs. Ellison opines that Booth is being unreasonable, Amelia responds, "Pardon me, madam, I will not suppose Mr. Booth's inclinations ever can be unreasonable," and Mrs. Ellison comments, "If I had been told this, I would not have believed it."

Despite Amelia's unquestioning obedience, this refusal generates the only incident in the novel where Amelia voices any annoyance directly to her husband. She asks him what had caused "so great a passion" (249). When he replies, "I would rather you would not ask me," she responds, "I will appeal to yourself whether this is not using me too much like a child," quickly adding, "If you still insist on keeping the secret, I will convince you I am not ignorant of the duty of a wife by my obedience; but I cannot help telling you at the same time you will make me one of the most miserable of women." Booth does then tell her of his suspicions that the donor of the tickets has too warm an interest in her. Amelia, incredulous, assures him, "No man breathing could have any designs as you have apprehended without my immediately seeing them." Her reply shows Amelia's guileless innocence, but, significantly, she is quite wrong, thereby demonstrating that a good woman indeed needs a man for protection.

Only once in the novel does Amelia feel anger toward her husband. She receives a note that contains a challenge to a duel from Colonel James to Booth because Booth has broken his promise and has "supped this very night alone with Miss Matthews" (490). She cries out, "It is too much, too much to bear," and throwing her arms about her children, exclaims, "You are undone—my children are undone!" When one of the children speaks of "poor papa," she says, "Mention him no more, your papa is—indeed he is a wicked man—he cares not for any of us." Amelia's distress is certainly understandable. She has cheerfully endured hardship, denying both herself and the children minor treats and pawning her clothes, while Booth gambled away their money, and now she learns that his life is imperilled because of his dalliance with another woman. Later that night she also learns that he has once more been imprisoned for debt. When she goes to see Booth the next day, however, she utters not one word of reproach. He confesses his affair with Miss Matthews, but she tells him that she has forgiven him long ago, having learned of the matter in a letter from Miss Matthews herself, a letter Booth thought lost. Amelia, after receiving the letter, had calmly dismissed the whole matter, explaining, "I made large allowance for the situation," and further believing that the letter itself, which was designed to make trouble, demonstrated that "the affair was at an end" (499). She indeed follows the conduct book advice for wives, which cautions against any remonstrances or upbraidings even when there is positive evidence of unfaithfulness.

Amelia is Fielding's picture of the ideal wife. Just as all the conduct books warned, Amelia's husband is not equally ideal—he is unfaithful, a gambler, sometimes a toper, financially irresponsible, selfishly proud—but the good wife is always ready to forgive masculine failings and to show proper deference to his judgment. A final example will illustrate the pattern. Booth has acquired a "debt of honour," that is, a gambling debt, which he cannot pay. We are told that when it comes to a choice as to whether he should try to temporize with a man he despises or pay the debt "by stripping his wife, not only of every farthing, but of every rag she had in the world" that "pride, at last, seemed to represent this as the lesser evil" (473). Amelia, learning of the debt for the first time, calmly agrees that it must be paid and pawns her clothes. Booth sets off to satisfy his creditor, but unfortunately he is not at home. He then meets an old army friend who insists on his joining him in a bottle, and, "heated with wine," Booth entrusts him with the money to bribe a "great man" in the hopes of getting a commission. The original purpose of Amelia's sacrifice is now irretrievably lost, but she utters not a word of doubt concerning this highly questionable transaction, telling Booth that "she would not presume to advise him in an affair of which he was so much better the judge" (476). John Sprint's marriage sermon could ask no more in the way of unquestioning obedience.

While the reciprocity advocated by Richardson's novels did undoubtedly characterize many happy marriages and was, as we have seen in the previous chapter, often the goal expressed in courtship, nevertheless it was seldom advanced as either the ideal or the norm for marriage. Sarah Chapone, who was in fact happily married, portrays the more usual view: "The husband in his judicial capacity must therefore be sufficiently qualified to be the regulator of his wife's conscience and to control all the mental faculties of the wife, that she may know nothing but through him and for him who is her *summum jus* [highest law]," annotating her statement with a footnote paraphrasing Milton's "He for God alone, she for God in him." She adds, "Neither shall it be any bar to his being her *summum jus* if it shall appear that he cannot be her *summum bonum* [highest good]," because "according to established rule, a wife is dead in law." Therefore, "it would be ridiculous for the law to consider the interests of a non–entity," which nonentity "may nevertheless be called into being occasionally at the pleasure and direction of the husband, who may dispose of her as he sees fit when so called, and then he may tell her what he thinks fit she should know, and order what he thinks fit she should do, and be a complete regulator of her conscience and actions also."

For Chapone, the authority of a husband did not rest in any intrinsic superiority of the male sex, but rather was a punishment meted out to women by God. "Permit me, Sir, to acknowledge that I admit not of any superiority in the male before the fall. Let it suffice at present to say that I humbly acquiesce to the sentence of the sovereign Arbiter of heaven and earth." She quotes from Genesis, "Since thou hast done this thing, thy desire shalt be unto thy husband, *He shall* rule over thee," and comments, "He who laid the burden well knew the weight and extent of it." And "who is he that shall reply against God! The authority of a husband is as clear and incontestable as any of the ten commandments." Even this vigorous contender for the equality of the sexes was willing to obey the dictates of scripture, although she wanted it made clear that a wife's obedience was a punishment, and a harsh one, not a divine ordinance intended for the benefit of women.

At another time Chapone argues that while normally authority is coupled with honor and respect because the person wielding the authority has demonstrated unusual capacities which work for the good of the governed, marriage is different: "There is one exempt case in which God has invested a particular set of men with great authority, and that by his *own declaration* not for the advantage of the governed, namely the authority of a man over his wife. That subjection was expressly denounced upon her as a punishment and a curse, and it has been well observed in other cases that the severity of the chastizement gives no dignity to the scourge." She conceded that "where the wedded pair do their duties on both sides it is a paradisiacal state; the burden consequently taken off," but she also notes that "where they do not, the struggle is intolerable and worse than the tumults and miseries of a civil war."

In a debate about the extent to which marriages should be arranged by families, Chapone's correspondent took the position that as long as a daughter did not actively dislike a suitor recommended by her family she should agree to the match, preferring her parents' judgment to her own. Her vows to love and honor should be seen as a promise for the future rather than a statement of present fact. Chapone disagreed. "I am not convinced that either of the contracting parties can escape the guilt of solemn perjury, provided they marry a man or woman whom they do not at that time love and honour." She explains that, while all contracts by their nature govern future actions, "these two points, affection and estimation, must and are understood in the present tense because they are the very principles on which the contract is professedly founded." She then argues that while fidelity and duty are matters of the will, love is not. "So no command of another, or resolution of my own could enable me to love him who appears to me quite unlovely or to honour him who appears to me no way estimable." Love, therefore, is essential to marriage. Not "what is called love by run-away girls and wiffle-headed fellows," but "true love . . . founded upon esteem, joined with an affectionate regard to the person." She notes, "You say truth, Sir, that suffering is the test of virtue, but you would not from thence infer that it would be advisable for a woman to marry a man because she thought he would make her suffer. As for the protection on the one side, and obedience on the other, they are duties accommodated to our present circumstances as sinners, and were not originally intended in the rite of marriage." In commenting on Richardson's *Clarissa* she condemns Clarissa's mother for being too dutiful toward her husband "to comply with whose tyrannical humour, she was culpably deficient in the duties of a mother, and abandoned her virtuous daughter." The true model of wedded love "is an appropriated kindness that is absolutely incommunicable to any other."

As Chapone's remarks indicate, the degree of love necessary to enter validly into marriage was a topic of dispute. It was generally assumed that older and wiser heads, that is, parents, could choose a mate better than an inexperienced young woman and that love would follow after marriage. Sarah Scott depicts such a marriage in *Agreeable Ugliness,* where the heroine's obedience to her father is rewarded by finding herself, after a time, truly in love with her husband.

Richardson also depicts a marriage which begins more in prudence than in love, but which nevertheless ends happily in the union of Charlotte Grandison and Lord G. The marriage of Charlotte and Lord G. provides a model quite contrary to the ideal of the conduct books and to the expectations of "common minds." Charlotte, Sir Charles's younger sister, is witty, outspoken, and willful. She is often chided by both Harriet and her brother for overstepping the bounds of propriety in not regarding "times, temper and occasions" (II, 338), but "she has principles" and it is not so much malice or "love of power that predominates in her mind, as the love of playfulness" (II, 330). Both Harriet and Sir Charles unreservedly love her for her high spirits and cheerfulness.

At the beginning of the novel Sir Charles helps Charlotte end an unfortunate entanglement with an unworthy suitor, entered into chiefly as a means of escaping her tyrannical father. She is now courted by Lord G., a good-natured, worthy man who adores her, but who is not as bright as she is. Harriet comments on Charlotte's situation, asking, "What can a woman do, who is addressed by a man of talents inferior to her own? She cannot pick and choose, as men do. She can only have her negative" (I, 230). She notes that it is said that women "must encourage men of sense only. And it is *well* said. But what will they do . . . if the men of sense do not offer themselves?" In this case Sir Charles advises Charlotte, "If you cannot have a man of whose understanding you have a higher opinion than of your own, you should think of one who is likely to allow to yours a superiority" (II, 99), and urges her to marry Lord G.

Charlotte finally assents, conceding that there is no man whom she prefers to Lord G., although she is painfully aware that she is not really in love. "For the man one loves, one can *do* anything, *be* everything, that he would wish one to be" (II, 340), she says, but, as she herself proves, "people may be *very* happy, if not *most* happy, who set out with a moderate stock of love, and supply what they want in that with prudence" (III, 228). Forced marriages are condemned in this novel and Sir Charles is adamant that he would never bring pressure to bear to make Charlotte act against her own will, but the novel also shows that a successful marriage need not be built upon passionate love and need not follow the prescribed patterns of the conduct books. The countess of D., a wise woman, explains what is meant by "that love which we vow at the altar"

(II, 547). It is not "adoration" but rather "a *preferable choice* (all circumstances considered) as shall make us with satisfaction of mind, and with an affectionate and faithful heart unite ourselves for life with a man whom we esteem." As Harriet assesses Charlotte's position, "She hates not Lord G. There is no man whom she prefers to him, and in this respect, may perhaps, be on a par with eight women out of twelve, who marry, and yet make not bad wives" (II, 347).

Whether Lord G. is going to prove a man Charlotte really can esteem is for a time questionable. Harriet reports, "I overheard the naughty one say, as Lord G. led her up to the altar, 'You don't know what you are about, man. I expect to have all my way: Remember that's one of my articles of marriage'" (II, 340). Lord G. returns "an answer of fond assent." At first the marriage is indeed stormy. In Lord G., Richardson has created a very lifelike portrait of a good-natured, well-meaning man who nevertheless can be extremely irritating chiefly because he is not sensitive enough or bright enough to see that his mannerisms exasperate by their silliness. Charlotte explains, "I do not, in my heart, dislike him. . . . But he is so important about trifles; so nimble, yet so slow: He is so sensible of his own *intention* to please, and he has so many antic motions in his obligations; that I cannot forbear laughing" (II, 417). As Harriet remarks, "Could but my Lord G. assume dignity, and mingle raillery with it, and be able to laugh *with* her and sometimes *at* her, she would not make *him* her sport" (II, 330). Unfortunately, he tends to sulk instead. Charlotte confesses, "I am afraid I think as *well* of my own understanding as I do of Lord G.'s. I love to jest, to play, to make him look about him" (II, 506).

Reformation finally comes. Charlotte's own intelligence persuades her that the course she is following will lead to unhappiness: "Charlotte, thought I, what are you about? You mean not to continue forever your playful folly. You have no malice, no wickedness, in your sauciness; only a little levity" (II, 518). She tells herself, "Make your retreat while you can with honour; before you harden the man's heart," and assures Lord G., "[My heart] is yours, and yours *only*." She explains to Harriet, "I have told him, in love, some of his foibles: And he thanks me for my instruction, and is resolved to be all I wish him to be." On the other hand, she notes, "I have made discoveries in his favour—More wit, more humour, more good sense." Far from tamed, she concludes, with an ironic dash, "He allows me to have a vast share of understanding; and so he ought, when I have made such discoveries to *his* advantage"

(II, 543). Some months later she writes to Harriet, "But here, I, Charlotte G. who married with indifference the poor Lord G.; who made the honest man, whenever I pleased, foam, fume, fret and execrate the hour that he first beheld my face, now stand forth, an example of true conjugal fidelity, an encouragement for girls who venture into the married state, without that prodigious quantity of violent passion, which some hare-brained creatures think an essential of love." She concludes, "You, my dear, left us *tolerably* happy. We now are almost *in*-tolerably so" (III, 402).

The success of Charlotte's marriage indeed shows the reader that "violent passion" on both sides is not a prerequisite for happiness, as several other marriages in the novel also demonstrate. It also suggests that marriage should be based on the temperaments and capabilities of both partners, often producing a quite different, but equally acceptable, pattern from that of the conduct books. The good result of the marriage justifies Sir Charles's insight that a woman like Charlotte, who will find it difficult to marry a man who is really her superior in understanding, should marry one who will "allow to [hers] a superiority." While Charlotte's excesses of willfulness are condemned, the basic structure of the marriage is not. It is only "common minds" who insist that the husband's intelligence should surpass the wife's and that the wife's role should be that of decorous submission.

Anna Howe, Clarissa's good friend, is another example of the problems an intelligent young woman faced when contemplating marriage. Anna and Charlotte have much in common. Both are witty, assertive, outwardly bold, but good at heart; both are courted by bland young men. At one point in *Clarissa,* Anna comments on the qualifications of Solmes and Lovelace, Clarissa's suitors, and Hickman, her own decorous "dangler": "That you and I should have such baboons as these to choose out of, is a mortifying thing, my dear" (I, 244). As Harriet remarked in reference to Charlotte, it is fine to say that a young woman should choose a suitor who is her intellectual equal, but where is she to find him?

After Clarissa's death, Belford, as her executor, writes to Anna Howe, reminding her that Clarissa's will expressed the hope that Anna would marry Hickman. In reply, Anna explains her hesitations. "I have such an opinion of your sex that I think there is not one man in a hundred whom a woman of sense and spirit can either *honour* or *obey,* though you make us promise *both*" (IV, 477). She continues, "When I look round upon all the married people of my acquaintance, and see how *they* live, and what *they* bear who live *best,* I am confirmed in my dislike to the state. Well do your sex contrive to bring us up fools and idiots, in order to make us bear the yoke you lay on our shoulders." She declares that if women were educated like men, they would despise men "for your *ignorance,*" as much as they already do "for your *insolence.*" Having these notions, she asks, "*Do you think I ought to marry at all? Why must I be teased . . . when I wish only to be let alone to do as best pleases me?*" (IV, 479).

Anna does marry, "and she then made Mr. Hickman one of the happiest men in the world." We are told that the union of "a woman of her fine sense and understanding" to "a man of virtue and good nature" could hardly be otherwise than happy, especially when his "behaviour to *Mrs. Hickman* is as affectionate as it was respectful to *Miss Howe.*" It seems probable that this marriage, like Charlotte's, owes its happiness to the granting on the part of the husband of a much greater degree of equality to the wife than was generally accorded, or consonant with the prescriptions of the conduct books.

Richardson's fictional picture of marriage was unusual. Much more common in novels was the portrayal of a happy marriage in which the husband is the wise mentor who protects and guides. Sarah Fielding presents two happy couples in *The Adventures of David Simple,* David and Camilla, Valentine and Cynthia. Cynthia is exceptionally intelligent, while Camilla is praised more for her goodness of heart. For a while the two couples keep house together, forming an idyllic society in which "cheerfulness and good humour [are] looked on as the chief ingredients" and where the women manage household tasks so well that the men enjoy "much of their amiable conversation" (316). In this happy group Cynthia contributes "sprightliness" while Camilla is known for "softness." As the novel continues, Cynthia and Valentine depart for the West Indies and we learn of them only by report, while Camilla and David become the focus of the work. The marriage that we see described in detail, therefore, is that of Camilla and David. Cynthia and Valentine might provide a different model, but we are not permitted to observe it.

Camilla and David exemplify the century's concept of the proper marital relationship. David is the protector and guide, albeit always a kind and generous one. "As the modest mind of Camilla ever fled for protection and refuge to David's understanding, so under his kind directions she walked securely free from fear or guilt" (341).

Their marriage is often compared, approvingly, to Milton's picture of Adam and Eve in Eden. David is always there to support his frailer spouse, "and as he never despised any little weakness which had unguardedly crept into her mind, he consequently always generously removed any such weakness" (363). Camilla is always grateful: "She had such a sense of her indulgent husband's kindness, that her mind yielded to the strength of his reasoning" (362).

Familiar Letters between the Principal Characters in David Simple also gives an account of an ideal marriage, that of Constantius and Fidelia. Constantius is characterized by good judgment and even though "he liked Fidelia . . . he did not choose her till he found her worthy to be loved" (II, 106). Now, "he is at once satisfied with and improves her understanding, admires her person, and loves her heart." (The progression of "satisfied with," "admires," and "loves" neatly indicates the relative importance of mind, beauty, and tenderness.) He is kind enough that he "never contradicts her to show only his power," but were "she to desire anything that would be a hurt to herself, he would have resolution enough . . . to resist his own inclination of indulging her" (II, 106). Like a good child, "she, by his instructions, improves herself," and "her inclination to do whatever he desires makes her obedience so perfect, that she spares him the pain it would cost him to deny her any request" (II, 107). Indeed, "if she can imagine anything to be his will she never hesitates a moment before she puts it into execution." Fidelia "has a very good understanding" and, "what is almost a miracle, is thoroughly satisfied with it," not "from a vain affectation, and believing it greater than it is," but because it is "enough to satisfy the only man she wishes to please" (II, 106).

These pictures of marriage at least suppose a wise, loving, and faithful husband for the wife to honor and obey. In *The Countess of Dellwyn* Sarah Fielding gives a picture of a perfect wife with an erring spouse. Mrs. Bilson is both charming and intelligent. The marriage is a love match on both sides, but after six months her husband tires of domesticity, spending more and more time in public places of entertainment. Mrs. Bilson is distressed, but she always receives him home with affection and "her great study was not to convert his indifference into aversion" (I, 164). His pursuit of pleasure plunges them into debt, despite her own frugality, and when he is imprisoned she learns that he is supporting an illegitimate child who is only three months younger than their eldest. Discovering that her husband had been "so frail, so void of delicacy, at a time that his fondness for her appeared at its greatest height, was a sensible affliction" (I, 172), but she never reproaches him. "Her only difficulty" is bringing the child to live with them because "she feared he would be distressed at finding her acquainted with this transaction" (I, 182).

In the same novel, the countess of Dellwyn is an ambitious woman who marries an old man for money and a title. She is unfaithful more from motives of pride than of lust, is divorced by her husband, and ends up with a "life [which] was a continual mortification" (II, 277). The moral is clear. Mrs. Bilson's history "gives so strong a proof of the efficacy of religious principles towards extracting the sharpest sting from the highest adversity, in as great proportion as Lady Dellwyn's story illustrates the power of vanity to bring to nothing every real advantage" (I, 215). What is also clear, of course, is the conduct books' model for wifely behavior. No matter what the husband's offenses may be, a dutiful wife continues to love and obey with uncomplaining cheerfulness. Although Lord Dellwyn is stupid, dull, and self-centered, Lady Dellwyn "was a memorable instance of the great imprudence a woman is guilty of when she fails in due respect to her husband." Such conduct can only bring dishonor on herself, and "the scorn which falls on her . . . is always deserved" (II, 162). Mrs. Bilson, on the other hand, by ignoring all her husband's offenses and giving uncritical devotion, wins through to a happy marriage with a reformed husband.

A discussion on the merits of marriage, jocular in tone, took place between Anastasia Fenton, a lively young wife, and her unmarried friend Catherine Stubbs. Here the chief issue is the relative merits of the married versus the single state. Stubbs had evidently disparaged matrimony on the grounds that it had adversely affected her friend's letter writing. Fenton replies, "With the necessary apparatus of best paper, new pen, and ink as black as anything except the defamation with which you chose sometime since to bespatter the matrimonial state, I intend to let the first part of my letter show you I can write as clear from blots as I could have before I was married (and as witty and prolix)." Further on, in what is indeed an ironically long and wordy letter, she compares the cares which preoccupy each in her present role. "I really believe if you and I were each sat down to write our best, and news was brought that a bottle of my best ale was burst and swimming about the cellar, if, on such a surprise I should lift my eyes off my paper and thereby discover and inform you that your locks were dropped curl, I am apt to think our entertaining, witty thoughts would be equally stultified."

She continues the comparison: "There are indeed you may say very great apprehensions and fears to employ our thoughts after matrimony, such as I at present experience." Then she turns the reference to her pregnancy to her own advantage. "But then too you must allow there is a period of time though not so nigh at hand when pink ribbons will less become you unmarried than they will me in a lying in." In a deliberately long peroration, she concludes her letter, "These are things to be thought about and no doubt but you do think of them and no doubt they sometimes intrude upon your thoughts when you are writing and no doubt have spoiled many a good letter and no doubt will do many another if not timely prevented by a husband."

In a letter written a few years later the two friends continue their mock contention. Fenton, after chiding her friend for complaining about the lack of wit in her letters, advises, "Dear Kitty for your own sake give up philosophical studies, for while you keep poring over the nature of insects you will still expect that your correspondents should in one line creep like a snail, in the next fly like a butterfly, in the third shine like a king fisher, in a fourth sting like a gnat etc. etc." And she assures her friend, "These things, take my word for it, will not be, especially from us married people who have not time (*as is supposed*) to wrack our brains for witticisms." She jokingly continues, "No, no, Kitty. In the married state there is a husband to be observed and talked to, children to be washed and combed, meals to be ordered three times a day, and I think a wife a great economist that can find time to sit down and enquire after an unmarried woman's health, and I think she ought to receive longer letters in return together with thanks and applause and not short scraps and criticisms."

In other letters Fenton abandons her advocacy of marriage. Replying to her friend's dismay about the waning marriage prospects of Harriet Byron in Richardson's novel *Sir Charles Grandison,* she writes, "If you mean to be grave about your Miss Byron and her Charles, I have really no reason to be of your opinion. You know I talk about matrimony sometimes and I really think it a most courageous act to give one's self and liberty away and swear to do as one is bid all one's life. Those women that marry to please themselves and of their own free will sometimes find will very strong in them after, without the epithet free annexed to it." Her letter concludes, "So much for the better state as you call it which I study this morning more gravely than common as Mr. Fenton is equipping himself to be a bearer to poor Mrs. Beard who died in child-bed on Thursday."

In another letter Fenton again cites evidence against the desirability of marriage. "You speak prettily of matrimony," she writes her friend. "You know we have had many learned disputations on that topic. To illustrate my side of the argument consider poor Mrs. Davison's case. She married well, met with a good husband, she has been a wife thirteen years, in that time she has had eleven children, she has buried nine of them and is now dying of consumption, the consequence of breeding and confinement." She concludes, "What greater hardships the old maids meet with, let the old maids tell."

Pregnancy was in most cases the inevitable and often continuing corollary to marriage. Fear of the dangers of childbirth, as much as a desire for emotional maturity, probably lay behind the reluctance of many parents to have a daughter married too young. Philip Elliot, for example, discusses his nephew's difficulties in courtship, noting that the parents of Miss Harford consider her too young to marry until she reaches twenty-four. Our information about knowledge of methods of birth control in the century is meager and uncertain. We know from Boswell's *London Journal* that he had a condom, but the journal makes it clear both that it was ineffective and that he viewed it as a protection from venereal disease rather than as a preventer of pregnancy. Breast feeding does, of course, usually prevent pregnancy but it was often avoided by middle- and upper-class women who hired wet-nurses.

There is no discussion of avoiding pregnancy in the letters or journals of the women themselves, but one does encounter a fair number of families with, say, three children. This argues some effort at birth control since two or three pregnancies is evidence of fertility, and, with most women marrying in their twenties, these couples would have a good twenty years in which to produce children. The number of unwanted pregnancies, however, is presumptive evidence that prevention was by uncertain methods, or relied on methods which are difficult to sustain such as sexual abstinence or interrupted coition. The records of the Foundling Hospital contain petitions from married couples asking that their youngest be admitted because they are unable to maintain another child. Elizabeth Rogers writes, "Your petitioner hath a husband and three small children in very poor and low circumstances, the youngest of her family being but seven months old, all supported by the industry of her husband, a bricklayer's labourer," and she "most humbly prays your honours to admit the youngest of her children to the benefit of this hospital."

Referring jokingly to the almost inevitable association of pregnancy with marriage, Anastasia Fenton writes, "I believe the town is quite free from the fever, but there is another frightful disorder begun . . . matrimony." She encourages her friend to brave the danger: "Think of the disorder as I do; like the small pox it is a thousand to one but one time or other it happens to all. To be sure in one case a face is often spoiled, in the other a shape but as the intellects are seldom hurt by either I don't think it's much matter."

The birth of her second child left her in a much less light-hearted frame of mind. She apologizes for not having written and explains, "My lying-in left behind it a weak habit of body and spirits." She comments that happiness "is not to be met with in this world without imperfection. You know my husband and I are now possessed of a hearty lively boy and a pretty little girl that has been well ever since she was born, so that were my own health perfect I should be too perfectly happy." Sadly, two months later her little girl was dead. She writes, "I shall . . . not attempt to tell you how much I have been afflicted. . . . I hope I don't wish to recall what God has ordained. . . . it is my desire to think it a mercy to have a check put upon a series of happy events." She admits, however, that she has not "submitted as I ought," and "cannot talk on this subject. I am frail and touched in a sensible part." She is so ashamed of her weakness that in a postscript she directs her friend, "Burn this lest it should not be fit for any to see but those who have just lost a child."

Both infant and child mortality were high, and the dangers of childbirth combined with the hazards of rearing children must have often made motherhood seem a dubious blessing. The extent to which women attempted to shield themselves from the overwhelming grief felt by Anastasia Fenton is indicated by a letter from Mary Foljambe. She is a happy young matron, enjoying a house party, "a tolerable large company of four and twenty" with "both music and dancing" together with "weather favorable for the sportsman." She writes of her little son, "Jacky is vastly happy and seems to enjoy the good society as much as any," explaining that "little Mary was too young to bring from home in this cold weather. Another year she will be old enough to have some enjoyment in it, if she lives and is well." This pessimistic reservation is evidence that even a young mother who is obviously in a cheerful frame of mind remains always aware of the uncertainty of her child's life.

The catalogue of troubles which might make a woman unhappy in marriage differed little in the eighteenth century from our own time, but the authority of a husband and the dependent position of a wife, both in law and in the accepted conventions of society, made it difficult to resolve these problems in a manner satisfactory to the woman. She was generally entirely dependent upon the good will of the husband, the very person causing the difficulties.

Unfaithfulness among husbands was considered a common frailty which wives were supposed to treat with "large grains of allowance." Mary Cowper found it impossible to follow this dictum. "You know, it is my misfortune to think I have no part of your heart if I have not the whole," she writes to her husband. "Since it is my very hard fortune to outlive your love, I beg that, without diminishing the small remainder of esteem you have for me, I may have leave to write freely to you." She reminds him, "You know the constant, sincere, nay violent love that I have ever had for you, which indeed has so clearly appeared in every action of my life that there is no need of saying anything upon the subject. You cannot be ignorant of the many unhappy minutes I have passed through the fear of losing the share I have formerly had in your heart." She refers to "the bitter instance" he gave her when she first came home to him of the "little constancy" she was to expect, and recalls, "You have since then told me often that you would never think of anybody but me and you have as often swore so to me. I now live to see that all those assurances were only to keep me silent, for I now live to see you keep correspondancy with people not at all fit for you if you design to be faithful to me."

Referring to a recent quarrel, Cowper writes, "Nay more, I hear you swear and storm at me because I won't believe that a little dirty letter writ in a woman's hand upon a single quarter of a sheet of paper is from the Duke of Montagu." Fearing that she has gone too far, she apologizes: "Forgive me if I repeat this again—but my heart is so full that I'm forced to give it a little vent, and after having loved you as you're conscious I have I can't part without endeavouring to persuade you that I am not altogether so much in the wrong as you believe me." She assures him, "I wish to God it was in my power to die to leave you to somebody that could make you happier," but "My religion teaches me that it is my duty to await God's affirmed time and that it is not lawful to shorten my days, be they never so miserable."

Since she can "never live with you to see you another's," she suggests "the only remedy I know of. It is with great violence to myself that I say perhaps it will be more to both our eases that we should be separate. Let me then go into the country and spend the remainder of my poor unhappy days in praying for your safety and happiness." This country retirement will demonstrate "that the world nor all its pleasures could by no means lessen to me the affliction of losing your love." Her life will be dedicated "to the education of my poor child in a perfect retirement," and she pleads, "I hope you will not deny me the privilege of carrying her with me." She assures him, "I love you to distraction in spite of everything" and "I love you now at this very minute as much as, nay I think more, than ever I did in my life. Though you can't bestow love upon me, think of me as of the lovingest, faithfullest wife that ever man had. Indeed I deserve it, nay more, could you see the bottom of my miserable heart." The similarities between this letter and the scene in which Pamela pleads with Mr. B. to be allowed to retire to the country are striking. The Cowper letter was written before the publication of *Pamela* and Richardson, of course, had no access to the letter, so no direct influence is possible.

A reconciliation was effected, for a series of loving letters follows this one. The next year Cowper writes, "My dear Angel, I assure you I can never have any real satisfaction when I don't see you." She is at court serving as a lady-in-waiting, but she asserts, "Even being with a Princess whom I love and ought to love so much . . . can't recompense the being from you so long."

Casual promiscuity causes little comment in letters and is taken for granted. Mary Papillon writes to her brother Phillip who is away at school, "I thought you had known the proverb about the nuts—a great many nuts, a great many b—s—d—s." Another sister, Anne, casually relays local gossip, writing, "They say Mr. O—df—d the b—ks—h has a chance child coming at Lymings. He denies it, but not with a very good grace, so most people think it true." She tells another bit of news: "Isaac Bubbure, who once lived here, will be out tomorrow, asked so he may be married, his child christened and the woman churched all at the same time, if he does not run away first as some people say he will."

Desertion was for some men an easy solution to marital problems. Three petitions to the Foundling Hospital are typical of the many received from deserted wives. Margaret Turner submits "The humble petition of a poor distressed woman," declaring "that her husband is gone and left her and she have been obliged to part with almost all that she had to support herself and child, not being capable of doing anything, her time being taken up with nursing." She therefore "sees that she and her child must infallibly be starved if not timely assisted," and asks that the foundation will "take her poor child off her hands that she may be enabled the better to provide for herself." Another petitioner explains that she "belongs to Trigony in Cornwall and was left young with child by her husband who under pretence came to London for servitude." She continues, "She followed him, but to her grief and distress can hear no certain account of him unless he's gone abroad." Now, she relates, "Since she came to London was brought to bed of a helpless infant that she cannot support." Rachel Larham recounts, "Her husband lived with her till such time as all her money and clothes were spent, then left her in a most wretched condition unable to assist herself."

A particularly outrageous case of desertion is related by Lydia Vernon: "Ever since poor Mrs. Dewar's vile wretch went off, joined with the brutality of the Father's treatment, it has had such an effect on me that I am to this day excessively ill." She should seek a cure at Bath, she continues, but she can't find it in her heart "to leave her and her child in the starving situation they have been in this six weeks past," for "the old Father has refused to give her anything," and, although it is March 19th, "nor has she had more than fifty pounds since her villain left her, which was a fortnight before Christmas." While leaving his wife "without a single farthing, he was building fine equipages and buying diamonds for his strumpets." Furthermore, "he has left the poor woman in the same vile situation as before, that is, I mean with the cursed disorder which she was again ignorant of," having been "fool enough to believe his protestations." She declares, "I thought he was less pardonable for murdering the woman in this manner (as he was killing her by inches) than if he shot her through the head," and believes him "now the basest of murderers." After "he and his party appeared about town in the equipage made for his lady" they have gone and "now are in Paris." Of the father, she says, "The old villain knows the poor woman can have no redress, so he has a mind to starve her."

Anne Warde, on the other hand, writes with what seems almost grudging admiration rather than indignation about "the person that broke into the cottage at Hagginfield five years ago," a man who makes John Gay's Macheath in *The Beggar's Opera* pale by comparison. He has just been hanged for "a great number of rob-beries," and, she relates, "I am told he had five wives who have all been to see him since his confinement. He appears to have been a curious genius throughout."

Drinking was nearly universal at all levels of society, and excessive drinking was another masculine foible which was tolerated by custom. Lord Rochester's statement that for five years he was never sober perhaps represents an extreme, but drunkenness was certainly a problem commonly confronted by wives. Anastasia Fenton writes mockingly of the festivities during the Christmas holidays: "The evenings have some of them been concluded among the gentlemen with swearing, fighting, spoiling furniture, breaking windows, snoring and such like masterly performances. Among the wives some have added a wrinkle in their foreheads, which I condemn, for if by any chance a drinking husband should die, a disconsolate widow would certainly look better with a smooth brow than a furrowed one." She concludes with a degree of smug-ness about the virtue of her own husband, "But as . . . [he] has taken care to keep himself sober, the cross wives (were they to see this) might call it theory." Drunkenness was often far from a jok-ing matter. Mary Fox writes, "The chief thing I desire is to live as I do: I mean a boarder, for I would not be forced to live with Mr. Fox again. I suppose you know his failing—seldom sober. I suffered very much when we lived together." She speaks of "his extravagant way of drinking" and betrays her fear in a postscript: "I hope you will not let him know what I have said of him to you, nor mention it to anybody." Fox's account of suffering and her fear of her husband suggest that she was a victim of physical violence.

Wife beating and other forms of physical coercion are not, of course, a problem confined to any one century. It does seem prob-able, however, that the parental authority vested in the husband in the eighteenth century might have given some tinge of moral justi-fication to physical discipline. John Sprint's admonition that husbands should endeavor to promote their wives' "spiritual good and welfare" could be variously interpreted. "I hear Mr. Langley's young wife is but fourteen and very small," Anne Chaytor writes. "He chose her purposely to manage her as he pleased." She con-tinues sarcastically, "We shall see what an extraordinary bringer up of young wives he will prove and how nicely he will teach her her duty, and by seeing how she behaves herself we shall learn the art of catching such nice gentlemen." She adds what may be a wishful thought: "Had he read the *London Cuckolds* he would have found the husband of the young girl to have had no better a fate than the others."

Chaytor writes of another husband, "He is thought to be one of the worst humoured men in the world. He says if his Lady be a good-natured woman he will break her heart, and if she be ill natured he will break her neck." Therese Parker writes of a recently widowed friend who has just refused an offer of marriage, commending her decision. "Her answer to his proposal was not a bad one if she has resolution to stick to it. She said that at home her Mother pinched her, when she married her husband horsewhipped her. She was now her own mistress and very much at her ease." Understandably, the widow "would not subject herself to the like treatment, particularly with a man of a jealous disposition."

Mary Trenchard writes of visiting her cousin: "I went Monday to visit my poor dear Belinda who I found abed, she having lain senseless the night before in a fit for near two hours. She and Sibella were exceedingly rejoiced to see me, but the rest of the noble relatives behaved with the utmost coldness, especially the tyrant yahoo who scarcely spoke. The occasion of this sullenness was from his generous usage of Belinda and I in opening our letters. My share of his disquiet proceeds from saying in one of them that I hoped the happy man who called her person his right would in time grow more worthy of her heart." She states, perhaps disingenuously, "I thought I spoke a good word for my cousin, but it seems his pride induced him to think he deserved her heart and the good opinion of the world besides."

With a husband all-powerful, not only physically but legally, one purpose of marriage settlements was to give some measure of financial protection to the wife, with regard to protecting her dowry from the imprudence or venality of a husband. However, as Mary Astell noted, covenants between husband and wife rested on shaky ground since in an arbitrary government "the will of the sovereign is all in all." Pressure was often exerted through the wife's affection. Frances Cawthorne writes to her father, explaining, "I am very sure Mr. Cawthorne is not able to pay the money for the Lincoln election. And as it makes him very miserable, I wish to know if my giving up more of my income in addition to the two hundred already stopped for interest would enable you to raise money. In that case, dear Papa, I am both ready and willing to do it." She declares that she will not regret "parting with my house in town and I will try to give up every luxury with fortitude and cheerfulness to pay you and to make Mr. Cawthorne happy."

Anne Cole, recently married to the baron d'Ongnyes, writes to her mother, "My want of money . . . has been the cause of misfortunes that I fear can never be repaired. Had I had money I might have engaged the Baron to stay with me and quitted Gland, which I had many reasons to desire." But "when the Baron came here . . . I had it not in my power to do anything to gain upon his spirit which is so great. My not offering to assist him with money, as indeed I ought to do in return for all his generosity to me, has had a very ill effect." She tried to explain to him, she writes, that her inability to assist him "was occasioned by the death of Mr. Curwen and the dispute about my writings," but "he was far from believing me and I doubt not thinks me a great cheat." He returned to Gland "with more appearance of melancholy than anger," she reports, "but what afflicts me most is the fears of his giving himself up to all sorts of debauchery in the melancholy humour he is in, to the entire ruin of his health, which is but bad." The baron has already squandered his own fortune, and now his loving wife is trying to set aside the legal settlements designed to protect her so that she can provide him with sums from her capital.

Her mother, Barbara Savile, replies in an angry letter, "Are you not yet sensible that all his pretences, his protestations of love to you are now plainly discovered to be love to what you had only? Cannot you see his different artful ways to prevail with you and attain from you what he married you for? And if he treats you thus while in pursuit of what is yet your own alone, how will he treat you when by his honourable stratagems he has got it?" She answers her own question, predicting, "Get it he will, and when you are in necessity in that strange country from his extravagance, who can you reasonably expect will pity you? Malicious spirits will laugh at you." While, she maintains, "I love not to meddle between man and wife, thus far I think it my duty to remind you that the wise think all extremes faults," and, cautioning her daughter against passion, "what you call violent in yourself, if you suffer it to govern you, in all probability it will destroy you." The baron has accepted a colonel's commission as a partial remedy to his plight, and his wife is distressed. Her mother writes, "I am unutterably afflicted to find that, considering the Baron's dishonorable falsehoods and sullen behaviour, you can be so much concerned for his leaving you. There lives not one that ever knew you that wishes you well but will think it the blessing that can be desired or wished for in your present circumstances."

Obviously Cole's mother did everything possible to make sure that "her writings," the marriage contract, continued to protect her fortune, and Cole writes sadly to a cousin, as she is planning to return to England, that her husband is much maligned, explaining that people "sport themselves with making bad things worse," and because the baron had "some sad faults, and those very public ones," they then "give him all sorts, even those he's farthest from." She explains, "My dear Mother's concern for me now makes her so angry at him that she will not suffer me to say the truth in answer to the many lies reported of him." "Marriage," Anne Cole philosophically observes on another occasion, "is certainly the happiest or the unhappiest state of life. There is a chance for the first, but my marriage that was so much occasioned by the melancholy posture of my affairs has a greater chance to be the latter."

Sometimes gentle suasion yielded to stronger methods. Ann Chaytor writes to her father about the terrible ordeal of Lady Brooks, whose husband and his two sisters are trying to force her to give up her "writings," the legal settlements. They compel her to write to her relatives asking them to send her the documents, but she manages to send another letter contradicting the first. When her husband and his sisters discover the deception, they are furious. She is now kept a prisoner in her chamber, allowed no pen or paper, and deprived of all her good clothes. (The situation resembles the Harlowes' attempts to intimidate Clarissa.) Chaytor writes her father, "I think it fit [her relatives] should know Sir James and his ill natured sisters' designs which I had from a good hand." She reports, "They've got Mr. Lampton's advice who advises that Sir James never consent to his Lady's going from him, and to show his dislike rather to lock her up, but if she will go, then never to own her more." The strategy is then revealed. Mr. Lampton "assures them if she goes in that manner, the law will not give her a groat," and Mr. Lampton comments that "he wishes he had her to manage and he would make her do what he pleased." Chaytor and her father became intermediaries and later she forwards a letter to him, noting, "I had the enclosed from the Lady Brooks with a request to send it this post. The poor Lady is in the greatest concern imaginable for fear of her sister [in-law]. Sir James swears her death and how things will end God knows." One has the uneasy feeling that the affair could well have ended in Lady Brooks's death, but fortunately her family intervened.

The philanderer, the drunkard, the spendthrift, and the tyrant obviously tend to produce an unhappy marriage. Then as now, however, the causes for unhappiness were often less dramatic and more difficult to define. Mary Trenchard writes, "I was in hopes when my pretty friend had gained her point in getting rid of the mother and sister that she would have been contented if not happy, but she is far wide of it." She gives her opinion that, "I doubt it will always be so," for "their minds are framed as opposite to each other as light and darkness, for which reason it is impossible there should be that tender sympathy and mutual esteem for each other which ought to render marriage the greatest blessing, and without which it is certainly the bitterest curse."

Frances Vane uses another metaphor for her own marriage, explaining that "setting us to rights together will be but patchwork, for we are oil and vinegar and never can unite." She does not leave her husband "from malice, nor passion, but because I cannot do my duty by him from the strong and settled aversion I have to him, which he daily increases by his behavior." A friend, Mrs. Jolliffe, cautions her "to remember, whatever may happen, that our suffering can never justify our doing wrong" and suggests that she "reflect on the solid satisfaction and true pleasure which always accompanies a consciousness of doing right whatever return it may meet with." This pleasure "amply makes amends for any it denies" and furthermore "it is the power of no person or circumstance to deprive us of [it]." Frances Vane replies, "We are very peaceable and very indifferent, the best and only lasting footing we can ever be upon."

Barbara Savile, in a letter to her daughter, gives advice which epitomizes the century's counsel to unhappy wives. "My dear child, there is certainly a deeper foundation for your disturbed thoughts. It is without doubt your expecting more from the world than it can give. I entreat you, do not understand this as a reproach or chide but as a necessary memorandum from a mother who truly loves you and truly sympathizes with you in all your sorrows, and who finds it necessary to speak to herself what she writes to you." As a final comfort, she suggests, "You must be more indifferent to the world and fix your expectations upon God."

Sarah Cowper in a diary which she kept for sixteen years gives an extensive record of the almost daily trials of an incompatible marriage. She writes of her husband, Sir William Cowper, "Certainly Sir W, who is ever opposing and contradicting the most indifferent harmless desires that may be, must render himself but an uncomfortable companion. O Lord give patience." The diary gives ample evidence to support her statement. "After dinner Sir W rebuked me before servants for giving my neighbor a few gillyflowers without his allowance," which "imprudence of his disturbed me much." The entry concludes, "My body suffers."

On another occasion she records, "Having been without company two months I expected Mrs. Ash this day. She is a person to whom I have been many ways obliged and for that reason could not but desire some opportunity to return it." She is afraid, however, that there will be "circumstances to make it uneasy" and continues, "And so it fell out. For I had not sheets to lay her in but what were in Sir W's custody which he refused to let me have. It provoked me exceedingly." On another day she notes, "Made uneasy by Sir W. . . . The dispute was about tableclothes," and "we are ready to sit at the bare board. To mention details were too tedious, but on the matter I suffer much wrong." She concludes, "Assist me O Lord to bear my burdens."

Another quarrel arose from her husband's objections to Cowper's expense for tea and cocoa. After recording that a quarter pound of tea lasts her six weeks, and a half pound of cocoa serves thirty-two days, she writes, "The base inhumane expressions that burst out upon this occasion are not fit nor possible to write." In describing their entertaining, she notes, "Sir W hath so ordered matters that at table we see not the face of a gentleman or woman in an age but the most despicable people one can imagine," because "none that wants not a dinner cares to see the uneasiness we are in. . . . If I carve . . . he bids me let them help themselves, if I let alone he calls on me to do it, and if I put them upon calling for a glass of wine, he saith sure they best know their own time . . . and so on in every like instance. In very solemn fashion I have desired him not to have me so perpetually under correction, but to no purpose. He persists even before my sons which makes me chagrined and uneasy that they should see us so silly."

In another entry Cowper remarks, "It is marvelous to hear him talk how much he is for liberty of conscience and setting people at ease to do as they list, when at the same time there is not a more absolute tyrant. . . . He restrains me in all my due privileges. . . . I just now met with a note that tells the difference between a wife and a concubine. The wives administered the affairs of the family, but the concubines were not to meddle with them. Sure I have been kept as a concubine not a wife." His preempting even her proper authority in the household was a continual aggravation: "A good husband maintains the propriety of his wife in feminine affairs . . . not so much as permitting an appeal to himself, that their juristictions may not interfere." In maintaining her authority over the servants, a good husband maintains his own, but "such husbands as bait the mistress with the maids and clap their hands at the sport, masters who protect their faulty servants hinder the proceeding of justice in a family." On another day she writes of going visiting "where they tell of ladies that manage their domestic affairs in such a manner as argues they have much power: Then home I come a humble mouse gnawing on the thought that in forty years I have not gained the privilege to change a cook maid on any account whatsoever. Who can help being uneasy at these matters? Though I keep silence my heart doth burn within me."

On another occasion Cowper notes that the way the house is run often grieves her, "but it is not always in the wife's power to prevent any faults in the manage of the family. For her authority is but subordinate if the husband who is supreme suspend her power." She amplifies on the subordinate relation of the wife, declaring, "Whatsoever is duty to the husband is equally so be he good or ill. It is not their defects that can absolve the wife, for she has by solemn contract renounced her liberty and taken him for better for worse, and it is too late after vows to make inquiry. How uneasy soever the perverseness of the husband may be, that cannot make the duty less."

Cowper's lack of authority over the servants sometimes led to insolent aggravations, as when she records, "I must be cloistered up, being told by my servants the horses will not go when my lady is in the coach." More importantly, her impotence made the household "the epitome of hell." Not only do the servants exhibit "the sins of men as cursing, swearing, whoring, cheating," but also "the devil of envy, wrath, hatred, malice, lying reigns here without due control." Once after "a day of most bitter provocation" when "Sir W affirmed that all people's servants were so profligate as ours," she observed that "masters were to blame for neglecting the word and worship of God in their families." He replied that he found nobody the better for going to church and that he thought whoring the least of sins. "I could not forbear to say," she writes, "that he ought not to reproach religion but love the effects," declaring that only religion has kept her a faithful wife, although he did not deserve one.

In another entry Cowper observes that in marriages, especially unhappy ones, "the great cause of evil has proceeded from slight occasions," and thus, "it is the first maxim in a married condition that you are to be above trifles." That this was easier to say than to do is made clear by her bitter description of her own marriage, which echoes the words of Mary Astell: "To be yoked for life to a disagreeable temper, to be contradicted in everything, and bore down not by reason but by the authority of a master whose will and commands a woman cannot but despise at the same time she obeys them is a misery none can have a just idea of but those who have felt it." She continues, "If this be a woman's hard fate, she is as unhappy as anything in this world can make her. A man in the like case has a hundred ways to relieve himself, but neither prudence nor duty will allow a wife to fly out: her business and entertainment are at home and though he make it never so uneasy to her she must be content and make her best on it. Indeed, the provocation is great, yet nothing can justify revenging the injuries we receive from others."

When their eldest son received the prestigious appointment of Lord Keeper of the Privy Seal, she reported Sir William's remark that "it is a wonder these little things can disturb me now that I am the Lord Keeper's mother. But I rather think whoever is his wife may be the sow-gelder's mother and it would do every jot as well. Never met two more averse than we in humour, passions and affections; our reason and sense, religion or morals agree not. If vexation would kill, I had never out-lived so many tedious weary days and nights."

She records in a list of foolish women a spinster of fifty who is contemplating marriage and is "about to fling away her never to be enough valued liberty." One Sunday, she narrates, "going to church early, I chanced to be present at a wedding, the most melancholy sight one can see." She has recently lost the sight of one eye with a cataract, and she muses, "For the loss of my eye I never shed a tear, but this melts me into weeping. . . . To hear a simple woman promise to love without cause and obey without reason is amazing." She asserts that she cannot imagine anyone past sixteen entering into marriage, and concludes somberly, "Such as are come to years of discretion should be well advised of what they undertake, for vows though rashly made must be kept so far as possibly they can." On another day she reveals, "When I hear the Bills read at church for any disease or distress whatever, it shocks me less than the Banns of Matrimony. Could I forty years ago have foreseen what hath since happened, I should sooner have chose (were it no sin) to leap into a whirlpool than suffer as I have done in that state. However, we must do good by forgiving injuries."

When commenting on the story of a woman who has run away from her husband, Cowper observes that the runaway has forgotten "this command of the Lord: Let not the wife depart from her husband," and adds, "A certain person I could name was helped by this consideration to resist abundance of tempting causes to have eloped." Despite the unhappiness of her own marriage, Cowper condoned no undutiful conduct in wives, and condemned a visitor who "represented her own ill nature" by telling of her "insolent treatment of the best of husbands, whom it is plain she loves not." She writes, "I have often wondered at those imperious wives who can extravagantly spend what their husbands get with indefatigable toil and labour. Methinks a good woman would be very sparing of what comes that way." She took care to appear cheerful in company so that her friends would "be apt to believe that I have endured nothing." She describes "the method providence has put me in" which is "to fill my head with the good thoughts of the best men, and thereby to lay by my own that are troublesome." This, she writes, "I have found effective." At home, also, "I am outwardly peaceable and silent, thought not inwardly so patient as I earnestly wish to be." On her wedding anniversary she notes, "Our wedding day thirty-eight years since, never yet kept with any ceremony, but now is remarkable, for on it Sir W. hath yielded we shall dine at one o'clock, so that I have gained a point. It is the first time I ever did prevail (to the best of my remembrance). Sure it is an omen of my approaching death, or perhaps, happening in the reign of Queen Anne, it is a sign the power of women will increase."

Later that year, troubled by her failing eyesight, Cowper determined not to leave London to go to Hertford for the summer. "This is the first time (I may truly say) that ever I designed to contradict his will." She prevailed, and their brief separation led to an exchange of letters. Cowper records, "Came the first letter (I think) that ever I received from Sir W since we were married. The truth is we have been but little asunder." Her reply poses a problem in form. She explains in her journal, "It being the first occasion I ever had to answer any letter from Sir W, I was at a loss how to subscribe myself." She solves the problem in this way: "The common form of words your loving, affectionate, etc. I omitted and said your most faithful consort which sure I am was perfectly true having with compassion been the partaker of all his adverse fortune." Sir William writes lovingly in reply, "I am very sensible my faults are great and many and that I have failed very much in my good intentions toward you," but "I can truly say that I never did or spoke anything designedly to disturb your peace, and I can as truly say that I am your truly affectionate husband." Cowper conveys her pleasure in his letter in her diary, writing, "A good word maketh the heart glad," and noting that she has replied, "I have more hopes of you now than ever," and that his amendment "shall produce its due effects with all grateful returns from me."

When Sir William returns to London they have another quarrel. Cowper notes that this "is all the effect of those lovely expressions I lately by letter received, which yet perhaps were sincerely meant when said." Her ingrained truthfulness extends to her account of her husband's death: "On the 20th of November Sir W came home seized with an apoplexy and dead palsy over one side, struck speechless and never spoke more, continued so till the 26th and then died." Her next entry notes, "Sir William Cowper was decently buried with his forefathers in the parish church at St. Michael Cornhill," and then adds her only comment on his death: "This surprising providence has put us in astonishment." She was a serene and cheerful widow who got on especially well with her daughter-in-law, Mary Cowper, whose marriage initially was troubled by her husband's unfaithfulness but later became a truly loving match.

Both Charlotte Lennox and Clara Reeve give striking fictional pictures of the daily strains of an unhappy marriage. In *Euphemia,* Lennox's last novel, her heroine yields to her mother's deathbed entreaties and marries Mr. Neville so that her mother can die happy, knowing that her orphaned child will be provided for. Euphemia soon realizes, "I have drawn a blank in the great lottery of life," but "there is a state beyond this, in which my hopes aspire to a prize," and "it is the Christian only who can endure the present with fortitude" (I, 58). Religious faith sustains her, as she declares, "I am a wife; I know to what that sacred tie obliges me: I am determined, by Heaven's assistance to fulfil the duties of my station." She does act as a wife should, following her husband into the wilds of Albany and Schenectady when his debts force him to accept a commission in New York, but she writes to her friend, "I perceive all the hardships of my situation" (I, 59). The novel gives an interesting account of life on the frontier with descriptions of Indian ceremonials, blizzards, and the hardships of this then remote region. Eventually Euphemia and her husband return to England where Euphemia's intelligence and virtue impress Neville's uncle who makes her his heir, imposing conditions in the will which put her fortune out of the reach of Neville. She now has the satisfaction of being able to educate her son, rescuing him from his father's attempt to debauch him. At the end of the novel she has achieved some happiness, with her independent income giving her control over her life.

Euphemia's marriage is realistically portrayed. Neville is both foolish and pig-headed. He "cannot bear the least touch of blame," Euphemia declares, and "whenever the event shows that he has determined wrong, either totally forgets that it was he who had determined so, or defends the measure in spite of conviction" (IV, 24). She adds, "I never, on such occasions, contradict him." Despite her obvious good sense, she never succeeds in influencing any decision affecting the family: "I sometimes venture to throw out hints," she writes to her friend, "but this he considers as advice, a liberty not to be endured in a woman and a wife" (IV, 5). Relative domestic peace is purchased with submissiveness; in this novel we experience the daily aggravation the century's model for marriage could produce for an ill-matched wife. Euphemia's marriage has common ground with that of Sarah Cowper in its daily petty irritations. In *Euphemia* the reader feels the constant strain for a wife in trying to carry out the marriage vows when absolute power is vested in a husband who is inferior in intelligence, wisdom, and even common sense and yet is overweeningly egotistical, jealously guarding his prerogatives.

The friendship of other women is very important to Euphemia. Her correspondence with Maria helps sustain her spirits, as does the company of her former governess, Mrs. Benson. In America she finds in the company of intelligent, good women some of the social pleasures so lacking in her marriage. When Neville goes off to Philadelphia or Boston "to provide amusements for himself," she is perfectly happy "in the enjoyment of domestic happiness" (IV, 5). The novel makes it clear that she could live a contented life if only her husband would always be absent. After her inheritance gives her independence, she looks forward to a quiet but cheerful existence in the company of her children and women friends. The many lively and confiding correspondences between women that are quoted in this book suggest that Lennox's depiction of the emotional support women gained from each other is realistic, and that when patriarchal structures tended to suppress women's autonomy in relation to men these friendships were especially valuable.

The School for Widows gives Clara Reeve's most detailed picture of marriage. Rachel Strictland and Frances Darnford are both unhappily married, but for contrasting reasons. The first has a miserly tyrant for a husband, while the second is wed to a weak-willed spendthrift. The story of Frances Darnford is a conventional exemplum, showing the evils of vanity and the corruption that follows on fashionable vices such as gambling. She is rushed into marriage by her father, who "was transported with joy at the prospect of so handsome an establishment" (I, 63). Her husband does have a fine estate, a pleasing manner, and a good appearance. She finds herself "pleased with my husband" while "he was extravagantly fond of me" (I, 65). Soon, however, she learns that "pride and indolence were his leading qualities"; the first leads to lavish spending and the second to inattention to his affairs. He even tries to stave off ruin by offering her as mistress to a wealthy friend. She runs away, writing him that his "infamous proposal . . . has cancelled all ties between us" (II, 229). Darnford dies soon after, and, scorning his lecherous friend's offers of help, she opens a school to support herself. Frances Darnford's flight is, in fact, one of the only instances of wifely rebellion which was actually condoned by the conduct book writers, who did not extend a husband's authority to sinful commands.

The marriage of Rachel Strictland is a much more realistic account of the daily unhappiness of an unsuitable match. Here, as with Lennox's Euphemia, we are in the presence of the kind of misery that Sarah Cowper recorded in her journal. Rachel Strictland, neither rich nor especially beautiful, allows her guardians to arrange a suitable marriage, chiefly so that she will have a secure livelihood. This economic motive was indeed a powerful force impelling young women to marry. Mr. Strictland is recommended as "a young man of uncommon prudence and sobriety, one who would increase my fortune" (II, 103), and she marries "without any reluctance, and without passion," aspiring "to nothing higher than a state of tranquillity" (II, 105). She is, in fact, doing just what the conduct manuals counseled—following the judgment of her elders and dismissing any frivolous, unmaidenly notion of amorous love.

Rachel Strictland soon discovers she has married a penurious, ill-tempered man who "will not bear any kind of opposition" (II, 115).

Looking back on her own experience, she advises, "Let every woman take care to know the temper of the man she marries," and "of all the requisites let good nature be the first; it is the basis upon which woman must build her happiness" (II, 136). Although she has no desire to be a dominating wife, a type she detests, desiring only "a kind and gentle master, who would indulge my reasonable demands, and check me in what was improper and unreasonable" (II, 137), her days are a series of painful humiliations. Finally, after a quarrel, she suffers a miscarriage and her life is in danger. She is thinking of asking for a legal separation, but, at the suggestion of the old housekeeper, she draws up a set of "articles" listing minimal demands: her allowance should be paid, she should have a servant, she should be allowed to make and receive visits, she should be permitted to write letters, and she should be treated with courtesy. Strictland agrees, and the marriage settles into an uncomfortable truce. She is still "never sure of the temper he was in" and "obliged to guard every word," confessing "it was always a holiday to me when he went abroad" (II, 184). A son and a daughter bring her some happiness, and, like Sarah Cowper, she constantly tries to "reconcile my mind to what I knew to be my duty" (II, 180).

When Strictland dies, Rachel recounts that she "could hardly understand" her own sensations. "I felt compassion and concern for the father of my children" and "I wish that I had loved him more!" (II, 284). Again, one is reminded of Sarah Cowper's enigmatic journal entry about her husband's death—"this surprising providence." To Rachel's surprise, since "Mr. Strictland had a mean opinion of women" (II, 286) she is made executor and residuary legatee in her husband's will. She is to receive the income of the estate and act as her children's guardian only so long as she remains single, however; if she remarries, she is to be given a small settlement and the children are to be taken from her. Finding this will "most generous, just, and prudent," she declares, "I subscribe to the conditions with my hand and heart, and wish more men were as wise as Mr. Strictland in guarding their property for their children, and restraining their widows from . . . buying themselves husbands" (II, 290). She is, in fact, later courted by a wealthy, handsome, and altogether compatible man. When the will is explained to him, he proves his disinterest by declaring "fortune was no object with him" (III, 242), but she will not give up her children to the care of another. Although she is prevented from enjoying a potentially very happy marriage, she does not repine, and echoing the dictum of *The Ladies Calling* that one venture into marriage was enough for a lifetime, declares, "if all these considerations could be set aside I had resolved, for reasons respecting myself, never to marry again" (III, 243).

While Reeve presents the reader with two marriages in which a good, intelligent, and compliant woman is made miserable by her husband despite her wholehearted attempts to please him, in *The School for Widows* she seems to make no real protest against the established code of wifely submission to the authority of her husband. The lesson that is drawn is one of caution, and carefully assessing the true character of a future husband. However, both Frances Darnford and Rachel Strictland have followed the advice of parents or guardians in the most approved fashion, and Rachel notes that her husband's "mean and sordid mind" (II, 115) was never evident in courtship, so the advice of caution does not seem especially applicable. Reeve seems to draw back from the real dilemma that her novel presents—that of the miserable plight of a woman who is, through no fault of her own, trapped in a life of unrelenting unhappiness. In fact, rather than challenging the legal and social codes which made such situations possible, the work seems closer to a practical guide, reminiscent of the conduct books, giving counsel to those in like marriages. Accommodation and submissiveness, barring only sinful behavior, make life barely tolerable, and one can always hope to be a widow. Even more surprising is the explicit approval of a restrictive will which effectively binds Rachel Strictland to celibate widowhood. The tyranny of her ill-tempered husband continues beyond the grave.

Sarah Scott also shows an unhappy marriage through the life of Mrs. Morgan of *Millenium Hall,* forced to wed a man for whom she "had a very strong dislike" (93). The union is doomed to failure; he "admired her beauty, but despised her understanding . . . for his ideas and conversation were so low and sordid that he was not qualified to distinguish the charms of her elegant mind," while she "suffered less uneasiness from his ill humour, brutal as it was, than from his nauseous fondness" (107). She carries out all her wifely duties, however, nursing him faithfully through his last illness, and she is finally rewarded with widowhood and a large inheritance. Scott's portrait of marriage here is designed to show the evils of a forced marriage, an imposition universally condemned by the fiction of the period.

Given the strong religious and social feelings against separation or divorce and the prevailing belief that marital harmony was almost entirely the wife's responsibility, it is very difficult to assess the percentage of unhappy or happy marriages. Divorce was a possibility only open to the rich and influential, since it required an Act of Parliament, and it was primarily a method for a politically powerful husband to rid himself of an erring wife. Certainly there were strong motives for a wife to present a contented facade to the world, since any other aspect was apt to gain only disapprobation or derision. Within the marriage all of a woman's training and belief inclined her to be submissive, and in the practical realm, since both the law and greater physical strength gave the husband dominant power, passive acceptance and docility were often the only courses possible.

Fortunately, however, the mutual esteem and companionship joined to love cited as the ideal did often exist. Sarah Savage writes in her diary on the anniversary of her wedding, "The return of the year minds us of the mercy of God in our marriage—brought together, taught, kept, increased, comforted on every side—how much are we indebted. 'Tis now thirty years, yet I remember . . . that morning." She recalls from a happy distance her "solicitous thoughts" and the attempts of friends to divert her. Each year of her diary marks the day, with similar comments: "Now thirty-one years, a time to be much remembered, the good providence of God having made it so comfortable to us."

Jane Pateshall's journal records a similar uneasiness before the marriage and a similar happiness in marriage. "I had refused other good offers and did design never to be married," she writes. "I was afraid of altering my condition for so great an uncertainty." She had prayed to God that if she does marry, "it might be to one I might live happy with, and to Him be the praise for the blessings he was pleased to bestow on us. We lived in peace, free from quarrels, never gave ill words, never knew jealousy or mistrust, had the same interest, but above all endeavoured to promote the true interest of each other in a future state of happiness."

Similarly, Elizabeth Shakleton in a memoir tells of her first attempts at schoolteaching: "I was favoured with understanding and knowledge of the business beyond what I could expect, my careful, industrious husband assisting me in many things belonging to my department as well as his own so that we were reciprocally helpful one to the other, sympathizing and bearing burdens one for the other in our arduous calling."

Letters of the period also testify to marriages not only happy but passionate. Jane Lennard heeds neither the conventions of feminine aloofness nor those of punctuation as her words tumble out: "Nothing can love like me for in you is the only joy and satis-faction of my life but dear life if you have any kindness for me make haste home for I am sure I have been in so much trouble for parting with you that I have not had the least minute of pleasure since." She adds, "I write this with tears in my eyes." Pen Foley writes more restrainedly, "I hope my dear love this will find you quite rested after the fatigue of your journey, but can't help being so spiteful as to wish you may find absence and the great distance from me very disagreeable, so that you may in some measure guess at what I feel for want of you."

The letters from Jane Papillon to her husband Thomas during a summer of separation provide a glimpse into another loving and happy marriage. She was at their newly acquired country house in Kent with their four children, supervising the renovation of the property. He was compelled by concerns of business to stay in London. In May she writes, "That you desire to see me I take a secret content in. You will never come before you are desired, but I could wish to know a day or two before, for indeed I have not yet hung a curtain about a bed." The delay is "by reason of mending the ceilings" which "might long since have been done, but that the workmen come for a day or half a day and leave me a week." This "has been so vexatious to me that I every day contrive to bear with what is rather than have more to do with them when they have finished what is begun."

By July the renovation project was apparently causing unease to Thomas Papillon also, for his wife writes, "I shall observe your order as to the sending for the particulars you mention in [your letter]. I shall be careful to my utmost not to heighten your ex-penses. Methinks that word is expressed by you in some discon-tent, but I hope God will persuade you that I esteem your interest so much with my own that your heart may trust in me." She con-tinues to assure him of her carefulness, and states, "I often think I am now in a thankless office, but it was your will to expose me to it, and could I but enjoy you as I hope I shall another summer, a month or two at a time, ourselves alone, the content of it would pay you all your disbursements, for I believe that through the goodness of God we shall have a sweet accommodation." She warns him, however, "This summer we are likely to be unsettled to the end," for "I cannot by any means procure a carpenter." Her letter concludes by advising him that the "court day" has been postponed, "but if you can spare the time I hope you will . . . spend it with her that thinks no enjoyment this side heaven so desirable as the enjoyment of yourself in the Lord. This is the heart language of your most affectionately endeared Jane Papillon."

Her next letter begins, "I had a full expectation of you this day and find the disappointment very ungrateful, yet the less because you do affirm you still retain a desire of my company." She tells him, "I am with you night and day," and fears that "the East India company had drawn you into some new employ for them. So now, said I, indeed, I may be anywhere for we shall never have time to enjoy each other's company." She asks him to write "of your concerns and let me not be surprised with anything." As the summer moves into August, she writes, "I find the harvest very toilsome. Most days we have seventeen men to feed with five meals a day, and they are lords for the time." She "cannot get a maid fit to leave in trust" and she regrets that "it will be necessary enough for me to be here every year in harvest." She tells him, "You cannot want me, but I am sure I find it very harsh to be abandoned the comfort of your society. Your absence is the top of all my troubles and the bitter in all my sweets." She continues, "I often think my long absence will make my company a burden to you at my return, for then you have lived in so fine a serene way that you will think the family I bring with me a disordering burden, and nothing so well with me as without me." She admonishes herself to dismiss these "troubled thoughts" and to place her faith in God "to order all for the best for me," and hopes that "He that has hitherto given me favour in your sight will for His own glory continue it."

In Papillon's next letter she echoes this thought: "Were I not conscious of my own incapacity to be any addition to your delight and comfort I could a thousand times regret my absence from you. I could not be comforted were it not in confidence that the God that has given you grace will still persuade you to express it in a compassionate affection to me." She concludes, "He has made me hitherto dear to you and I will yet hope this mercy shall be continued." At the end of August she writes, "I am now every day contriving how to return with the greatest speed I may to the enjoyment of my choicest worldly comfort, thy dear self, but yet I fear it will be after Michaelmas." She tells him, "I am sure I shall not stay a day with content after I have settled things here." A short letter explains: "This is to go through divers hands before it comes to post which makes me unwilling to offer you anything in it but the assurance of our healths," with "thanks that I am not forgotten by you although at so unhappy a distance."

Papillon's letters continue to give details of household management: "I have received the sack and brandy and know where the claret is but cannot send for it till the dung be carried out." "I have now brewed four barrels and a half of beer in which I have saved clearly thirteen shillings and have better beer." "We have paid off all our harvesters which is a great ease to me." In October she writes, "I have received yours of the third to my heart's content and the filling of my soul with joy even to running over and when I read your love to me . . . thy continued love makes me sense God's goodness afresh." She thanks him for sending the money she needs for boards, lime, bricks, lead, and trees for planting: "I might have served a hard master that would have expected bricks without straw; blessed be God for the contrary. Truly I have to the best of my understanding been a faithful steward." On 13 October she writes joyfully, "I have received thine by which I perceive I shall be welcome to thee, the greatest worldly content I am capable of." The series of letters concludes with her heartfelt assertion, "I am sure I can never choose to leave thee so long again."

About ten years later the tenor of the Papillons' letters is much the same. She writes thanking him for his "thoughtfulness to provide" for her on a journey, and explains, "I could not think but that it might have slipped your thoughts, your mind being filled with so many things of greater weight, but I see nothing makes you forget me. I therefore bless my God for you. Oh, how many years has God given us solace in each other and given us to see his love to us in ours to each other. Goodness and mercy shall follow us I hope still." Thomas Papillon writes to his wife, "I have received one from you this day which was very grateful being the first I have had from you since my coming hither [London], for I know not how to call it home in your absence." He chides her, "But my dear, why do you so value me, a poor worthless sinful nothing? I stand more in need of your prayers for quickening grace and a spiritual frame than you do of mine." He urges her, "I beg you would sit more loose from any dependence on me, not that I would have you love me less, but that I desire you may so live while I am that when I am not you may not be at a loss."

And eighteen years after that summer, Thomas Papillon writes from Holland, "I have received thine and find thy affections still working towards me as mine to thee and that we cannot be content without the enjoyment and society of each other." He begins to look for a place to live, relating, "I am going tomorrow to Utrecht and shall consider how I like that place. As to this place, it may be convenient in reference to trade, but . . . there is no good Christian society; getting of money and saving money is the only business." His frequent letters repeat, "Your absence is my greatest trouble" and assert, "I love you as my own soul." From Utrecht he writes, "As I wrote you, I cannot live comfortably without you; all the world is nothing to me in comparison." He laments that he lives like "a prisoner," like "one out of this world." Deciding that he cannot tolerate her absence, he declares, "This has engaged me to think of taking a house where you may be with me, and I think I shall agree for one this day." Twenty-five years after the first series of letters Thomas Papillon writes to his wife from London, "As it hath been with you so it hath been with me. I have not slept well since you went, but by degrees it begins to be somewhat better and I hope it will be so with you and that the air will do you good." He assures her, "I bear you still in mind and cannot do otherwise having you in my heart and in all my prayers."

Another series of letters that gives insight into the life of a happy wife is the letters of Elizabeth Amherst Thomas to her brother, then Sir Jeffrey Amherst, the commander of His Majesty's forces in North America. The letters are probably especially numerous and especially full of ordinary household detail because she was raising his son together with her own. She therefore tried to give him frequent news of the family. The tone of the letters, naturally, is quite different from the Papillon correspondence.

Elizabeth Thomas was married to a clergyman, and they were in constant financial difficulties. In one letter she relates that although her brother had loaned them money to settle bills, it was not enough and she had secretly borrowed £150 from "Mr. Delabere a very honest attorney." He is now pressing for its return and she has been forced to confess the debt to her husband. She writes, "You will believe it hurt his spirits who thought his circumstances almost clear of any encumbrance. He blamed me but not so much as I deserved, for concealing it so long from him." They have set about new schemes of economy, she reports. They will keep no horses and therefore will only need one manservant, and they plan to discharge one of their two maids. As an economy, they will drink tea only in the mornings. Good livings in the church were distributed largely through influence. She reports, "My Brother has been so kind as to ask for the vacant prebend at Worcester for us, but it was too late; it was promised, and whether we shall ever attain to so much as a promise of anything God knows." The brother spoken of is her husband's brother, and she now brings some gentle pressure on her own brother. "It is my opinion that if his majesty knew how very happy some addition to our income would make us, he would be readier to bestow something on Sir Jeffrey's relations than the ministry are." She continues, with an ironical reference to the dubious grounds for many ecclesiastical appointments, "and I must say that by our relationship to him we seem to have a claim to be considered, and I think it is a very great slight done to Sir Jeffrey's services if we are not provided for, and if they don't behave better I'll write libels on the A—n [Administration?] whenever I am out of humour which will be whenever I am cold or hungry." She concludes, "I joke, but it is seriously very hard."

The necessity for frugality seldom dampened Thomas's spirits, however. In one letter she relates how one of her economies has come to set the fashion in her village. "You may tell all your Sevenoaks ladies that rose colored yard stuffs are all the fashion at Northleach this winter, and petticoats of the same, patterned in scallop shells." She explains, "I happened to see a piece at Mr. Charles," and "the whole charge of gown and coat and making was one pound. It is well glazed and looks like satin." As a result, "the Duttons and Mrs. Wallis must all have the same, it is so handsome, and Charles is writing every post for more rose-colored stuff." She jokes, "You little think that I buy rose colored gowns and set fashions. It is a sign I am very young and handsome and above all remarkably genteel."

The letters tell of various household economies, all in the same cheerful spirit. After the cider is pressed, she reports, she distills the "pummice," the crushed apple mash, into brandy. After fortifying the cider by adding two quarts of brandy to each eighty gallon hogshead, the rest is aged and, she brags, "kept a year will be equal to French brandy, as I have experienced."

She is a good manager with the children's clothing also. She writes her brother a careful account of his son's wardrobe. She has bought fifteen yards of Irish linen "at two shillings nine pence a yard to make Jeff six shirts," she reports, and at the same time she is giving his old ones new wristbands. She writes of his clothes, "His eldest are but shabby and he was very unwilling to own he had them when he came here, but I found them out." She has cleaned and mended them, "excepting the old leather breeches which were too bad to wear or mend and I bought him a pair for seven shillings six pence." Now, however, she asks, "Shall I get him a suit of clothes and let him make the best he has now his everyday ones? My way with Jack is always to keep a best and a worst suit in wear." She gives details of waistcoats, hose, and pocket handkerchiefs, and concludes, "If you approve this system, I'll manage the same for Jeff."

Thomas and her husband took care in supervising the boys' education. "Mr. Thomas says," she relates, "that he would by all means advise both Jeff's and Jack's sticking to on Latin, English writing and summing for a year or thereabouts, as he thinks French would but interfere at present and little heads cannot take many things at once to any purpose. To be competent Latin scholars he thinks of use to any gentleman of any profession, though dancing all the while he says he approves of, as it will employ their heels and keep them upright and clever."

Thomas writes that both boys are making good progress in Latin. Their personalities are complementary, and the shy one is spurred on by his more venturesome companion, while the steadiness of the quiet boy is a useful check on the impetuousness of the other. Jeff "is naturally of a sweet temper and will make a very clever man." During January she writes, "We detain our boys from school because the weather and roads are bad yet, but their time is not lost as they daily learn Latin, geography etc. of days, and in the evenings I teach them to play at whist or cribbage." She shows a rather modern approach to education when she explains, "You may laugh at these accomplishments but whist teaches them gravity and conduct, and cribbage, as they keep scores, plays them insensibly into arithmetic." She is also concerned with the social graces. "These are not the only branches I instruct my nephew in. They also make the tea for me and do the honors of the table," and "I am sure I have not a niece that can do it so well."

Thomas had a reputation in the family for a talent for writing. At one time she and her husband apparently proposed to write an account of Sir Jeffrey's campaigns based upon his journals. She writes that they will be a good combination; he has the "solid erudition" and her "flying genius" will serve to "embellish the style with a little female currency." On another occasion she jokingly laments her lack of a proper response to one of his victories. "I could sit down and write an epic poem on your victory, but it is market day and Mary is coming to me, 'Madam shall I buy some eggs, madam the butter woman is come, madam do you want a couple of ducks? Madam the maltman has brought his bill.' Simon Hughes has visited me, 'How do you do good madam,' then comes Mary, 'Is the note ready to go to Nutgrove, madam'!" She voices the feelings of many housewives enmeshed in daily routines in concluding, "Now . . . you'll say it is very true I have no time to write poetry."

Good humour is pervasive in Thomas's letters despite occasional impatience with her circumstances and her role. She writes offering her brother "a very fine picture," explaining, "It is a large one and more proper for an officer's house than a clergyman's the subject being a lady stepping out of a bath into a grotto to dress, and as she has no clothes on she shows her bum and has the finest bum and the finest heel that ever was seen." On another occasion she reminds her brother, "You have heard of Cousin Grace Catt whose mother was an Amherst, who wore men's clothes partly and drove her own team to market with corn and once thrashed three men who attempted to take her gun away when she was shooting crows in her ground." She claims kinship, telling her brother, "And whenever you catch your sister Bess at deviating a little from the rules of feminine delicacy, you must attribute the lapse to a grain of the masculine spirit inherited from the same source."

Thomas enjoyed their rather rare social excursions, and reports of the generous hospitality during a visit, "They all recommended victuals and drink to me," adding, "I could not but taste of all, but took care about liquor." She records that her caution allowed her only "one large glass of very strong beer and three of wine which were Moselle." On another occasion, she was at a dinner where her brother's victories are being celebrated and toasts are drunk to each of the Amhersts. Finally a guest exclaimed, "Good God what a number of Amhersts! Are there any more to come?" She replied, "Yes, you may drink my health in a bumper for I am sister to them all four." She tells of a pleasant round of parties during a visit, writing, "Very merry we were, and where ever we went the General's health was drunk in bumpers. I was in high spirits, and laughed like a girl of fifteen, but now I am returned to our own fireside, doubly enjoying the tranquillity of it. I am the grave matron again with my boy Jack saying his catechism at my knee."

How happy was the average eighteenth-century marriage? It is certainly true that the religious teachings, the social mores, and the legal codes of the period created a highly authoritarian model for marriage in which power resided in the husband and submissive obedience was expected of the wife. Even feminists of the period, such as Mary Astell, agreed that once a woman had taken solemn vows she was obligated to honor and obey her husband, no matter what enormities he might be guilty of. (The only exception, conceded even by John Sprint, was a command to engage in sinful behavior.) Such a pattern undoubtedly both caused and exacerbated difficulties for many wives, and so prevailing was the ideal of wifely submissiveness that a woman's protests would gain little sympathy in the court of public opinion. Legally, she had no recourse at all, although in extreme cases her family sometimes intervened and secured a separation. Divorce was only possible by an Act of Parliament, and in practice was granted only to petitioning men. The life of a woman wed to a tyrannical man was a life of daily humiliation in the best of circumstances, and of dangerous brutality in the worst.

The ideal proposed for marriage, of course, stressed that the power of the husband, tempered by love, was used only for the benefit of his wife. The man's greater strength of both body and mind provided a secure refuge for the weaker sex. Each partner brought certain qualities to the union: he provided reason, stability, and subsistence; she contributed tenderness, grace, and housekeeping. The extent to which any couple actually reflected the image approved by the conduct books varied widely with the personalities and beliefs of the partners. It also seems to be true that the ideal of a companionate, cooperative marriage as opposed to rigid patriarchy gained adherents during the period studied here. Jane Papillon, writing in 1667, while undoubtedly a happy wife, conveys a tone of deference in her letters which suggests she subscribes to a very traditional view of her role. Elizabeth Thomas, writing a century later, conveys a much greater sense of independent equality, even borrowing money without her husband's knowledge. However, while the image may have changed, there was virtually no change in laws or in other structures that might help wives; therefore, those who most needed help—those married to tyrannical husbands—were not benefitted. The extent to which a marriage was patriarchal or companionate depended entirely upon the husband's willingness to cede the power society granted him.

Novels almost all gave a happy marriage as a reward to their heroines. The novels considered in this study universally stressed that marriage should not be entered into without love and that courtship should be a time when the couple got to know each other well, forming a relationship based on mutual esteem and common interests. Caution and intelligence were necessary when choosing a husband who would then assume absolute power over one's life. Most of the novels suggest that the ideal pattern is that of loving cooperation in a framework where the husband is a wise, kind mentor who will be guide and protector. The majority of novels end with the marriage of the heroine, but a few depict the daily reality of marriage itself. Of the portraits of marriage, the works of Sarah Fielding and Henry Fielding are notable in reinforcing the conduct book model of wifely submissiveness, while the novels of Richardson suggest a radical departure from the model.

Sarah Fielding, as we have seen, presents her ideal of marriage as that of David and Camilla, where "the modest mind of Camilla ever fled for protection and refuge to David's understanding." David is a good man, but even when a husband proves to be a profligate, as with Mr. Bilson, the good wife carries on cheerfully, never taking notice of either his absence or his extravagance, and, in the novel at least, she is rewarded by the return of his love. A wife, on the other hand, no matter what the provocation, may never stray, and if she does is rightfully consigned to "continued mortification." Henry Fielding's *Amelia* also strongly supports the image of wifely submissiveness as the chief virtue of women. Despite Booth's unfaithfulness, gambling, and general incompetence, Amelia never offers a word of protest, cheerfully pawning her clothes to pay his debts. While some of Booth's actions are condemned, Amelia is consistently praised. She is presented as the ideal wife.

Richardson's novels all offer radically different ideas about marriage. The Amelia-like submissiveness of Clarissa's mother is expressly condemned in *Clarissa,* while both the continuation of *Pamela* and *Sir Charles Grandison* depict marriages in which the husband grants more than full equality to the wife, pledging to be guided always by her wishes. In *Pamela* Mr. B. grows into this role, beginning as a highly patriarchal husband but, under the influence of Pamela's virtue and good sense, gradually changing until he declares, "And now, my Pamela, from this instant you shall be my guide." The recommended conduct-book response of appearing to ignore a husband's unfaithfulness nearly results in disaster for their marriage, and openness rather than feminine wiles is presented as effective in preserving it. Sir Charles and Harriet, from the first, have a marriage of equality in which he pledges, "Your will, Madame, will ever comprehend mine."

Even more radically, Richardson's novels present models for happy marriages where the woman is clearly superior in intelligence and more forceful in personality. Sir Charles advises his sister Charlotte that if she cannot find a man who is her equal then she should marry a man who will recognize her superiority. Her match with Lord G. we see evolving into a happy marriage. Anna Howe, at the end of *Clarissa,* gives a telling summary of the dilemma of the intelligent woman confronting marriage vows when "there is not one man in a hundred whom a woman of sense and spirit can either *honour* or *obey*." She does marry, but it is implied that Hickman's "good nature" and "respectful behaviour" will result in a marriage rather different from the prescriptions of the conduct books. Throughout Richardson's novels the intelligence and virtue of men are inversely proportional to their insistence on masculine power.

Together with the depiction of the Harlowe marriage in *Clarissa,* two other novels, Lennox's *Euphemia* and Reeve's *School for Widows,* show with great force and realism the daily misery of an incompatible marriage. In each case, the marriage has been entered with reasonable prudence, so each is also a warning of the difficulties which might confront any young woman. While these works graphically demonstrate the inequity of the century's pattern for marriage, neither suggests rebellion. On the contrary, the wives virtuously and patiently put up with their tyrannical and unloved husbands. The journals of Sarah Cowper are evidence that such marriages indeed existed in actuality.

Fortunately, many marriages were happy, and most couples worked out a model which fit their own temperaments. Probably many would agree with Lady Bradshaigh when she writes, "The little rubs you speak of which must happen in a married state are what no doubt everyone sometimes has experienced, but what temper must they be who make such trifles their lasting unhappiness?" However, for the unhappily married woman the model created by conduct books was a nightmare. She had made solemn vows, "for better or for worse," and no enormity on her husband's part excused her from her sworn duty. Society, religion, even feminists like Mary Astell, all instructed her that her duty was clear—to honor and obey. Practical remedies were virtually nonexistent, and her only consolation was that her trials would earn her merit for the next world. The only novelist who offered an alternative model for marriage was Richardson, who depicted ideal marriges of absolute equality between man and wife. Richardson's novels may well have aided the movement towards companionate rather than authoritarian marriages; they certainly condemned patriarchal tyranny.

CHAPTER 5

Spinsters and Widows

S PINSTERS AND WIDOWS were each an anomaly in the eighteenth century because they were women unattached to a man who both dominated and protected. Neither, therefore, fitted the ideal of woman that the age had created, and both, in fact, were pitied. Whether their state was in actuality pitiable largely depended upon their financial position. An unmarried woman or widow of independent means certainly had far greater opportunities to determine her own course of life than a daughter who owed obedience to her father or a wife who was subject to her husband. When a sufficient income provided this autonomy many, especially widows, indeed did enjoy their new freedom. But when, as was all too common, the spinster found herself dependent on a grudging eldest brother or the widow on the generosity of a son, the position could be miserable, and the opportunities for a woman to obtain financial independence through her own efforts were meager and often demeaning. The century pitied the spinster and the widow, and sustained the conditions which made the single state unenviable. In this chapter the difficulties facing single women will be explored, and the lives of some typical spinsters and widows will be illuminated through their own words. Novelists seldom gave much importance to either category, except for Sarah Scott who created a utopian community of widows and spinsters in *Millenium Hall*.

Since marriage was considered to be the natural and desirable condition for a woman, that in which she could best exercise her social functions and best practice religious virtues, the unmarried woman was seen as a potential bride, as someone waiting to be fulfilled, until, alas, advancing age made this hope seem improbable. Marriage conferred status on a woman not only in the practical sense that it made her mistress of a household, but in a more subtle and pervading sense also. Lady Bradshaigh, speaking of her meeting with Catherine Talbot, a woman known for her learning and accomplishment, describes their mutual diffidence and hopes that her own shyness "will excuse for all my disagreeable and ill-timed reserves." Then, rather than pleading awe before a woman of Miss Talbot's reputation, she continues, "Thus far I am willing to take blame to myself," explaining, "the married lady *ought* to have made more advances."

The *Oxford English Dictionary* records that "spinster," which had long designated an unmarried woman, took on the pejorative meaning of "old maid" in 1719.[1] Significantly, spinning was at the same time becoming obsolete in most households, and changes in the economy and in the structure of the family during the century made the presence of an unmarried woman in the home much less desirable. While by modern standards a great many tasks, such as brewing, sewing, and baking, were still done at home, especially in country households, much of the household work of an earlier age, such as spinning, weaving, and butchering, was being done by specialists and formed part of the retail trade, especially in towns and cities. An extra pair of hands was no longer so useful in the household. Spinsters were seldom a problem while they were still also daughters, for an unmarried daughter almost inevitably assumed the care of aging parents, often with little reward after their death. While the term "spinster" technically referred to all unmarried women, it will be used here generally with the connotation the century gave it of "old maid."

Concomitant with the decline of household industry was a growing desire for privacy on the part of married couples. Elizabeth Wheeler replies to a request made to her to secure lodgings for a newly married couple, writing, "As to dear Mother's request concerning the marriage, I am not able to certify their being so very private. There is no house at present at liberty for them except they go to William Lucas, the same which cousin Joseph and Nanny were at when they first settled." Evidently, dubiously comfortable accommodations might be preferred for the sake of privacy. The same desire is expressed in Jane Papillon's letter to her husband: "Could I but enjoy you as I hope I shall another summer, a month or two at a time, ourselves alone." The couple had four children and a few servants, so "ourselves alone" actually refers to the absence of relations, not to a honeymoon idyll. This growing trend toward a household consisting only of the married couple and their children, together, of course, with the servants consonant with their status, was a hardship for widows and spinsters. It was often a greater hardship for spinsters, however, for the bonds of duty were much stronger toward a mother than toward a sister. A widow might also have some financial security from her jointure, while the chief financial provision that was likely to be made for a daughter was the stipulation that the heir provide a dowry. These provisions were often informal and unenforceable by law.

Some spinsters had enough self-esteem to refuse offers of marriage which they found unsuitable. Marthae Taylor was a very independent spinster who refused several offers of marrige. She comments to a friend, "Though the blue be off the plum, I'm so far from being humble therewith that I grow more and more extravagant in my expectations, if I can be said to have any," and on another occasion writes, "The old maid sets a high value on herself I assure you, nor will she 'bate an ace for age, nor is she conscious of any other cause for abatement." She resolves "to laugh at the skits the ill-natured world throws at old-maids." Nevertheless, she gives rather different advice to a young relation, commending her niece's refusal of an unsuitable match: "As to the affair you mention, your prudence has done you a good office in my opinion, and I have hope therefrom that you'll not be too easily caught." She continues, "Yet I'd have you consider, my dear, that a female of your father's numerous stock cannot hope to be so amply provided for but that in the decline of life, if she reach that time single, she may possibly be somewhat desolate if not disconsolate." Referring to her own experience, she notes, "you see how lightly regarded I am by kindred, how I've been tossed from wig to wall as the phrase is, how distressed for a home when years and infirmity made it necessary." She says bitterly of her relations, "Their regard and affection seem wholly confined to husband, wives and children. Hence let

200

that prudence that bids you decline one offer prevail with you to accept a better when Providence points it out."

She suggests a very practical rather than a romantic approach: "If a man has good principles; is sober, honest and religious; has good sense and good nature, with competent fortune to provide in a decent way for you and the children you may be blest with, refuse him not, for you can't miscarry. Endeavour to be duly qualified to make a good wife, a good mother, a good mistress, a good neighbor and a good christian. Your own understanding will instruct you to regard the essentials and overlook trifles in the man you choose." The pragmatic nature of the choice is indicated by her rhetorical question, "What if his face be coarse, his bow awkward or his air ungenteel?" She concludes with an analogy which stresses creature comforts: "You may be as warm, as clean, as easy and cheerful hearted in a plain silk gown as in one adorned with fringes."

Mary Allsopp, writing to a friend, illustrates the plight of the aging spinster. Her health is failing, and she reports, "Indeed I am a poor creature and have not a relation that assists or comes at me. I meet with such slights as affects my poor mind, and I can't help but wish I had never come to this place, but I did not think when I had lost my dear sister that I had ever behaved to my relations as to have them quite neglect me in my distress." Her nephews, she relates, "seemed deaf" when she told them "the miserable situation I was in."

Martha Dashwood describes what one hopes was a more typical situation. She writes that her sister is "treated with great respect by Mr. & Mrs. Whalley" and that "next summer I expect she will return to us." She explains, "Mr. Dashwood, who is one of the best of husbands, endeavours to make her situation as agreeable to her as he can," but "her dependent state has given me and still does vast uneasiness as it is entirely out of my power to free her from it." She concludes, "I trust in God that she will never be destitute of friends."

The uncomfortable nature of this kind of dependent life is expressed by Mary Knollis: "I have no thoughts of returning this Winter as for many reasons it is judged best for me sometimes to be absent, as my good Brother many years ago often declared that he never would have a relation to constantly live with him." She relates a further complication: "He has a sister of his own unmarried." (In the period the expression "in-law" was very seldom used. One's mother-in-law was simply mother, brother-in-law simply brother, and so on. This verbal formulation often reflected actual feeling.) Knollis declares, "As for me, I owe him the greatest gratitude; his kindness I cannot express," but, despite this, "my dependent state is so truly affecting to me that it requires all my fortitude not to sink under it. Were it not for the appellation of Lady Mary, I would have gone to service years ago. But alas had I anything certain I should be happy. Nine years already have I known myself a dependent for every necessary." She was at least in a somewhat happier condition than Miss Dutton, of whom Samuel Richardson reports, "We have a lady with us also, Miss Dutton, who is likely to resign her breath with us: a most worthy person of long acquaintance whose heart has been broke by a barbarous and most sordid Brother-in-law with whom it was her hard fate to live." She was, in fact, cared for in her last illness in Richardson's house and died there.

Boarding with a family was one solution for homeless spinsters or widows with sufficient funds. Mary Buller writes to her cousin, Gertrude Bampylde, "If I may advise I should take the forty shillings a year, for that will be of more advantage to you than the twenty pound to be laid out in annuity: The greatest wonder to me is how your relations whose ample fortunes might afford you a support without their feeling it, more than sufficient to make the remainder of your life easy, can suffer you to be under obligations." Further, "you was mentioning of settling yourself in some good family. Is there any good neighbors thereabout that would let you be with them? If there is, I think it is the best thing you can do. Suppose it was at a good honest farmer's—there you might live at your ease and the servants that they have might assist you in what you wanted."

Of course, some spinsters were no doubt genuinely troublesome. Letitia Barnston writes to her steward asking him to "enquire of Mr. Gwynn Millener if he knows whether Aunt Vaughan is duly paid." She continues, "She torments me with letters and complains of Mr. Gwynn though I verily believe without reason. It was my own request to him when in London that when a quarter was due he would take the trouble to enquire of the persons she lodged with what was owing to them and to discharge them and pay her the remainder." Aunt Vaughan "complains that he pays them too much" but this "is nonsense, for I know she would gladly receive all, live merrily while it lasts, and shift to new lodgings when she could not pay off the old ones." Barnston concludes,

"As she pleases to live in London she may jog on as she pleases for me, for I know she has an income from her friends and myself that would maintain her in a genteel manner out of London, but she absolutely refused to leave it."

Parents usually tried to make some provision for unmarried daughters, but if, as was often true, the estate was entailed, the carrying out of these provisions largely rested with the eldest brother. This was true whether they were stated in legal documents or merely expressed in letters or verbal instructions. Anne Chaytor, the sister of William Chaytor whose daughter Ann's letters appear in chapter 2, illustrates the difficulty in her letters to her brother. In an early letter she writes, "You talk of changing my condition. I'll assure you one great reason which made me think the less of it before you married was the fear of putting you to too much inconveniency. I never could speak to you anything concerning my fortune before you married, but always relied on your good nature which I always found and still do"—she adds what was to prove a prophetic statement—"though it is generally seen that people's kindness is much taken off from their relations when they have once got a wife." She concludes, "I hope you will be just to yourself and me, which is not at all doubted by your affectionate, loving, sister."

Chaytor does find a suitor who pleases her, and writes her brother, "I hope I shall have no cause to repent for he is a sober, good humoured man and one that I like and have reason to believe he loves me," adding that he "is industrious and in a way to get more and as to quality it is the best of that name in Northumberland which everyone knows is not mean." Her prospective husband "is steward to my Lord Chine and his Aunts" and she relates, "I do not doubt by God's assistance but we may live very happily," giving details of the farm they will have "almost as good as free land" together with his salary of "fourscore pounds a year beside what other advantages are to be made of the place." She then says, "And now dear brother, as you have always told me that I need not fear but to have my portion paid me, I hope you will not grudge it to him no more than if it were to a man that had a great estate, and for what additions you have mentioned several times, I will not expect that." She explains her husband's position: "He is much concerned for me to have me live well and to leave me in a good condition if it should please God he should die. The better my portion is, the better it will be for me every way."

Her brother's response was not satisfactory, evidently, for she writes bitterly, "I cannot imagine what should change you so of late for when you were newly married you wrote several kind letters to me (which I have still) wherein you expressed I need not fear my fortune secured to me with the addition of brotherly kindness. And now I must have but half my fortune and you pretend you give it as a gift." A few months later she writes again asking for her money and declaring, "It would come very seasonally now for I have put Mr. Ogle [her husband] to charges several ways and he has got nothing with me yet which I am much ashamed of." She complains that even if the match is considered a bad one, "One little to another would help much, for I have added nothing to him, which if I had it would be a great deal better for use." The brother upon whom Chaytor depended had financial troubles of his own. He eventually became a bankrupt, and her portion was never paid.

Susanna Clark writes to a friend about her troubles after the death of her parents: "I am still ignorant what I shall have for support. We are moving for an annuity, but nothing is fixed." She describes her plight, noting, "The world grows thin, spirits fail, I am fallen four inches in size," and "my daily fatigue without any assistance reduces strength to a low ebb." She congratulates her friend, "I hear you are amply provided for in a genteel manner which gives me great pleasure (as I hope it is really so)." Her expectations are evidently not unduly high, since her letter gives news of Sally who "expects to be well married to one who gets fifteen shillings a week."

Mary King also had trouble with her brother. She writes that she has been informed that a debt contracted by their father has now been owing for three years, and her brother refuses to pay it on the grounds that it is her debt. She asserts, "My father never did make me pay for my physic in his life out of my allowance," and "besides I had no allowance from him for three quarters." She explains, "The gown and other things my brother and sister can witness he gave me order to take." Evidently her brother has refused to pay her promised dowry, for she states, "And truly brother my fortune to poor Mr. King has been very bad. I am sure it is a very great hindrance to me." She notes also that it would be "a great advantage" to her little boy. Sarah Perrin records the career of her brother who not only lost his own fortune but the fortunes of his two sisters, speculating in the famous South Sea Bubble. Fortunately, she managed to marry well anyway.

The plight of unmarriageable spinsters caused many writers of the period to regret the loss of nunneries. Mary Astell, in *A Serious Proposal to the Ladies,* suggested the founding of a sort of Protestant convent. The ladies would take no vows, but they would dedicate themselves to piety and learning, avoiding the frivolities and temptations of the world. "To avoid giving offence to the scrupulous and injudicious by names which though innocent in themselves have been abused by superstitious practices," she writes, "we will call it a Religious Retirement" (60). It will have a double aspect, she continues, "being not only a retreat from the world for those who desire that advantage, but likewise an institution and previous discipline to fit us to do the greatest good in it. Such an institution as this . . . would be the most probable method to amend the present and improve the future age" (61). It would not "exclude the good works of an *active* from the pleasure and serenity of a *contemplative* life, but by a due mixture of both retain all the advantages and avoid the inconveniences that attend either" (73). The women would endeavor "to expel that cloud of ignorance which custom has involved us in" and "to furnish our minds with a stock of solid and useful information" (75). Their chief practical work would be the education of girls, "to stock the kingdom with pious and prudent ladies." And, of course, there would be an immediate practical advantage: "Nor can I think of any expedient so useful as this to persons of quality who are over-stocked with children, for thus they may honourably dispose of their daughters without impairing their estates" (158). The capital sum which a woman would pay upon entering would be five hundred pounds. George Ballard reports in his life of Mary Astell that she had found a benefactor who was going to establish such an institution, but he was dissuaded by Bishop Burnet, who thought it was too close to popery. Anglican convents were not founded until the nineteenth century, when they were in large part a response to the women's movement and an effort to answer the same needs that Mary Astell articulated. In *Sir Charles Grandison,* Sir Charles plans to found an institution for spinsters on Mary Astell's model.

The Ladies Calling also laments the disappearance of convents: "I think it were to be wished that those who suppressed them in this nation had confined themselves within the bounds of a reformation, by choosing rather to rectify and regulate than abolish them." The work suggests that while these societies no longer exist, "there may be nuns who are not professed," and that a woman still has the option of devoting her heart to God, and intending to pursue a virgin life which will admit no human love. It then declares that the case for nuns "does not much need stating in our clime," because "women are so little transported by the zeal of voluntary virginity, that there are but few can find patience for it when necessary," and expressing the contemporary aversion to spinsters, states, "An old maid is now thought such a curse as no poetic fury can exceed, looked on as the most calamitous creature in nature" (II, 3).

Sarah Scott's *A Description of Millenium Hall,* as its title suggests, presents a utopian community, in this case one created and managed solely by women. Two travellers, Sir George Ellison and his somewhat frivolous young friend Lamont, discover this Eden when their carriage breaks down nearby. The two are kindly received and introduced to Millenium Hall and to its inhabitants, learning the stories of their several lives before they came to this refuge. The two founders, Mrs. Morgan and Miss Mancel, are the survivors, respectively, of an unhappy marriage and a tragic love affair, traditional reasons for women to flee the world, but the hall also shelters a surprising number of voluntary spinsters. Miss Trantham had been the belle of the London season, but she rejected all offers and now finds true happiness in this country retreat. Lady Mary Jones, a highly eligible heiress, has rejected the glitter of society and the prospect of marriage to join the company of women at the hall. Mrs. Selvin has also refused proposals of marriage. Although, she declares, "it was impossible Lord Robert could fail of pleasing," she tells him that "it could not be advisable to marry," explaining that "enjoying perfect content, she had no benefit to expect from change" (205). She tells her suitor, "Were you endowed with all the virtues that ever man possessed, I would not change my present happy situation for the uncertainties of wedlock" (210–11). As we have seen, actual women such as Marthae Taylor did sometimes share this reluctance to risk the loss of freedom that marriage entailed, but it was nevertheless usually assumed that "old maids" had no other choice. Scott is deliberately stressing here that the single state could be the preference of some women and that it could offer a rewarding life.

Millenium Hall shows women to be highly capable, practical, and businesslike. They also live together in great amity. The charities managed by the ladies of the hall include schools for the young and cottages for the old, a home for genteel women reduced in fortune, a "manufacture of carpets and rugs" that gives employment to a whole village, and even a special community for freaks where they can escape exploitation and be sheltered from curious stares. The education of girls is intended to prepare them so that they will

never suffer "the wretched fate of those women who . . . are reduced to become dependent" (80). These poor creatures, we are
told, are "the most unhappy part of the creation" largely because
"they are ignorant of everything that might give them superior
abilities" (81). Young married couples are given furniture and
"some sort of stock, which by industry would prove very condu-
cive towards their living in a comfortable degree of plenty" (140).
This method of giving seed money to encourage people to make
their own way is typical of Millenium Hall, where much is accomplished on slender means and the women "are such economists,
even in their charities, as to order them in a manner that as large a
part of mankind as possible should feel the happy influence of their
bounty" (140).

The History of Ophelia, by Sarah Fielding, also presents single
women leading rewarding lives but its fairy tale atmosphere makes
it a dubious exemplar. Ophelia, an orphan, is raised by her spinster
aunt who, betrayed by a lover, has fled the world and lives in pastoral isolation. The opening of the book does show a utopian existence independent of men, but it is clearly eccentric rather than a
model. It is based on a disappointed love affair rather than conviction, and its contentment largely depends on a conveniently orphaned child. Later in the work, Ophelia herself is a curiously passive heroine who only manages to escape from the predicaments
her naiveté produces by the help of a man, the good clergyman,
Mr. South. She marries the rake who abducted her, now reformed,
and, the reader is led to assume, will therefore live happily ever
after.

As we have seen, women did refuse offers of marriage, choosing
to remain single. Mary Cowper writes to her husband, "You say I
don't tell you what made me take up the resolution of living single.
I won't trouble you with the particular reasons of my making it,"
but "I shall content myself in general to tell you that I was so perfectly sensible of the ease and happiness of my condition . . . that I
was fully resolved to preserve that happiness and never to change
that condition of life which was so agreeable to me." She continues, "For the unlikeliness of its being preserved you must pardon me for not agreeing with you in thinking it so. Nobody but
you could have talked me into breaking that resolution. I have
given proof that I could resist all other inducements."

Anne Warde voices a similar sentiment in her response to con-
gratulations sent by her uncle on her marriage. "I have no right to
accept them," she writes, after thanking him for his good wishes,

Figure 12. Domestic Employment: Washing. Phillip Mercier. Washing was one of the most onerous employments open to women of the eighteenth century; it was also a normal part of the lives of all lower-class women. Reproduced by courtesy of the Trustees of the British Museum.

"as I still retain the name of Anne Warde. And to own the truth I have at present no inclination to resign that and my liberty." She jokingly notes, however, that while she is "still a spinster, yet matrimony is much in vogue." Lady Bradshaigh depicts the more usual view of spinsters in writing, "I have known two or three good natured old maids in my life and no more," but "wives and widows without number."

The financial problems of spinsters were directly related to the few opportunities for remunerative employment open to women, while social and psychological problems undoubtedly followed from the nature of these opportunities. Sewing and laundering were two traditional occupations for women, but they were both so poorly paid that it would be difficult for a woman to maintain herself in them. More commonly they were pursued as a source of supplementary income by wives or daughters who were partially maintained by husbands or families. Laundering especially was also arduous and carried a distinctly lower-class connotation which would mean it was not a real option for a woman with any claim to gentility. Shopkeeping required some capital, unless a daughter or widow inherited a going business because of the lack of male heirs. Commerce was often impossible for a woman because of guild regulations and in general would not be thought of unless there was some family tradition.

Sarah Fielding, in *The Adventures of David Simple,* gives a picture of the difficulties two young women encounter trying to earn a living. Cynthia, an exceptionally intelligent young woman, becomes a lady's companion when she is left penniless. Although "she seemed as if she loved me, and I was ignorant enough of the world to think she did so," Cynthia relates, her mistress delights in humiliating her and she soon learns through the unrelieved misery of her position what the phrase "toad eater" (113) means. (In Charlotte Lennox's *Henrietta* the heroine also discovers the difficulties of such a job as well as that of lady's maid.) Camilla, trying to earn subsistence for her dangerously ill brother and herself, finds it impossible. "Alas, sir," she tells David, "there is no situation so deplorable, no condition so much to be pitied, as that of a gentlewoman in real poverty" (169). She describes improper advances from men while fine ladies ignore her and resentment from tradespeople if she attempts competition, while her landlady berates her as unwilling to work. "In short," she explains, "persons who are so unfortunate as to be in this situation are in a world full of people, and yet are as solitary as if they were in the wildest desert; nobody will allow them to be of their rank or admit them to their community" (170). She even puts on rags and goes begging, but at the end of the day she is set upon and robbed by a gang with the warning that she is not to dare to return for "that street belonged to them" (168). David Simple rescues her at the point of starvation.

The two chief practical alternatives for women who had to be self-supporting were entering service and school teaching. Marthae

Taylor, requesting a place for her niece, writes, "I have long been bringing myself to this boldness, to ask the favour of your ladyship to take one of my poor widowed sister's daughters into your service. I think the girl I would wish your ladyship to take will make a good servant," for she is "of an honest ingenuous disposition without gall or guile, good natured, quick, active and industrious." Her training is described. "The school learning she has are reading, writing, knitting, sewing plain work and a little shades [embroidery], pastry and dancing." Furthermore, Taylor adds, "The Mother, seeing her daughters were to earn their bread, hath put them early to do all the offices in the house except the very drudgery," and, therefore, "she can wash small linen and get it up very neat, can spin flax or worsted, can mix a pudding, season a pie or dress a plain dish of meat with a frugal sauce very prettily." She gives a personal recommendation, saying, "She's been here some time, carried the keys, waited at tea and tended the children who would not willingly suffer any one to do anything for them but their bonny Annie." Taylor describes her as "a brown person neither ugly nor handsome, about as tall as me though not fifteen till April next."

Taylor continues, "I don't desire any wages for her, and she shall come clothed as your ladyship shall choose with money to uphold it for one year or further according to your ladyship's pleasure." A servant would, of course, be fed and housed, often in a greater degree of comfort than at home, but the real reason for this offer to work without wages appears when her recommender writes, "And if after that your ladyship should choose to part with her, her being thus initiated into service will make way for her elsewhere, for the difficulty lies in entering these young persons who are unknown to all but their kindred." She concludes by asserting, "I shall have not the least apprehension of her doing anything to forfeit your ladyship's honour, or to give me any painful sensation for having been instrumental in placing her well."

An employer was often willing to train a servant, valuing innocence and honesty over skill. Letitia Barnston writes to her steward, "If you know any of my neighbors that are stocked with children (more than they can well maintain) I should like to take one off their hands . . . to bring up a servant," stipulating that the child not "exceed in age eight or nine" and be "quick in apprehension and from honest parents." And, on another occasion, she directs her steward to "immediately enquire of Mrs. Harwood the just character of the young woman which you've mentioned." She explains, "I require one who is very diligent in her place, in her attendance on me, very neat in her person and things belonging to my apartment, and truly honest. She must otherwise know how to wash and get up my fine linen very well," but "as to her being ignorant of house affairs I can soon instruct her in as much as I want in that way if she hath good sense." She declares, "I teach all the young people that have lived with me enough in that way that they may not be quite ignorant in a house of their own, if they should ever have one." Her letter concludes, "If the person be good tempered and healthy and chooses to serve me, pray let her come. Read what I wrote to her."

Anne Woolrich writes offering a place to the "poor sister" of Henry Chaytor, a typical offer to a dependent spinster. "If she has not got a place or be unprovided for," she begins, "if she can like to come to live with me my work is very small." She continues, "I fancy she can make a bed and light a fire and wash muslins or small clothes. I can hire a washer and I will be as kind to her as I can, and if she does not like on these proposals she shall have her liberty to leave it when she pleases." The plight of such a "poor sister" is further explained in a letter from Margaret Blanchard, asking Henry Chaytor to meet his sister, who has taken the stage for London: "It was a very sudden resolution, being she had resolved to spend this winter with my Aunt Wawne at Darton," she writes, "but I believe when she came to consider that she could have no advantage but just getting her meat with my aunt, and of necessity must wear the clothes off her back and if a suitable place had offered in the Spring which are hard to be met with here she would have been at a great loss on that account." She discusses the position that a relation, Katey Blanchard, has found, and then declares, "But as for your sister, she's not capable of going through so much work as Katey is. But no doubt by the assistance of her relations and friends at London and thereabout, she may meet with one suitable for her." Being frail or delicate was no advantage to a dependent spinster.

Some insight into the life of a servant can be gained from a set of "rules which are expected to be observed by the women servants" together with "some advice which it is hoped they will think their interest to follow" drawn up by Lady Bradshaigh. She evidently kept four maidservants, for rule one is that "Two of you [are] to go to church every Sunday morning and two in the afternoon." Rule two reminds them to say morning and night prayers and to "live good and virtuous lives, being strictly just and honest and keeping yourselves from all sorts of wickedness." The third rule cautions against lying: "Anyone may be guilty of a small fault now and then, but if it is acknowledged you shall never hear more of it from me," whereas, "if once I catch a servant in a lie, I can never depend upon them again." The next rule admonishes, "Whenever you are ordered to do anything, do it without grumbling whether you think it belongs to your place or not, for willingness and good nature are half a servant." She advises that they should "always act as if they were in the presence of those they serve," and that this conduct will lead to being "thought worthy of being entrusted and valued." Rule five establishes the authority of the housekeeper who is "put over you by me and is to act in my absence as myself."

The succeeding rules give additional guides to behavior. They "are never to go out without the leave of my housekeeper, no, not for half an hour," and are cautioned against "gadding abroad, tattling, gossiping, private feasting or junketing." She writes, "Especially I warn you against taking *snuff* and drinking *tea,* two very pernicious and expensive things, and I do positively forbid it while you live with me, though you bear the expense yourselves." Dress is to be "plain and neat," and a maid should not "aim at things above" her. The keeping of late hours with any man will bring "certain ruin" and it is "absolutely forbid in this family." Furthermore, servants are advised to "never keep company unless you intend marrying." Men are never allowed into the laundry or into the bed chamber, and the order is given to "always lock your chamber door at night." Cheerfulness, neatness, and thoroughness are praised. The servants are to rise at six, retire at ten, and breakfast, dine, and sup regularly all together. The advice concludes, "Above all things, have the fear of God before your eyes and may He give you grace to do your duty to Him and you cannot fail in your duty to those you serve."

Some servants were indeed the paragons that Lady Bradshaigh's rules would create. Sarah Chapone reports to George Ballard, "I was lately at my sister Kirkham's and I found her very happy in a servant whose well-bred manner took my attention immediately." She continues, "I was informed she was your niece. I conversed with her, and, I must say, much to my satisfaction." Ann Peacock was a servant of the Chaytors who rose to a position of great responsibility, managing his country estate for Sir William Chaytor while he was in London. She writes of negotiations with tenants and other matters pertaining to his interest. Mary Brooke exercised a similar position of trust for Edward Walwyn, looking after his Hereford estate for him. She writes detailed letters about the management of both the house and the farm, telling gleefully in one letter of her cleverness in trapping a confession out of the thief who stole an elm tree.

Much more common, however, are complaints about servants. Sarah Cowper writes in her journal, "I resolve to leave off contending with servants, concluding that if they offend out of stupidity they cannot, if from obstinacy they will not amend. Either renders it fit to give over." And in another entry she asserts, "So enormous [outrageous] are servants in this age, that their keepers are forced to turn every stone as may fence against them." Anastasia Fenton writes to a friend, "My time and thoughts are a deal taken up about servants" and notes, "Am parting with all mine, not before it was time. They have used me worse than I deserved." Mary Cowper writes to her husband, "I'm sorry you have so much trouble with the servants. You see a little what puts me sometimes out of humour. I say a little because I am sure they restrain themselves as much as ever they can, now you are there." She continues, "I'm surprised at what you say of their lying three in a bed in the house, for I thought six maids might have lain in three beds without crowd. But I believe they do as in London: quarrel and then lie three in one bed and but one in the other."

The sexual peccadillos of servants are a common cause of complaint. It was axiomatic in the period that all servants were unmarried, presumably so they could give their full devotion to their employers. Widows were eligible as long as they had no dependent children, and such older women were considered desirable as housekeepers who would exercise authority over other servants. The requirement of being unmarried applied to men as well as women. Mary Rebow writes, of a house servant, "Andrew came to me on Wednesday and very readily acknowledged his having been married two years, but assures me it has been of great service to him for it has made him think properly." He pleads that "his wife is no kind of inconvenience, for she has been settled some years in Dean Street, Soho, and makes it a rule never to come near him when he is at service," and "they have no children." He evidently hopes the rule will be broken in his favor, for she writes, "He persists in not seeking after any other place till he has your final answer."

Both the care considered a husband's prerogative and the possibility of becoming pregnant made marriage even less acceptable for women servants. Lady Bradshaigh writes indignantly about the marriage of her housekeeper, "My spirits are rather in a flurry occasioned by my old housekeeper's being married in my absence. She did not think it necessary to even acquaint me with her intentions." When marriage was cause for dismissal and a number of young men and women lived in daily contact with each other in the same house, the inclination toward illicit sexual activity was, not surprisingly, constant. As we have seen, Lady Bradshaigh's rules enjoined maids to lock their doors, and forbade male servants to invade the feminine precinct of the laundry, let alone bed chambers.

Complaints about the licentiousness of servants are common throughout the century, with apparently no sense of there being any hypocrisy in creating the occasion and then criticizing the result. Sometimes an employer did sympathize, but the double standard usually favored the erring male rather than the female. Elizabeth Isham writes to intervene with her husband for the coachman: "Morpelt [the steward] I suppose has given you a large account of Betty's proceeding with the coachman. The particulars I leave to him, and shall only tell you the hard fortune of the fellow. If you turn him off he must be inevitably ruined." She cynically opines that Betty "has picked him out of twenty to swear the child to," and concludes, "not that I flatter myself that my interest with you or what I can say will anyways avail, but your own pity and good nature is what the man must depend upon."

Maidservants were well advised to follow Lady Bradshaigh's advice: "But above all, keep yourselves *honest,* for your soul's sake in the next world as well as for your reputation in this." Seduction was, in fact, one of the recognized hazards of going into service. Margaret Blanchard writes about a friend, Miss Last, that she wishes she could help her. "She's a very pretty woman. Has been so accounted at York to both her uneasiness and mine, for pretty women in her circumstances are generally admired to no purpose. I only wish I could have got her a good husband here. She then needed not to come to London to get a service. How dangerous it is for so pretty a woman as she to be without a maintenance, especially at London."

The records of the Foundling Hospital give evidence that female servants were indeed in a vulnerable position.[2] Elizabeth Thomas petitions the hospital to accept her son "begotten by my fellow servant Richard Kent who left me destitute and incapable to provide for the said infant." A jeweler, John Henderson, adds testimony that Elizabeth Thomas has always behaved honestly and soberly. May Hendrie, another petitioner, is described as "descended of honest parents which are both dead." The petition relates, "She has been for some years a maid servant in different families in which character she behaved well, till unfortunately a gentleman lodging

214

in a house in Edinburgh where she was last a servant . . . got the advantage of her when there was none of the family in the house and got her with child." Another story is told of Elizabeth Hale, who "was a nursery maid in a family near Gray's Inn to which place she was every day sent with the said child. . . . being constantly in the gardens she had the misfortune to become acquainted with one Mr. Featherstone, a young gentleman belonging to the said Inn who under the pretence of marrying your petitioner seduced her and got her with child." She has now "expended all her money and sold part of her clothes" and is "quite destitute." Ann Smith tells the commissioners that she has been "a servant in a creditable family" and was seduced by "a man whom she has found since to be a married man." Her employer is understanding, for she writes, "if your petitioner could provide for her child her mistress would receive her again into her service."

As Ann Smith's letter indicates, an illegitimate child was not only a social stigma but a practical problem, since there was no place for children in the supposedly celibate world of service. Ann Brown explains the difficulty in her petition, declaring, "Your petitioner always bore the character of a sober, virtuous and honest young woman by all who knew her," and "she always behaved as a honest and faithful servant." She has been "seduced by a young man under promise of marriage" and after having got her with child he has absconded. "She therefore humbly prays etc." for her child to be accepted at the hospital "as her nursing deprives her of the means of getting her bread."

Employers were, of course, often aware of the dangers and did adopt quasi-parental roles. Sarah Chapone writes to a friend in London, "My maid, Mary Ballinger, attended Miss Norwood in the stage to town and is to return in the Winchcomb waggon," and "as she is an innocent, inexperienced country girl . . . I am fearful of having her lie at the Inn. I therefore presume on your goodness and that of all your family so far as to beg a lodging in your hospitable house for her." So also Deborah Jennings writes to a friend in Bath, "I have a favour to beg of you if it is not too inconvenient, that if we do not arrive at Bath the same day she does that you will let our maid . . . lie with one of your servants. She will not know what to do with herself at an Inn and also it may keep her from contracting a bad acquaintance."

Employers, especially in large households, felt a responsibility to supervise the lives of the servants, insisting on morning and evening prayers, for example, and tending to view them as somewhat like children. Deborah Jennings writes an amusing and colorful account of the panic that resulted when, after a previous tremor, an earthquake was predicted in London by "a crazy man" on 5 April 1750. The rich fled to country houses, the middle class to suburban inns, the poor camped out in the parks and fields of London, "some very earnest crying and praying, just by them people selling gingerbread and gin which went in great plenty." She continues, "As to myself, we sat up till one o'clock, as all our servants were so terrified that they would not go to bed, I thought it best to sit up too, for I thought that if a mouse but stirred they would all run out of the house, and it may be leave the door open in their fright. So I carefully stayed till their fears were over and the house shut up."

From the servant's view, life below stairs looked rather different. Eleanor Potter writes to her friend, Mary Farrin, "By that time I hope to hear of you being happily married, for I don't suppose that you can have much more satisfaction with fellow servants than myself, for Mr. Joseph told me about Mrs. Ann. I am sorry to hear that such a one as she should have so much power." She declares, "I wish you much joy if you got married; I have heard say that cures all diseases," and "I have often been advised to try it." Far more common than troubles among the servants, however, were troubles with the mistress. Mary Needham reports a happy situation: "Sister Richards has been at Marlebrough to see Nelly who has been there these three weeks and she likes her place vastly," for "her Mistress is very kind to her." The sister of Henry Chaytor hesitates before accepting an offered position in "the north," saying, "I am willing to take any sort of place here rather than run so great a hazard as not to please when I come there."

Ellen Hope in a series of letters to a friend gives an account of her feelings. In September she writes, "I have been at Devizes at the fine concert and ball, and I danced till five o'clock in the morning. There was a great deal of fine company, but now I must bid farewell to pleasure," explaining that she is "to set out tomorrow morning for Bath" where she will "stay three months to wait on Mrs. Colman." She adds the reassuring fact that "My aunt knows her very well," and says that "if we both agree I am to go with them to their home which is at Ipswich in Suffolk." Her first report is favorable: "I like my place very well and hope I shall keep it. Mrs. Colman is a very good lady so in her I should think myself very happy." She has, however, a reservation: "It is very indifferent living in lodgings."

A month later her account is a bit more harried. "My time is very much taken up," she writes. "My place is not like waiting on a single lady," and "I am obliged to buy everything in and see to the serving up of dinners and suppers." She has been offered the post of housekeeper in Ipswich, but reports, "I have made no bargain as yet: My master is a young gay gentleman and keeps a great deal of company, so that I am afraid it will not do." Evidently, she grew accustomed to the responsibility, for two months later she speaks confidently of future plans, relating that they will not "go into Suffolk before May" and that they will pass through London, staying at the Three Crowns in Whitechapel. "I don't know whether I go in the coach with them, or in the stage, but will let you know." She refers to a letter from her friend, noting, "You were pleased to banter me about going abroad," but "though I like England very well yet I should like to see some foreign parts. I believe I shall soon for my master and mistress talk of going to Holland next summer and tell me I shall go with them."

In contrast to this happy success story is the fate of a woman who serves an ill-tempered and imperious mistress. Marthae Taylor writes to a friend in just such a position: "I'm concerned for your unhappy situation. The only consolation I am capable of administering at this distance is to advise you to make a virtue of necessity, to take the edge off misfortune by resignation." She cites as example the fable of the reed and the cedar in which the gently pliant reed receives no damage from the wind, but the lofty cedar is torn up by the roots. However, she declares, "The time will come when these haughty ladies who learn to forget that their dependents are of their own species shall boast this vast disparity no more, and if they persist in grinding the faces of their fellow Christians and divest themselves of that humanity, charity and benevolence which the station providence has placed them in requires, how can they hope that it shall not . . . be ever so."

In the meantime, Taylor's well-meant, pragmatic advice to her friend indicates some of the virtues necessary to sustain the role of a servant or of a lady's companion in the century: "Not that anything on her side can justify the neglect of duty on yours, therefore do the best you can by all fair and honorable means to oblige her." She suggests, "When she grows angry at any of those trifling occurrences which only can happen in your affairs, and which perhaps may often appear to you as very unreasonable, here is an exercize for your humility. Let that instruct you to submit in silence, or by a soft and civil reply so intimate your future care to avoid the like occasion. Let it not ruffle or discompose even the inmost thought of your heart, nor the serenity of your countenance." This rule is to be adhered to "whatever previous occasion or succeeding return you meet with," and "you'll soon feel the sweets of this, not only in the tranquillity of your own bosom, but it is odds that it disarms your lady's anger."

Taylor offers hope that this method will "by degrees incline" her friend's mistress "to conceive an advantageous opinion" of her friend's "understanding." But, she writes, "If you miss of this you have, at least, the merit of obeying that precept where servants are bid to obey their masters and that not only to the kind and gentle but also to the forward." She enlarges on this argument, urging, "Murmur not that God's providence hath necessitated you to be a servant," and asserts, in what seems a bit of understatement, "There is in that station a larger field to exercize virtues than is generally imagined." She concludes, "I would not dissuade you from an endeavour to get a more comfortable being when a promising occasion offers, but be not anxious about it; let it not embitter your life," for "no state or condition of life on this side of the grave admits of content."

On a different occasion Taylor offered advice to a mistress who was having trouble with her household. "The modern way of educating ladies makes most of them strangers even to the theory of economy in their families, and fewer yet, even with fine understandings, know anything of the practical." This is the root of the general complaints about servants, she believes and, "in order to remedy this effectively, it is necessary for a lady to choose a person [as housekeeper] bred a housewife in a middling station of life." She should have "such abilities natural and acquired as shall qualify her to govern with wisdom and prudence," including "a sound judgement, a knowledge of all the parts of every particular servant's business, an industrious watchful eye and that good nature which is the effect of good sense. Not a milky softness that may expose her to contempt, but a discreet affability in exerting her authority such as shall command love, respect and obedience." Taylor continues her prescription, "Justice and integrity I should have laid as the foundation, and added a generous candour and genteelness of spirit to the superstructure." All this will "secure your Ladyship's ease and interest as well as honour." She advises, "Let this woman act as your proxy or representative in your family, invested with a power suitable to that denomination," for, without this, "you can no more rule your family well than can the Generalissimo rule the army without inferior officers."

Taylor then admits, "I confess it is difficult to find a person thus qualified who has added to the rest experience, a necessary qualification," but "I am able to assign a good reason for this which is in the power of your Ladyship to remove. It is not because there are no such persons, but that those persons won't accept the place on those mean, I had almost said servile, conditions the generality offers them." She then comments disparagingly on the usual treatment accorded such a woman in three areas—salary, living conditions, and authority. "The man's wage who wears your livery," she writes, calling attention to the disparity in pay between male and female employees, "is by some deemed sufficient for the woman that ought to bear the burden of all your household cares." When it comes to a general standard of comfort, she declares, "the genteel accommodations of life are thought above anybody in the capacity of a servant" and furthermore, "the authority afore described is esteemed a distraction from that of the lady's." While such poor conditions prevail, "those posts will only be supplied by those fitter for kitchens or laundries, and the ladies will have just cause to complain of disorder, confusion and a slovenly consumption of their fortunes." Under ideal circumstances a life in service, especially at the upper levels of housekeeper or companion, could be pleasant and even psychologically fulfilling, but such posts were rare.

Schoolkeeping, the other common employment for women, was both arduous and difficult to prosper in because of the many seeking to support themselves in this way. In contrast to service, schoolteaching was possible for women with dependent children and indigent widows. Jane Ball writes to Sir Roger Newdegate describing her plight. She is the widow of William Ball, who had a place in the customs but died leaving her with five children, the eldest nine years old, and an income of only seven pounds ten per year. "Such is my unhappy condition," she writes. "Nor does anything occur to me that I can possibly do to help breed up my family, but keeping a school. This I am resolved to do either here [Cowes] or at Newport, from which however but little can be expected for the present. There are several school-mistresses already settled in both places."

Elizabeth Elstob, the Old English scholar discussed in chapter 2, tried for seven years to get a post in a school. When she was told of a possible opening in a charity school, she assented immediately. "I assured her of my readiness to serve . . . as far as lies in my power," she reports to a friend. She expresses diffidence about being fully competent to teach spinning and knitting: "The gown I

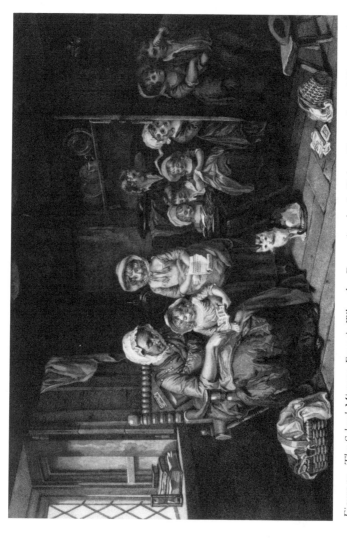

Figure 13. The School Mistress. Francis Wheatly. Engraving by J. Coles. Illustration of Shenstone's poem. Employment as a schoolmistress, often a drudgery, was one of the few options available for widows as well as for single women in the eighteenth century. Reproduced by courtesy of the Trustees of the British Museum.

had on when you gave me the favour of a visit was part of my own spinning and I wear no other stockings but what I knit myself, yet I do not think myself proficient enough in these arts to become a teacher of them. As to your objection on the meanness of the scholars, I assure you Sir I should think it as glorious an employment to instruct those poor children as to teach the children of the greatest monarch." She continues, "But I must acquaint you that mine may truly be termed a life of disappointment," and says she fears that "her ladyship is provided with a mistress before now." She concludes, "My only care is to endeavour for a small matter to support me." Her fears proved correct; the post was filled.

A few months later, however, Elstob was happy to write, "At present, after seven years patience and endeavours for a school, I have obtained such a one as I desired." She has "met with a great deal of friendship and generosity from the good ladies in this place," and so must refuse an offer to translate an Old English text: "I should think it the greatest piece of ingratitude to neglect the dear little ones committed to my care." The rigors of the job are indicated in subsequent letters. "I must, Sir, acquaint you," she writes responding to a request for a favor, "that I have no time to do anything till six at night when I have done the duty of the day, and am then frequently so fatigued that I am obliged to lie down for an hour or two." Three months later things were still worse, for she writes, "I assure you, Sir, these long winter evenings to me are very melancholy ones, for when my school is done, my little ones leave me incapable of either reading, writing, or thinking, for their noise is not out of my head till I fall asleep which is often too late." On 12 September she notes matter-of-factly, "Yesterday being our little Fair Day, the only holiday almost that I have in the year, I designed to visit Mrs. Ballard."

Elstob no doubt did not possess the temperament and constitution essential to endure this kind of schoolteaching, but her reactions were not unique. The occupation was generally considered arduous. Mrs. Bampylde writes to a widowed friend that she is happy to hear that she "has found so many good friends" and urges her to follow their advice: "I think as they do, that a shop would be easier than a school, and you may depend upon my sending something towards it." The capital necessary to start a shop made this alternative inaccessible to most impoverished women, but if funds could be obtained, and if the woman herself had some knowledge of trade, it was clearly preferable to schoolteaching.

A variant of schoolteacher was the governess. The governess was in an anomalous position in the family, considered to be both a gentlewoman and a hired servant. She was neither the social equal of her employers nor of the other servants, being generally treated as below the one and almost always above the other. The post could, therefore, be a lonely one, but Elizabeth Elstob, at least, saw it as a blessed relief from schoolteaching. "I must acquaint you with the good fortune which has befallen me," she writes. "It is an offer from the Duke and Duchess of Portland to teach their children to read. There are only little ladies to teach at present, the eldest not four years old, the little Marquis not one, . . . children of a most charming disposition, and the character I have of the Duke and Duchess cannot be equalled by any of their rank, so that neither my best friends nor myself could have wished a more happy and honourable situation for me."

Elstob indeed was pleased with the post, writing to a friend the next year, "You will I don't doubt be glad to know that I think myself the happiest creature in the world." This, despite having begun her letter by apologizing for not writing sooner, declaring that she hopes the delay will not be imputed "to any neglect or disrespect." She explains, "My little ladies take up my time so entirely that I have not the least leisure to do anything. From the time they rise till they go to bed they are with me," adding with no apparent irony, "except when they are with her Grace, which is not long at a time." She gives enthusiastic details of teaching her pupils ("the eldest not yet four and a half years old" and her sister "not three years old till next month") the alphabet, "a great deal of the catechism," and "some little poems." That this life should seem the pinnacle of earthly happiness gives insight into Elstob's earlier struggles. Marthae Taylor while a governess similarly apologizes for not writing: "I devote so large a share of my time to the dear little cherubs that I've seldom more than the remains of an evening for my pen."

Mrs. Coke of Holkham gives details of what she expects of a governess. Her first requirement points out an additional disadvantage to the job, its relative impermanence. She writes that she "would wish to have a person as governess to her children who has had the experience of one education, and that education had turned out well." The candidate "should possess the strictest religious and moral principles, understand English and French grammar perfectly, and be able to read, write and speak both these languages with some degree of elegance and to know enough Italian to teach to read and understand it." In addition, "She must be genteel in her behaviour, tolerably well acquainted with ancient and modern history, heathen mythology and arithmetic, and well skilled in geography." And, as an afterthought, "If she were capable of keeping up the children's music and dancing when they are in the country it would be an additional recommendation, as well as her understanding any ingenious work."

The daily routine that this Renaissance woman will be required to follow is then outlined. "She is to rise early to walk out with the children winter and summer before breakfast when the weather will permit, and likewise they are to be a good deal out in the air the rest of the day." This is not to be looked on as frivolous recreation, however, for Mrs. Coke is "of the opinion that a judicious governess would be able to convey much useful instruction to her pupils in conversation during their walks," explaining that at this time "perhaps it might be better received and retained by them than when presented in the more questionable shape of a lesson." "The governess is to be inseparable from the children," who are two young ladies "just six and seven." The day will be even fuller than Elstob's, for the children are never to be alone with their mother; the governess "is to be with Mrs. Coke whenever they are." She assures her friend that they "are very docile and good tempered children and remarkably healthy."

The problems confronted by spinsters who had to support themselves were shared by widows in a similar plight, often with additional complications. Margaret Blanchard, asked to aid a spinster friend, writes bitterly, "I could advise her no way because I am in a much worse condition than she, for she is single. I've so many more to provide for than myself, that sure my case is worse than any single person's." Furthermore, a widow with children was barred from entering service. The Foundling Hospital received many petitions from widows seeking to place an infant there so that they could get employment as servants. Mary Butterford writes, "Your petitioner having had the misfortune to lose her husband in a voyage from Hull into the straights is left with a little one about a fortnight old," and "in the maintenance of herself and child she has exhausted her money and clothes." Mary Wright was a maid for two years, and left her place to marry the hostler. He worked as a porter for seven years, then left her "a widow with a young child which she is utterly unable to support." Her only recourse is to place the child in the hospital and return to service.

Many widows of soldiers and sailors petitioned the Foundling

Hospital. Elizabeth Wingrove asks for the admission of a child whose father was a "Lieutenant Fireworker in the Royal Regiment of Artillery and died in his majesty's service at Bombay," and Sarah Grainger explains that she "is left by the death of her husband who was a soldier in the army with a young child named Sarah entirely destitute of every means for its relief and support." The petition from William Wilder, a pensioner in Chelsea College, relates that "he has had the misfortune of having a poor young child left accidentally with him about five days ago by a soldier's wife from Germany whose husband was killed there." The mother, he explains, asked if his wife would mind the child while she went on a brief errand, but to his "great sorrow never returned, nor does the petitioner know where she went to nor nothing at all about her." Whether this last case was actually a virtuous soldier's widow is open to doubt, but the real problem was sufficiently common to cause the hospital to set up a preferential category for the widows of soldiers and sailors who died in service.

An indigent widow with several children might try to start a school, as Jane Ball proposed to do, but many were dependent on charity. Elizabeth Ball, the mother-in-law of Jane, writes a letter of petition to Sir Roger Newdegate a generation earlier, explaining, "My husband died five years ago and left me with six children and a small estate of forty-six pounds a year with debts amounting to above seven hundred pounds." She relates, "The creditors putting very hard upon me obliged me to mortgage this estate for that sum," and after "paying the interest, and five pounds a year land tax and ten shillings a year quit rent, I do not receive more than nine pounds a year."

Her troubles are not solely financial, for she records, "Soon after the death of my husband my eldest son died at the age of nineteen." Her next son, now fifteen, who had served three years on a man-of-war, had been taken ill and has been sent home "very sick, lame and naked." He "has been a great expense to me," she relates, "but I thank God he is now recovered again purely." She worries that her next son, aged thirteen, is "at home with [her] entirely unprovided for in any way of life or business, as are [her] two daughters." Vocational training indeed started early, since the daughters are ten and seven. The youngest son, twelve, "by the interest of a gentleman" is in a well-known charity school, "the Blue Coat Hospital called Christ's Hospital in London." She states, "Indeed I have known what it is to want the common necessities of life for some time," and "I may with truth venture to say that the people in the parish workhouse eat more hot meat in the week than my children or I," who last ate meat four months ago when a loin of veal was sent as a gift on Whitsunday. She promises prayers and gratitude to him if he can help her. Fortunately, he did.

As the charitable work of caring for abandoned, orphaned, and destitute children, begun by the Foundling Hospital, grew during the century, foster care became another job open to widows. At first, infants were only placed with wet-nurses, married women who promised to wean their own infant to nurse the foundling. Robert Dingley writes to the governess of the Foundling Hospital of the many problems which arose. "In general such as take foundlings are extremely poor and take them through pinching necessity. Most wet nurses are young, inexperienced and wrong headed, as many know who have had them in their families." He continues, "Suckling makes them thirsty and their own prescription is generally porter when they can get it or miserable small beer amongst the poor," and "from their bad food and various causes their milk is unsatisfactory." These women, he complains, "often overheat their milk by hard labour and catching cold etc.," and "many have irregular or bad husbands and by them often diseased." A further problem is detailed: "Nor can it be expected that though they promise to wean their own children that they do, or to be so unnatural as to give the least share of milk to her own child whose natural right it is." As a remedy, Dingley proposes the increasing use of dry-nurses, elderly women who would raise the infants in their care by artificial feeding.

As distrust of wet-nurses grew during the course of the century, breast feeding by the mother herself became more customary in the middle and upper classes. Marthae Taylor writes to the Countess of Orerry, "Now what would I give to see your Ladyship suckle the little lady and cherishing her in your bosom—the very idea can give me pleasure," and "it enhances, if possible, the high opinion I had conceived of your ladyship. Who will now presume to think that duty and proper office of a mother servile!" In Samuel Richardson's *Pamela,* the heroine's desire to nurse her first child provokes a quarrel between her and her husband. Mr. B. is allowed to have his way, and little Billy is consigned to a wet-nurse, but Richardson does not intend this to be exemplary except as an example of Pamela's willingness to bend to her husband's will at this stage of their marriage. In *Sir Charles Grandison,* Harriet, Charlotte, and Lady L. all nurse their own children.

Where the mother was unable to nurse, interest in methods of rearing the infant by various formulas grew. Thin gruels combined with milk and fed through devices made of thin cloth are recommended. It may be that only the most vigorous survived, but infant mortality was high in any case. The development of the concept and practice of artificial feeding made the care of infants by widows a possibility. Dingley gives some of the advantages. "Dry nurses may be of more advanced age, many are widows, not so poor and often take children for amusement and not entirely for the pay," he writes, adding that the infants get more attention since often the women "have no children of their own or they are grown up and out of hand and provided for." These foster homes were supervised, often by clergymen, and the nurses were paid a yearly maintenance for their charges as well as being provided with a standard set of clothing. Some took care of three or four children at a time. The system seems to have worked well, in some cases foster parents becoming so fond of their charges that they virtually adopted them. Conscientious supervisors tried to guard against abuse.

The financial problems of widows, as was true with spinsters, usually stemmed from the males who controlled the money. With unmarried women the dominant figures are the father or eldest brother; with widows the emphasis shifts to the deceased husband and eldest son. For example, Jane Pateshall writes of her sister's difficulties as a widow: "My brother Stanley died soon after," and "most of his debts were concealed from my sister. She was not liable to pay them and no law could compel her to do it, yet, being a good christian, she resolved (as I was glad she did) to pay them all, which she did to a farthing. She immediately sold the silver plate which my grandmother Allen gave her, and other things of most value, and sold an estate of her own which my Father gave her for a thousand pounds." She adds bitterly, "My Father at her marriage gave her as many hundred pounds as he understood would clear Mr. Stanley from debt in ready money," and "I can say of my sister she was very careful and contracted no debts, but parted with her own clear fortune to pay his."

Mary Clarke, on the other hand, owed her troubles to her son. She writes her lawyer, "I am sorry to be so troublesome to you, but hope you will excuse one that can safely say I have not had a mind at ease this twenty year, and God knows when I shall. Though my misfortunes have obliged me to so much lessen my income, yet I can be contented with a little. I was in hopes when the account with my son had been settled I should have been more easy in my mind . . . and that I should have had my jointure more regularly paid." A few weeks later she writes, "That two hundred pounds I paid of my own money for my son's fee farm rent sticks sorely in my stomach. If he would pay me some of that, and the rest of it, in half a year I would be easy." Evidently she is not on speaking terms with him, for she instructs the lawyer, "Pray tell my son I hope he will make no difficulty of it, but let it be finished. He may think I will do nothing hard by him, but he must consider I have nothing else to live on, and I hope he would do nothing hard by me," but "self preservation everybody must think on." Two months later she writes, "What I am to do I know not."

The next year Clarke records, "I declare I have not four pounds in the house," and "one dreads the being sick and wanting help. I believe I shall be sick for good and all if I lead such a fretting life as I do." She says, "I have writ a great deal of my mind by this post to my son and I hope he will think of what I have said," for "I am weary of my life to live at such a pass. When you have read this, burn it." Negotiations evidently continued, for six months later she compliments her lawyer: "I am sure you have done it in a very just manner, and I hope he will come to reason. It is sad he is so unwilling to come to. I am sure I have lived so long in this way that I am almost weary of it. Pray let what he signs in the book be done in a manner that he may make no disputes after, and then we will keep him to it every year."

Such cases serve to give ironic support to the conduct books' claim that women were better off when under the authority of a man, in Clarke's case a lawyer. "Yet sure God and nature do attest the particular expediency of this," declares the author of *The Ladies Calling,* "by having placed that sex in a degree of inferiority to the other." He continues, "It is observable that as there are but three states of life through which they can regularly pass, viz., virginity, marriage and widowhood, two of them are states of subjection, the first to the parent, the second to the husband," and "the third . . . we find by God himself reckoned as a condition most desolate and deplorable" (I, 40).

Many widows, if well provided for, gloried in the relative independence of their state. Elizabeth Phelips, for example, demonstrates considerable financial acumen in her letters and papers. She managed to reunite the family estates and left her son a much improved patrimony. Frances Hamilton of Wells was left a widow in her late thirties and seems to have thoroughly enjoyed the role. She managed with great competence the farm and estate that her husband, a doctor, had left her, keeping detailed records of every phase of the operation. The profits of different products—honey, cheese, butter, barley, wheat, timber, straw, reeds, potatoes— are all carefully assessed and a diary is kept of tasks performed. "William cut wood, Edward kept birds away." The date when each crop was planted and harvested is noted, along with rather perfunctory comments on visits paid, the mainstay of most feminine diaries of the period. Hamilton kept separate books recording wages and taxes and ran a stone quarry as well as the farm. Ursula Venner managed both her own finances and those of her widowed father. Her brother, Edward, was evidently happy to leave the family finances in her hands, and she shows her interest and aptitude in a large collection of letters written to him.

The status of widows was undoubtedly higher than that of old maids because they had once been wives and had therefore filled their ordained role as women. Remarriage, however, was frowned upon. *The Ladies Calling* declares that for widows "the conjugal love transplanted into the grave as into a finer mold, improves into piety" (68), suggesting that it is best that widows should retire from the world, devoting themselves to their children and to charitable work. "Marriage is so great an adventure," it asserts, "that once seems enough for the whole life" (80). For the widow who is so rash as to contemplate another marriage, the work lays down very stringent conditions, detailing that there must be equality of fortune and age. Under no circumstances should a widow jeopardize the interests of her children for selfish and ephemeral pleasure.

Since sexuality was considered indelicate in women, indeed, ideally nonexistent except for dutiful submission to the masculine desires of lawful spouses, remarriage could only be a foolish caprice or a confession of gross sensuality. Marthae Taylor writes to a widowed friend that she has "just now received a piece of news that disturbs my tranquillity not a little," that is, that the widow has many suitors. She continues, "Tell me, will she ever play the fool and make a man her master? Shall another revel in the fruits of industry that good Mr. — gathered for you and yours?" The catalogue of ill effects is expanded: "Shall those dear boys see a stranger rival them in your affection and hurt them in their fortunes? Shall a kind brother (I had almost said a yet living husband and father to your orphan children) be mortified and provoked to reverse his kindness?" And, finally, ridicule is brought to bear as she asks if "the prudent, the discreet Mrs. — shall forfeit that character and verify those skits the ill natured world throws at widows?" She answers herself: "Oh! No, it cannot, it must not be!" She hopes that her fears are ill-grounded, "perhaps only a joke." If not, "I shall hereafter say much more to convince you that no second marriage can make you so happy as is in your own power to be without it."

Deborah Jennings expresses a pragmatic attitude toward remarriage: "I can hardly pity any woman who marries three times if she is ill used," since "they can have no excuse for marrying so often but bad circumstances." This is a valid motive, and she declares, "I don't so much wonder at their giving up liberty," for "liberty and property are both very desirable, but there is no living without the latter." The conviction that money is the only good reason for a second marriage also lies behind Anne Kynaston's comment on the widow Jones, who is going to be married to Lord Hereford. "It must be pride if she does," she writes, "for he has five children and a small estate." Sarah Cowper is more emphatic when she records, "It is wondrous to me how any woman that has recovered her liberty can throw it away again."

Nevertheless, many did. The "ill natured skits" referred to by Marthae Taylor depicted wealthy and deluded widows who were preyed upon by fortune hunters, victims of their own vanity and lasciviousness. The social pressures against remarriage are evident in a letter from Mrs. Molesworth to her first husband's family: "I trust neither my friends or the world can disapprove of the choice I have made, as by marrying Mr. Molesworth, a man of family, character and fortune equal to my wishes, I think I have ensured my own happiness, and I hope to be able, as I am sure I shall be willing, to contribute to his." She apologizes, saying, "I hope my dear friends will pardon my not sooner acquainting them with an affair so very interesting to myself, and as so, not indifferent to them," but "as my determination was sudden and my resolution unalterable, to apply for advice which is seldom asked until too late to be taken I think is paying but an ill compliment to one's friends." With thanks "for past favours of every kind," she hopes that "the ties which united us will not now be broken but that you will still consider me as belonging to a family everyone of whom I affectionately love and truly esteem."

Louisa Oakeley tells of a somewhat unusual instance in which the deceased wife actively promoted a second marriage between her bereaved husband and a widowed friend. "I suppose you have heard of the Wattkins' wedding," she writes. "I think he might have stayed a little longer." She gives the circumstances: "He went to the lady on Friday evening and was married Saturday noon, brought her to Wynnstay in deep mourning. I hear he is now in a grey frock with white waist coat and stockings" and "she has two thousand pounds which he does not meddle with." Oakeley relates the history of the match: "His first lady wrote a letter to him and one to her to be read as soon as she was dead, and if he approved of the lady hers was to be sent by the post to her. It seems they both proved effectual."

As lack of money was to some the only understandable motive for a widow wishing to remarry, so the same motive was to many the only understandable reason why a man would wish to marry a widow. Ann Chaytor writes, "I beg my father will be very careful and cautious about widows," for "there is so much cheat amongst them." She warns him, "For nothing could be more positively reported than that Mrs. Godolphin had £90,000 and I believe she had not five," but "if you could get a great fortune it would do well." She advises her bankrupt father, "It would be best to keep it secret after you marry till you had agreed with those you mention [creditors] for if you agree before the lady may be lost by delay, but for God's sake consider well or else you may ruin us all." Marrying a widow for reasons other than financial gain obviously does not cross her mind. The many lampoons on widows victimized by fortune hunters shows that this, indeed, was a common view.

Sarah Scott's *The Man of Real Sensibility, or the History of Sir George Ellison* relates the life of a benevolent man. This idealized man marries not one but two widows—one seven years older than himself. Money is not a motive since Sir George is a wealthy plantation owner. After the death of his first wife, he marries a widow with a young child whom he adopts, and they enjoy "the utmost felicity the world can afford" (39). It seems probable that one of Scott's motives in writing this tale was to contradict the prejudice against marrying widows.

The old-maid spinster, then, was scorned and pitied, while the widow was honored only so long as she remained piously faithful to the dead. The subjective view, the actual state, of both categories was largely dependent upon financial condition. When a woman had secure independent means of support, she could fashion a tolerable and even interesting life. The possibilities of creating this independence by her own efforts were, of course, limited by general restrictions on the role of women. Business was not usually her field, except in the few instances where she continued to manage an enterprise or estate willed to her by a husband, nor could she become an explorer, lawyer, university scholar, member of Parliament, and so on through a list of the countless roles closed to women both by social mores and by the concomitant legal and educational barriers.

In assessing the degree to which lack of access to such fields was a severe hardship in itself, it should be remembered that the ideal of the eighteenth century was the leisured gentleman who was an accomplished amateur. Most men did not either covet or admire professional roles. Richardson's Grandison and Fielding's Allworthy each exemplify common values—the landed proprietor who devotes himself to the just management of his estates and of his family, to private charities and good works, and to rational amusement. In the last category the bias might lie toward the intellectual, the artistic, the social, or the sporting. In this context, the actual dissatisfaction felt by most women in being barred from commerce or the professions was certainly less than it would be in a society which saw these occupations as the most fulfilling. As long as a woman accepted this standard, she could, if financially independent, lead a satisfying life, developing her talents for literature, music, or art, enjoying the theater, concerts, and a round of social events, and managing her household affairs. The century demanded, however, that she remain an amateur and a dilettante. While a man might well choose this role, it was forced upon the woman. Serious commitment to any but domestic concerns courted hostility and ridicule. Dr. Johnson's famous reproach to a young man for choosing to spend the afternoon with an "un-ideaed girl" rather than in masculine company reflected both the general opinion and the ideal of the age. For some women (Elizabeth Elstob, for example), this represented an oppressive hardship, while many who seem basically content with their lives, such as Caroline Powys, nevertheless expressed a desire for more learning, for larger responsibilities, and for a role which would be both more demanding and more fulfilling. The women authors considered here are such women.

The restrictions placed on women in the eighteenth century affected all classes and all roles that a woman might play. They were most disabling, however, for the woman who had to make her own way—the spinster and the widow—and most painfully if she were poor. The age deprived these unfortunates not only of material means of support but also of the all-important psychological support of social approval and of an important, useful role to play. In many cases penury was exacerbated by disparagement and loneliness. Except in Scott's *Millenium Hall,* novels provided few models of contented spinsters, and Scott's model was not available to women in real life. Widows who are admired for wisdom in the novels, such as Mrs. Shirley in *Sir Charles Grandison,* have not remarried. While marriage might be indeed a courageous act on the part of a woman, it was still the role sought by most women and the reward given to most of the virtuous heroines.

The novels of the century provided virtually no models for happiness in the single state, although it is suggested, for example, that Richardson's heroine in *Clarissa* might have been happy living on the income of her inheritance had she been able to secure it, or that Burney's heroine in *Cecilia* could have contentedly remained single exercising good works, if Mortimer had not reappeared. Sarah Fielding's *Adventures of David Simple,* on the other hand, and Lennox's *Henrietta* graphically portray the problems confronting a young woman forced to earn her own livelihood. As we have seen from the letters of real women, these descriptions were all too accurate. While the plight of the poor spinster and widow was deplored in novels of the period, no viable alternatives, Scott's *Millenium Hall* excepted, were suggested. The novel as a genre, therefore, strongly reinforced the desirability of marriage, despite its risks, as the goal for all women.

CHAPTER 6

Reinforcement or Rebellion?

E A L I S M, in the sense of giving an accurate portrayal of the existing world, was assumed in the eighteenth century to be the hallmark of the new genre, the novel. Samuel Johnson voiced the general opinion of his age in *Rambler* number four: "The works of fiction, with which the present generation seems more particularly delighted, are such as exhibit life in its true state." Samuel Richardson, in a letter to Aaron Hill describing the writing of *Pamela,* emphasized another aspect of the new form. He declared that he hoped that this new species of writing would turn the young away from "the pomp and parade of romance writing, and . . . might tend to promote the cause of religion and virtue" (Carroll, 41). Indeed, the eighteenth-century novel gained respectability in large part because it was thought that its focus on the true rather than the fantastic made it an instrument for imparting knowledge and encouraging moral improvement. How realistic in fact were eighteenth-century novels in their depiction of women? What did they teach women?

The questions are of interest not only as criteria for judging these works—criteria that the age itself continually posited—but as a way of assessing the influence of novels on the behavior of women, on the ideals they formed for themselves and on the possibilities they were encouraged to pursue. Most of us need only turn to our own experience to confirm the effect that fictions, including now films and television, have had upon us, especially in youth. Fiction reflects the values of its time, to be sure, but just as importantly, it creates them. The novel, which, its eighteenth-century authors insisted, showed not the artificial or impossible but, as Sarah Fielding claimed, "characters [that] are really to be found in human nature," was an especially powerful cultural force. Sheridan's Lydia Languish and Lennox's Arabella satirize the power of reading in forming the expectations of young women. What were their real-life counterparts learning from the fiction they read?

Assessing novels from the standpoint of a rather literal realism presents immediate and unavoidable problems. For the modern critic, of course, such an assessment is so complex as to make such a search meaningless, but here we are adopting the naive standards voiced above by Sarah Fielding. Who, then, is the "real" eighteenth-century woman? How can we describe her? As we have seen in earlier chapters, she was in some ways as varied as her contemporary counterparts—sometimes docile, sometimes rebellious; sometimes happy, sometimes not; daughters, wives, mothers, widows, spinsters, all living different lives. However, the preceding survey of actual eighteenth-century women does, I believe, give us the basis for a general sense of boundaries. Remembering their own descriptions of their lives and feelings we can make some fairly accurate judgments about what would seem to most eighteenth-century women normal behavior and realistic standards. We will try to look at the novels through the eyes of these women rather than twentieth-century eyes. We will be asking: How believable, in the context of its own time, is the delineation of the characters of women in this book?

Even more important, what influence might these works have had on the behavior of women? That is, does the writer, by direct narrative comment or by words given to admirable characters, advocate modes of conduct? If so, what are they? Does the action or plot of the novel demonstrate that certain kinds of behavior are good or bad? What is rewarded and what is punished? What is shown as possible or impossible, successful or unsuccessful? Are the commonly held notions of women's capabilities reinforced or challenged? Are the boundaries set by society for women accepted or questioned? A final consideration is the importance of the role played by women in the novel. Are they seen as having value in their own right, as being worth the attention and concern of the reader, or are they seen chiefly in relation to men, as the cause of happiness or pain?[1]

The treatment of specific aspects of women's experience by each of these novelists has been discussed in chapters one through five. In this chapter the work of each will be considered as a whole, leading to an assessment of the influence each might have had on eighteenth-century women. (Criteria for the selection of novelists are discussed in the introduction.) The novelists are Samuel Richardson, Henry Fielding, Sarah Fielding, Charlotte Lennox, Sarah Scott, Clara Reeve, and Fanny Burney.

Samuel Richardson presented lively and believable women in his novels. He believed that their credibility was an essential part of their appeal and therefore gave them faults so that they might seem within the reach of emulation.[2] Each of his heroines is exemplary, however, and each radically challenges the century's picture of women. Richardson insists on women's parity with men in intelligence and in the assertion of self. In *Pamela* we see a young woman insisting on her own interpretation of the world against the combined forces of wealth and privilege; in *Clarissa* we see a young woman destroyed by the hypocritical morality of a middle-class culture which treats women like merchandise; and in *Sir Charles Grandison* we see an ideal world in which women can function in full equality. Richardson's novels all ask for fundamental changes in the society he knew.

Richardson's works assert the importance and the strength of women's friendship.[3] He declared, in fact, that one of his purposes in *Clarissa* was to show that women were capable of "the highest exercise of a reasonable and practicable friendship" (I, xiii). It was common to assume that while men form lasting bonds, women's friendships are only a substitute for what is really desired, male attention, and that they are therefore quickly discarded, especially when a man intervenes. Anna Howe remains Clarissa's loyal friend throughout the novel, despite pressure from her mother and despite the blandishments of Lovelace himself. In *Sir Charles Grandison*, Harriet has to face the probability, at one point a near certainty, that the man she loves, Sir Charles, will marry another woman, Clementina. Harriet says, "However hard it is to prefer another to one's self, in such a case as this; yet if my judgment is convinced, my acknowledgement shall follow it" (II, 366). She becomes convinced that Sir Charles *"ought* to love Clementina" (II, 181) and she yields to a woman "not *less,* but *more* worthy than" (II, 495) herself. Harriet's generosity of spirit, even to a woman with no previous place in her affections, shows that women can indeed act nobly toward one another. Her insistence that her judgment will prevail over her emotions also shows her expectation that women should act like rational beings, following intellectual conviction rather than the more suspect promptings of the heart.

Richardson's women are not only intelligent, they are characteristically shown, in normal circumstances, functioning as articulate, informed participants in discussions of general interest.[4] Much of the first part of *Pamela* and almost all of *Clarissa,* to be sure, depict an ambiance far from normative in which the heroine is under great stress. Both Pamela and Clarissa more than hold their own in debates with their persecutors in these special circumstances, and Anna Howe is a notably lively presence. Even more telling as an example for readers, however, are scenes from *Pamela II* and *Sir Charles Grandison.* The most typical setting in these works is the drawing room or parlor where men and women gather to enjoy music and the pleasures of conversation. The women take an equal part, and their opinions have equal weight with the men's. Pamela, in fact, assessing the relative merits of the couples they know, comes to the conclusion that in virtually all cases the woman is intellectually superior. "I dare not, Sir, conjecture whence arises this more than parity in the genius of the sexes, among the above persons, notwithstanding the disparity of education and the difference in the opportunities of each" (II, 416), she remarks. Mr. B. does not speculate either, but he does agree with her judgment.

When Sir Charles talks with women he refuses to adopt the artificial "appropriated language" about which Mrs. Shirley complained. Instead, he "addresses himself to women, *as* women, not as goddesses" and "does honour to the persons and to the sex" (III, 139). On one occasion Sir Charles attends a bachelor party, but his favorite amusements customarily are all found within the family circle, and all in the company of women. Far from the tea-table chat and scandalmongering which satirists attributed to women, the talk in Richardson's drawing rooms is on manners and morals, although seasoned with banter, to be sure, and not divorced from the pleasures of music and dancing. Harriet is typical of the group: "When she speaks, she never disappoints the most raised expectation" (I, 424), bringing to the conversation "a wit lively and inoffensive: And an understanding solid and useful" (II, 10). Catherine Talbot would not have to worry about being too talkative in this world. Significantly, it is Harriet's forwardness being depreciated at the party in chapter 1, where Talbot feels self-conscious about appearing to be a "perfect Phoebe Clinket."

As we have seen above, Richardson's model for marriage grants not merely equality but superiority to the wife. Pamela grows in wifely stature as Mr. B. more truly reforms, and at the end of the novel he has given over the direction of his life to her. In *Clarissa,* the authoritarian marriage of the Harlowes is seen as wrong, and Clarissa's dilemma is partly a product of her mother's bowing to men who insist on patriarchal power. Sir Charles, as the good man, proposes to give his wife not merely equality but the power of decision. Men who insist on the rights of a husband are portrayed as both foolish and tyrannical. In the marriage of Charlotte Grandison we see the happy outcome of a union where an intelligent woman marries a man who is willing to acknowledge her superiority.

Richardson's novels emphasize the intellectual and spiritual integrity of women as they try to function in a society which denies them their most fundamental rights.[5] *Clarissa* begins with the conflict between Clarissa and her family over her marriage. In this conflict, as we have seen, Richardson dramatically embodies the plight of women under the code of respectable eighteenth-century society with Clarissa's plea, "Only leave me *myself*" (I, 399), illuminating the fundamental powerlessness of women in the age. *Pamela* is also essentially concerned with the struggle of a young woman to maintain her own integrity, who claims, despite society's disparagement of her rights, "My soul is of equal importance with the soul of a princess" (137). As we have seen above, this claim is ignored by both the gentry and the clergy, the power structures in Pamela's world, but Pamela herself refuses to assent to any standards but her own.

In *Sir Charles Grandison* Richardson presents a picture of the kind of society a good man could possibly create—a utopian soicety that, far from denigrating women, accepts their values. Sir Charles always shows his complete acceptance of a single standard of judgment for men and women. In contrast to his age, he believes that "men and women are . . . much alike . . . put custom, tyrant custom, out of the question" (I, 455). Having a free choice as a wealthy, privileged male, Sir Charles shows by his choices that he both values women and the standards usually considered "feminine" in his society. In the created world of the novel, women function as the intellectual and moral equals of men.

Richardson's heroines, as we have seen, each insist that women must give their first loyalty to themselves, to their own integrity and to their own code of values. Their society is not willing to allow these claims, believing instead that a daughter's first duty is obedience and a wife's is submissiveness, seeing women as having a claim only to relative lives lived for the benefit of others, almost always men. Pamela gains happiness because Mr. B. converts to her system of values, while Harriet finds the perfect husband in Sir Charles who represents a utopian ideal of what a man should be.

Clarissa, however, Richardson's greatest imaginative creation, is destroyed by her refusal to renounce her own most deeply held beliefs. Clarissa's tragedy gains in significance when we recognize that her struggle, both with her family and with Lovelace, is not an aberration, but a natural consequence of following to their logical ends the century's most fundamental views about women. The Harlowes' actions expose the hypocrisy of a supposedly Christian society that used women like goods in a mercantile exchange while mouthing pious platitudes about duty and obedience. Lovelace's libertine code, as we have seen, is based upon the same assumptions as those of the Harlowes—that women are an inferior sort of creation, rightfully controlled by men, who will yield to their fate when violated by male power. Richardson shows that there is little to choose between the respectable standards of the middle class and the rakish code of the aristocrat—between them they destroy Clarissa. The century's most powerful feminist text, *Clarissa* is a revolutionary indictment of its society's view of women. Clarissa's passionate rejection of "the man, who has the assurance to think me, and to endeavour to make me, his *property*," speaks for her prototypes in real life.

The newly respectable genre began, then, with a fundamental questioning of the way in which society estimated women and the way in which women were treated. If Richardson's depiction of women had become the hallmark of the "new species of writing" the novel might have become a powerful instrument for changing the way society regarded women and the way women thought about themselves. As we have seen in the discussion of novels in the preceding chapters, this did not happen.

Henry Fielding, in his works, also presents lively and believable women. His view of women, however, confirms the traditional one.[6] They are portrayed as warm, loving, and emotional, rather than rational. They turn to men for strength and wisdom and see loyalty to a man rather than loyalty to themselves as their highest value. Fielding's novels occasionally protest abuses of the system but fundamentally endorse the view of women as rightfully dependent on men for guidance and protection.

Sophia, the heroine of *Tom Jones,* is perhaps Fielding's most appealing heroine. She is energetic and loving, ruled by her heart rather than by her head. When she is threatened by her father, Squire Western, with an unwelcome marriage to the odious Blifil, nephew and heir of Squire Allworthy, Sophia runs away to honor her promise to marry Tom. In depicting her escape, Fielding draws a courageous Sophia who pays no heed to the fears of her maid, Honour, about walking the countryside at night. (This may be intended as a deliberate contrast to Pamela who misses a chance to escape from Mr. B. because she mistakes a harmless cow for a fierce bull.) "There is a degree of courage," Fielding writes, "which not only becomes a woman, but is often necessary to enable her to discharge her duty" (559). At the appointed meeting place, when Sophia encounters a man instead of her maid, "she neither screamed out, nor fainted away." (He proves to be a messenger from Honour.)

Sophia is a truly romantic heroine, however, because she acts on the basis of emotion rather than rational thought. Honour advises her, "For Heaven's sake, Madam, consider what you are about" (564). Given the drastic step Sophia has taken, such a caution might seem superfluous, but in fact it is not: "Sophia had been lately so distracted between hope and fear, her duty and love to her father, her hatred to Blifil, her compassion, and (why should we not confess the truth) her love for Jones . . . that her mind was in that confused state, which may be truly said to make us ignorant of what we do." As we have seen above, Sophia's chief motivation for running away is her promise to Tom never to marry Blifil, and her knowledge that she would never be able to disobey a direct command from her father.

Squire Allworthy, who, as his name indicates, is usually an exemplary character, thinks highly of Sophia. She has many good qualities, he notes, but one especially which is "absolutely essential to the making of a good wife," that is, "she always showed the highest deferences to the understandings of men" (883). He has observed that "in the company of men she hath been all attention, with the modesty of a learner, not the forwardness of a teacher," and that she has "no dictatorial sentiments, no judicial opinions, no profound criticisms" (882). Once, he relates, he tested her, asking her opinion about a disputed point. Sophia passed the test with flying colors: she refused to speak and told him, "I am sure you cannot in earnest think me capable of deciding." He approves. "I never heard anything of pertness, or what is called repartee out of her mouth; no pretense to wit, much less to that kind of wisdom which is the result only of learning and experience; the affectation of which, in a young woman, is as absurd as any of the affectations of an ape." As we have seen, learned women are always satirized in Fielding's work. They are not only guilty of ludicrous affectation but are also defective morally.

In the preface to *Joseph Andrews,* Fielding declares that "the ridiculous only . . . falls within my province in the present work" (7). In reading the novel, therefore, one must guard against looking for realism in flat, stereotypical characters used to further Fielding's satiric purpose. Names such as Mrs. Slipslop or Mrs. Tow-wouse indicate that an analysis of these characters in terms of realistic exemplars mistakes the tenor of the work, and while Mrs. Slipslop's pretensions to a learned vocabulary are mocked, so is the ignorance of the local justice of the peace. Three women are presented as exemplars, however—Fanny, Joseph's sweetheart; Mrs. Wilson, who turns out to be Joseph's mother; and, at least partially, Mrs. Adams, the wife of Parson Adams, Joseph's friend and mentor. Although Joseph, a boy with no advantages of birth or education, has managed to learn to read and write, impressing Adams with his knowledge, Fanny is completely illiterate. This is not seen as a disadvantage, and Adams describes her as "the sweetest-tempered, honestest, worthiest, young creature," while Joseph declares that he does not "know a virtue which that young creature is not possessed of" (301). Fanny's chastity and her faithfulness to Joseph are her chief characteristics.

Mrs. Wilson's maiden name was Hearty, undoubtedly intended to suggest the first meaning of the word listed in Johnson's dictionary—"Sincere; undissembled; warm; zealous." (Fanny's surname is Goodwill.) She is indeed not only warm but generous. When she is left comfortably well off by her father, she rescues Wilson from debtor's prison and, freely confessing her love, marries him despite the contrast in their fortunes. The Wilsons live an idyllic life in country retirement, spending most of their time together, for, Mr. Wilson says, "I am neither ashamed of conversing with my wife, nor of playing with my children. I do not perceive that inferiority of understanding which the levity of rakes, the dullness of men of business, or the austerity of the learned would persuade us of in women" (226). Parson Adams, the classicist, agrees about the pleasures of family life but then laments that "his own wife did not understand Greek" (227). Wilson quickly makes it clear that his pleasure in his wife's company is not related to learning and that "he would not be apprehended to insinuate that his own had an understanding above the care of her family." In the Adams household, when Adams cites theology his wife characteristically refuses to pay any attention to such bookish nonsense, citing the judgment of common sense. She is, indeed, often wiser in the ways of the world than her quixotic husband, but the capacity of women for abstract thought is, nevertheless, denigrated. Fielding's ideal couples are shown spending their time at home together in contented companionship, at the cost of limiting their conversation to domestic concerns. In contrast, as we have seen above, Richardson's heroines are all well educated, and in his novels learned women are never deprecated.

Women's friendships are usually of dubious worth in Fielding's works. Mrs. Bennet does not hesitate to use Amelia to get a commission for Atkinson, and she herself has suffered from the jealous malice of her aunt. Amelia is betrayed by her sister. Sophia finds Lady Bellaston a treacherous ally, and even her maid Honour considers financial advantage as important as loyalty to her mistress. Miss Matthews, Amelia's rival, declares, "We women do not love to hear one another's praises" (90), and the narrator of *Amelia* assures us, "It may be laid down as a general rule, that no woman who hath any great pretensions to admiration is ever well pleased . . . to fill only the second place" (204). When a deceitful relationship is described, the same narrator comments philosophically that "such are the friendships of women!" (52).

While Richardson's heroines are all beautiful, their intelligence is their significant asset. In contrast, Sophia earns Allworthy's approval by her attentive silence. It is her beauty which receives the highest praise. Fanny's beauty, which attracts all who see her, is joined with "a sensibility . . . almost incredible; and a sweetness, whenever she smiled, beyond either imitation or description" (153). No claim is ever made for Fanny's mind, and in their marriage, "Joseph remains blest with his Fanny, whom he dotes on with the utmost tenderness, which is all returned on her side" (344). Amelia is most often seen engaged in domestic chores and cannot be viewed "in a more amiable light than while she was dressing her husband's supper, with her little children playing about her" (488).

Amelia, like Sophia, has great respect for the understandings of men. "You know doctor," she says to Harrison, "I have never presumed to argue with you; your opinion is to me always instruction, and your word a law" (504). She tries to persuade her husband, whose poor judgment generates the plot of the novel by plunging the couple into one difficulty after another, to confide in her, telling him that "though my understanding be much inferior to yours," nevertheless, "I have sometimes had the happiness of luckily hitting on some argument which hath afforded you comfort" (179). In the context of the novel, it should be noted, Amelia is not portrayed as using feminine wiles to gain information but as completely sincere. One is reminded of Sophia's promise to Mrs. Fitzgerald that rather than see any fault in her husband's understanding, she would forfeit her own.

The key to Amelia's character is love, not logic. When Dr. Harrison attempts to comfort her with sensible arguments, "Amelia . . . more than once flattered herself, to speak the language of the world, that her reason had gained an entire victory over her passion," but soon "love brought up a reinforcement . . . of tender ideas, and bore down all before him" (105). When a doubter asks if Amelia's virtue is "so very impregnable," a friend replies, "Her virtue hath the best guard in the world, which is a most violent love for her husband" (455). Again, she resembles Sophia in basing decisions not on a sense of right and wrong or on considerations of self-respect, but rather on her loyalty to a beloved man. She is portrayed throughout the novel as being ruled by emotion. On one occasion, "though there was no kind of reason for Amelia's fright . . . yet so tender were her fears for her husband, and so much had her gentle spirits been lately agitated, that she had a thousand apprehensions of she knew not what," and "she ran directly into the room where all the company were at dinner, scarce knowing what she did or whither she was going" (524).

Amelia's lack of logic or of any very penetrating intelligence is portrayed not as a defect, but on at least one occasion an advantage. When Booth has succeeded in concealing his unfaithfulness, "So happily, both for herself and Mr. Booth, did the excellence of this good woman's disposition deceive her, and force her to see everything in the most advantageous light to her husband" (179). Both Booth and Harrison often treat her like a child. When the truth about Amelia's mother's will finally comes to light, giving Amelia an inheritance which will solve all their difficulties, she is not immediately told. "Having been set down at their lodgings [Amelia and Booth] retired into each other's arms; nor did Booth that evening, by the doctor's [Dr. Harrison, the clergyman, not a medical doctor] advice, mention one word of the grand affair to his wife" (525). The news, of course, is of great importance to Amelia not only because it solves their financial problems, but also because it vindicates her mother, demonstrating that she did indeed love Amelia.

The next day Booth plays games with Amelia, causing her great distress by pretending to accept a loan from Atkinson, taking advantage of friendship. When she finally learns the truth, Amelia tells Booth, "It is upon yours and my children's account that I principally rejoice" (529), managing to cope with the shock with no more than a glass of water. It is just as well that Amelia sees her acquisition of fortune in this light, because Dr. Harrison, telling Booth the news when Amelia is absent, has said, "My child, I wish you joy with all my heart . . . the estate is your own" (522). The ambiguity of English pronouns makes it impossible to pronounce definitively whether the "you" and "your" are intended as singular or plural, but the context suggests singular, with Harrison immediately giving over Amelia's estate to Booth, as would, in fact, happen in law unless special provisions set up a trusteeship.

Richardson and Henry Fielding, then, conventionally considered the century's first novelists and the founders of the newly respectable genre of realistic fiction, each created believable women and heroines which their readers might emulate. Fielding's heroines, however, encourage virtually complete adherence to the codes of the time. They are admired most when they are warm, loving and emotional. They need the guidance and protection of men, and women who assert independence are either "unfeminine," corrupt, or both. Intellectual achievement in women is consistently ridiculed, and the good wife is seen at her most charming in the kitchen or the nursery.

Sarah Fielding created a body of work in which women are central, as the titles of her works usually indicate: *The Governess, or The Little Female Academy, The Lives of Cleopatra and Octavia, The History of the Countess of Dellwyn, The History of Ophelia*. Even her first work, *The Adventures of David Simple*, and its sequel, *Familiar Letters between the Principal Characters in David Simple*, actually pay as much or more attention to their two heroines, Cynthia and Camilla, as to their eponymous hero.[7] Most of Fielding's works are moral tales, and by narrow standards *David Simple*, together with *The Governess* and *Lives*, might not be included in the category of novels. Fielding herself, however, implicitly asks the reader to judge by standards appropriate to the new fiction when David Simple, an admirable character who can be assumed to speak for the author, declares that "the only way of writing well was to draw all the characters from nature." David further states that good characters should be drawn so that "the amiableness of their actions incite men to imitate them" (86).

Most of Fielding's admirable women are intelligent. It is Cynthia's intelligence, in fact, which has aroused the envy of her sisters, bringing her to distress when we first meet her in *David Simple*. Cynthia tries to earn her own living, securing a position as a lady's companion and learning what misery such a job entails. She is rescued at last by David Simple, fortuitously finds her lost true love, Valentine, and marries happily. The narrative makes it clear that Cynthia is to be admired and that the conduct both of her sisters and of her employer is to be deplored; nevertheless, the plot demonstrates that being intelligent is not of much benefit to a woman. This ambiguous attitude toward wit or learning in women is true of all Fielding's narratives. In *Familiar Letters,* for example, Leontina is described as the sort of wife who ought to make any man happy, having "a heart formed . . . for unaffected love" and "withal a head capable of making her a good companion to a man of sense" (II, 115), but, although her husband is said to have "an understanding much above the greatest part of mankind" (II, 112), he cannot accept her intelligence, growing peevish even when she exercises the utmost decorum and shows "deference to [his] opinion" (II, 116). Again, the reader is asked to admire Leontina and ridicule the excessive egotism of her husband, but one might also absorb the lesson that as society was then constituted, Cynthia's family were correct in discouraging learning or any sign of intelligence in women—such achievements produce only trouble. In *The Governess* Fielding shows Mrs. Teachum inculcating lessons of obedience rather than of intellectual substance. Both Mrs. Teachum and Fielding's own narratives teach deference to the opinions of men and reliance on their strength.

In Fielding's narratives happiness for women is found in marriage. Both Cynthia and Camilla in *David Simple* fail miserably in their attempts to support themselves, and any feminine assertiveness, such as Cleopatra's in *The Lives of Cleopatra and Octavia,* leads to unhappiness. What picture, then, does Fielding create of marriage? The ideal is stated as a happy cooperation between husband and wife, but the examples presented in the novels tend to show the husband as the wise mentor who protects and guides. Editorial comment always indicates that a wife is obligated to fulfill every marital promise absolutely, no matter what her husband's conduct may be.

Camilla and David exemplify Fielding's concept of the proper marital relationship. David is the protector and guide; Camilla profits from his kind instruction. The relationship depicted here is not necessarily improbable. The letters of Jane Papillon suggest that she regarded her husband in just such a light, and the marriage was certainly a happy one. If a wife did indeed regard her husband as wiser, her role, as prescribed by the conduct books, would certainly be easier to play. In *The Countess of Dellwyn* Fielding gives a picture of a perfect wife, Mrs. Bilson, whose spouse is neither wise nor faithful. The marriage begins as a love match on both sides but her husband soon tires of her company. Although he neglects her completely and spends their substance in gambling and keeping a mistress, Mrs. Bilson remains a model wife, always greeting him affectionately and finally following him into debtor's prison uncomplainingly. The patience of a loving wife toward a bankrupt husband is possible, as the letters of Peregrine Chaytor to her husband demonstrate, but Mrs. Bilson's lack of anger in the face of not merely improvidence and unfaithfulness but total neglect while her husband's "days were passed in public, and his evenings at the tavern" (I, 164) is highly improbable and also sets an impossible standard of wifely behavior. In the same novel, the countess of Dellwyn is the negative exemplar. She "fails in due respect to her husband" and "the scorn which falls on [such a woman] is always deserved" (II, 162).

What pictures of eighteenth-century women, then, can we say Sarah Fielding's work presents? First, her fiction gives an important place to women who are seen as worthy of interest and concern in their own right. She also approves of intelligence in women, sometimes indicating a critical view of the social attitudes which inhibit its development and disparage achievement. Her attitude here, however, is curiously ambivalent. While Cynthia's family and Leontina's husband both are said to be wrong, the reader is left with the feeling that, given the prevailing mores, each woman would be wise to conceal her wit. Furthermore, extreme diffidence is specifically praised, with Leontina in *Familiar Letters* described approvingly as making so little "show of her understanding . . . that it passes generally unregarded" (II, 114), while women of pseudo-learning who push themselves into the limelight are satirized. The diffidence felt by intelligent women about expressing ideas, such as those expressed by Catherine Talbot in chapter 1, would scarcely be ameliorated by the exemplars Fielding proposes.

Most of Fielding's women are unable to achieve happiness, or, indeed, even to make a living without the help of men. To be sure, society is criticized for the conditions which lead both Cynthia and Camilla to desperation, but the message is nonetheless clear. The one exception, a woman who has created a happy existence without men, is found in *The History of Ophelia,* the work of Fielding closest to the pernicious romances decried by the novelists, although the author insists in the "advertisement" that "it contains many incidents that bear so much the appearance of reality, that they might claim some share of our belief." While the novel does show women leading independent lives, it is too eccentric to be exemplary and the idyllic beginning seems simply a device to create a suitably naive and unworldly heroine.

Marriage for Fielding is clearly the route to fulfillment for women, and the picture of marriage, as we have seen, is highly patriarchal. Ideal marriages are those in which the kind, wise, and strong husband guides the wife, whose loving heart prompts grateful obedience to her protector. In less perfect marriages the wife can gain eventual happiness only through devoted submission, and no matter what his failings may be she is obligated to respect her husband as well as her marriage vows. Like Jenny Peace in *The Governess,* a woman is well advised to remember that man's "superior strength might assist" her and, therefore, she ought in return to use her "utmost endeavours to oblige him." That strength is, by implication, not merely physical but mental, and the endeavors, for a virtuous woman, are never grudged but constitute the basis for a truly fulfilling life.

Charlotte Lennox lays greater stress on the intelligence of her women, with all of her novels centering on a notably intelligent heroine. The intelligence of her heroines, in fact, constitutes their chief charm, and the narratives emphasize that empty-headed beauty is no match for the animation that wit lends to the countenance. Her protagonists are also well educated, with this learning admired by suitors as well as by wise older characters who sometimes become spokespersons for proper values in the novels. Mothers, however, are usually depicted as supporting false values of vanity and frivolousness. Even the deluded protagonist of *The Female Quixote,* Arabella, is shown as basically intelligent despite her foolish notions of romance.

Furthermore, the plots of Lennox's novels show the wit and learning of her heroines as a positive advantage to them. Intelligence gives them charm and they attract suitors who are immune to the appeal of mere empty-headed beauty. *Sophia* is really a parable about the advantage of education to a woman. While Sophia's beautiful sister Harriot is given every advantage of a fashionable but frivolous education, Sophia educates herself through a careful course of reading, aided by Mr. Herbert, a wise old friend of her father. This both "enlarged her understanding and confirmed her in the principles of piety" (I, 6), substantiating the claims of Mary Astell and advocates of education for women. She easily captures the heart of the eligible suitor her more beautiful but foolish sister has set her cap for, and while he only sought to make her sister his mistress, Sophia's wisdom makes her eligible to be his wife. Mr. Herbert declares that while "justly might it be called infatuation and folly to raise to rank and affluence . . . a handsome idiot," it is fitting "that a man of sense should make the fortune of a woman who would do honour to his choice" (I, 47). Despite her lack of a dowry, her future husband pledges to make the same marriage settlements that were made for his mother because "Miss Sophia in virtue, wit, good sense, and every female excellence, brings [him] an immense portion" (II, 32–33).

Lennox's heroines also tend to be more active in securing their own happiness than Sarah Fielding's. Harriot Stuart, for example, forces a confrontation with her lover which dispels a misunderstanding, while Henrietta runs away to avoid an unwelcome marriage, managing to earn a living for herself, even if somewhat precariously. However, as with Sarah Fielding's heroines, true happiness is usually the gift of a man. Henrietta is an interesting case in point. Toward the end of the novel, Henrietta and her employer, the frivolous Miss Belmour, are traveling incognito when they meet two young men also, it develops, traveling under assumed identities. "Mr. Melvil" falls violently in love with Henrietta. When a fever, the result of unrequited passion, endangers his companion's life, "Mr. Freeman" tries to persuade Henrietta to become Melvil's mistress. Eventually, it is revealed that Mr. Freeman is Henrietta's long-separated brother who is acting as tutor to Melvil, the son of a duke.

After true identities are revealed, Henrietta's brother offers only the most perfunctory of apologies for having tried to debauch her, and in a ferment of anxiety lest he betray his trust to the duke by allowing his son to become allied with a penniless commoner, insists that Henrietta reside in a French convent for safekeeping.

HENRIETT

E. F. Burney, del.

Milton sculp.

Figure 14. Illustration from Charlotte Lennox's *Henrietta*. Edward Burney. This illustration emphasizes that the heroine of the novel *Henrietta* is both intelligent and learned and therefore attractive. Reproduced by courtesy of the Trustees of the British Museum.

Henrietta assents, declaring, "To be sure I can have no objection; dispose of me as you please, you are in the place of my father [they are orphans], I will obey you as such" (II, 228). This submissive behaviour is incongruous, not only because her brother's behaviour has scarcely suggested that he is a moral exemplar, but also because Henrietta is the elder and has been shifting for herself since their parents' death with no help from her brother.

Henrietta's behavior is rewarded, however, although the novel presents the denouement in an ironic tone. Through the agency of her brother, she is reconciled with her wealthy aunt who develops "a prodigious fondness" for her nephew, for "women are ever readier to discover merit in the other sex than in their own" (II, 280). The guarantee of an inheritance for Henrietta makes marriage possible with the duke's son and she lives happily ever after.

Any lack of femininity is criticized in Lennox's novels. In *The Female Quixote* the daughter of a neighbor is described as "a great romp" who "delighted in masculine excercises" (71). She spends "a great part of the day in riding about the country, leaping over hedges and ditches, exposing her fair face to the injuries of the sun and the wind," and through all this has acquired "a masculine and robust air not becoming her sex." Curiously, her later fate is to become a wanton with two illegitimate children. In contrast, Arabella, when her father is ill, shows such "extreme tenderness" that her suitor's "affection [is engaged] more strongly" (58), and at her father's death she suffers prolonged fainting spells.

Lennox's first four novels, *The Life of Harriot Stuart, Henrietta, Sophia,* and *The Female Quixote,* all show energetic, intelligent heroines who try to control their own destinies, although they are not always successful. The novels also suggest, however, that a good marriage is the true, indeed only, route to happiness, and that, in general, men are better able to cope with the world. Female friendships are denigrated; in *Henrietta* the wealthy aunt favors her nephew over Henrietta and Henrietta's friend Miss Woodby betrays her "without reflecting on the baseness of the part she was acting, and only sensible to the pleasure of engaging the attention of a man" (I, 190). The young women whom Arabella meets are catty and envious, while Harriot, Sophia's sister, together with other women in the novels, is selfish and shallow. The novels suggest that Lennox's attractive heroines are the exceptions rather than the rule, although they also encourage emulation of these heroines.

Euphemia, Lennox's last novel, is different from her earlier work in several ways. First, Euphemia's story begins with her marriage, which, far from the usual happy ending that rewards the virtuous heroine, proves to be miserable. Second, one of the chief themes is female friendship and the satisfaction that women can find in their own company. Third, Euphemia's husband, unlike Sir Charles in *Sophia,* is not reformed by a virtuous wife; instead Euphemia is left an independent fortune by his wealthy uncle who admires her good sense. (The striking depiction of an unhappy marriage in *Euphemia* has been discussed in chapter 4.)

Euphemia also echoes motifs that appear in the earlier novels. Intelligent women are more attractive than empty-headed beauties, but "the learned and scientific Lady Cornelia Claffick" is satirized for "talents so masculine, and so ostentatiously displayed" (II, 159). In contrast, "the wise, the pious, the virtuous Eleonora," although superior to most males in learning, "engages in discourse with timidity and is surprised, confused, to find her superiority acknowledged" (II, 167). Indeed, she is so diffident that "one may converse with her for whole years . . . without discovering her to be a great genius." Also criticized is "the fearless huntress Miss Sandford," who should be warned that a "woman who . . . leaps every five-bar gate . . . must not expect to inspire a delicate passion" (II, 166).

Lennox's heroines show energy and intelligence in trying to control their lives. While wit and learning are not only admirable but also beneficial to women, Lennox reinforces some of the conventions of the age by ridiculing any ostentatious display of either, advocating quiet diffidence. Tomboys are also criticized, and feminine decorum praised. In general a wedding is the proper reward for virtuous heroines, and a married life "lived in great harmony together" is the feminine ideal. Lennox does not radically challenge the standards of her age, but she does realistically show the strains this model could produce. Her novels also present women who are competent and equal intellectually to the men in their circle, although they must never flaunt their gifts. As models for young women, Lennox's heroines would encourage learning and the development of intellectual powers, but principally to attract and capture the right man. With the right man, a man who would value his wife's intelligence more than mere beauty, a life of quiet and inconspicuous domesticity brings happiness and fulfillment. Since opportunities for women outside of marriage were almost nonexistent, Lennox's models for women were realistic.

Sarah Scott's body of work presents surprisingly disparate conceptions of the proper role for women. Some of her novels, notably *The History of Cornelia, A Journey Through Every Stage of Life,* and *A Description of Millenium Hall,* radically challenge the conventional view of women, while *The Man of Real Sensibility, or the History of Sir George Ellison* suggests that the century's prejudice against marrying widows is wrong. Others, however—*Agreeable Ugliness: or The Triumph of the Graces* and *The Test of Filial Duty*— reinforce in a very stringent way the obligation of daughters to obey parents, especially fathers, even at the sacrifice of future happiness and, indeed, of conscientious scruples. Except in *The Man of Real Sensibility,* the focus of each novel is a woman, and, with the exception of *Filial Duty,* whose protagonists are not described as in any way remarkable, a woman of marked intelligence and practical good sense.

The History of Cornelia has a plot as improbable as any romance, starting with an escape from a wicked, lecherous uncle, continuing through abductions and imprisonments, and ending with marriage to Cornelia's true love. Cornelia herself, however, is highly capable and her actions are always believable. She not only manages to engineer several escapes, but also to support herself. She has been well educated by her father, and, as with Lennox's heroines, her intellectual gifts attract approbation from suitors. Mr. de Rhone admires her "spirit of independency" and observes that "instead of common entertainments, to which vanity generally leads women . . . her sole recreation was in books" (51). She rescues a milliner, Mme. de Miteau, from bankruptcy by teaching proper methods of bookkeeping and inventory control, while "her ingenuity enabled her to extend their trade" so that soon the shop is doing "more business . . . than ever" (49).

A Journey Through Every Stage of Life uses the fairy tale format of a banished princess to whom, to while away the tedium, a wise governess tells stories. The framing device allows Scott to interject comments from the naively innocent princess and from the worldly-wise older woman. While most of the eight tales are short and highly stereotyped accounts of disappointed love or of the rewards of faithful virtue, the first story, "Leonora and Louisa," is quite fully developed, accounting in length for almost two-thirds of the book. The narrator explains that this is a true account of a lady she knew well in England, and that she gives precedence to this history because "she was almost the only woman I have ever met with who endeavored to conquer the disadvantages our sex labour under, and who proved that custom, not nature, inflicts that dependence in which we live, obliged to the industry of man for our support, as well as his courage for our defense" (I, 6).

Leonora disguises herself as a man and successfully pursues careers as a clergyman, a portrait painter, and a schoolmaster, proving that a woman, if allowed the same education as a man, can function well in these presumed masculine roles. Eventually, she resumes her feminine identity, and although her lover delights in "the sprightliness of her wit, and the solidity of her judgement," now "she took care to conceal her learning, as she had been accustomed to do while in her female habit" (I, 149).

In an ironic ending, the governess declines to continue the tale after the union of the happy couple, declaring that "a story would make but a bad figure continued on beyond marriage," but, even more importantly, because she "began Leonora's history in order to show, by an uncommon example, how capable our sex might be of preserving independence" and therefore "could have no excuse for continuing it after she had done so common a thing as marrying" (I, 160). The princess objects to this interpretation, exclaiming, "A melancholy moral!" and declaring, "I must rejoice in the manner in which it concludes." She adopts a traditional view of women, asserting that "it would be a disgrace to our sex if one of them, after succeeding in every other attempt, conquering fortune, prejudice and custom, should find her power insufficient to vanquish the heart of a man," and advocating the route to feminine power often proposed in conduct books: "She who holds his heart in chains has no reason to fear he will lay any very heavy fetters on her will" (I, 160). The governess seems not to have succeeded in converting her romantic young charge to the cause of women's independence.

A Description of Millenium Hall presents a utopian community created and managed solely by women who are highly intelligent and practical, as well as capable of living together in friendship. The theme of lasting female friendship appears in many of Scott's works—Cornelia finds a good friend in Mme. du Maine, and is a good friend to Julia; Leonora and Louisa support each other in their troubles, as do Emilia and Charlotte in *The Test of Filial Duty*. In general, these novels present a group of very independent women who are intelligent, resourceful, and capable. They manage to make their own way in the world, and while a happy marriage is the destiny of Cornelia and Leonora, the women of Millenium Hall live without men by choice, not necessity.

Despite the unusual independence of her heroines, Scott insists on the great importance of reputation for a woman. Cornelia, for example, refuses to assent to a secret marriage with the man she loves, a man who is in every way worthy of her hand, because "concealment must destroy my reputation, for the loss of which, innocence is not a sufficient comfort, nor the greatest happiness, the company of a most tenderly beloved friend, a sufficient recompense" (31). Her concern for reputation leads her into all sorts of difficulties that marriage to Bernardo would have prevented, but even when the couple are eventually united it is never indicated, either explicitly or implicitly, that her decision was faulty. Similarly, Mrs. Morgan of *Millenium Hall* agrees to a repugnant marriage rather than allow her name to be defamed. Scott is also curiously insistent on filial obedience for daughters in *Agreeable Ugliness* and *The Test of Filial Duty*.

Scott, then, in many ways presents a picture of women who are more independent than most women were in fact, and certainly far more independent and capable than the models offered by conduct books. Leonora is explicitly offered as an example to demonstrate that the limited roles allotted to women are culturally imposed, not the result of any lack of intrinsic ability. Women are generally seen as equal or superior to men in intelligence and in managerial ability. While Scott's plots are often improbably filled with romantic adventures, her more rebellious heroines are themselves down-to-earth young women who generally convince us of their common sense. In two areas, however, Scott reinforces the century's code of conduct for women: they must always be solicitous of reputation even if they are innocent in behavior, and they must give absolute obedience to parents, especially to fathers.

The Old English Baron, Clara Reeve's first and best-known novel, originally titled *Champion of Virtue,* is, as the author herself declares, "the literary offspring of *The Castle of Otranto."* As such it is of little interest to the present study, since it makes almost no attempt to be realistic. The women—Lady Lovel, the idealized dead mother; Margery Twyford, the loving foster mother; and Emma, the faithful sweetheart—are all stereotypes of feminine roles, but this is also true of the men. As one might expect, it is the knights who dominate the action, while the women are largely passive. The novel is so clearly removed from the everyday world that only Lennox's Arabella could take it as a model for conduct.

Reeve's other works, *The Two Mentors, The School for Widows,* and *Destination: or Memoires of a Private Family,* are set in the modern world and are clearly intended to be exemplary. In *The Two Mentors* a young man, Edward Saville, is the center of the action as the two mentors of the title contest for his future—will he become a virtuous clergyman or a worldly-wise rake? Women, however, function as major characters in the novel, and they are portrayed as important in their own right, not merely as relating to Saville. *The School for Widows* tells of the unhappy marriages of two school friends and focusses entirely on the lives of its women protagonists. *Destination,* on the other hand, virtually ignores women and concerns itself solely with the education of boys.

Reeve's women are usually intelligent and accomplished. Saville admires Miss Melcombe, whom he eventually wins as a wife, for her achievements. "I find new accomplishments rise upon me every hour," he writes, enumerating that she "plays sweetly upon the harpsichord; she sings like a virgin of Paradise; . . . she speaks French, she reads Italian, she has been taught the elements of several sciences." However, far from flaunting her talents, "she conceals them with as much care as most ladies take to display them" (I, 172). Furthermore, the ladies of the household where Miss Melcombe lives are constantly employed in worthy feminine tasks, making childbed linen for the poor and doing other needlework. Saville approves. "Such women as these do honour to their sex and to human nature. May I obtain a wife of this school, as the completion of all human happiness!" (I, 195). Another woman, described with approval as "a good wife and mother" (I, 113), while not "a shining character in the conventional way . . . is all that a man ought to wish for in domestic life, an excellent manager without any ostentatious display of it." On the other hand, a "bold woman is shocking," arousing "mingled indignation and contempt" (I, 145).

Rachel Strictland and Frances Darnford, the protagonists of *The School for Widows,* are both far more intelligent and capable than their husbands. Their abilities are of no help to them in their marriages, but after they become widows Mrs. Strictland proves to be a very good manager of her husband's properties, avoiding the penuriousness which often hindered him in his dealings, while Mrs. Darnford, in order to support herself, successfully founds a school. A former pupil says of her, "She deserved knowledge because she made wise and good use of it; she taught us our duty, and set us an example of the practice of it" (I, 27). In contrast, *Destination* deals only with the education of young men and strongly implies that the education of women is of no consequence since their

254

destiny is solely to "make some honest man happy in a wife" (106), and the ideal wife is "modest and unassuming" (II, 88).

Reeve does question some attitudes toward women. In *The Two Mentors,* for example, Miss Jones, a woman who has had an illicit affair but who is determined to reform her life, marries happily with a respectable naval officer. The clergyman who is the virtuous mentor observes that "there is a great difference between a concubine and a harlot" (I, 72), which, considering the century's strictures regarding chastity in women, is a fairly liberal attitude. In the same novel, parents' favoritism for sons over daughters is criticized. Miss Melcombe is virtually abandoned by her father when his second marriage produces a son, proving true the prediction of a friend: "Alas! . . . thou art of no consequence in the scale against a son; thou wilt be forgotten by thy father" (I, 297). When she herself is expecting a child, a friend offers himself as sponsor for a son. A lady interjects, "It seems that you are certain for a son, but if you should be mistaken?" and the man replies, "Then we will reserve ourselves for another time" (I, 255).

On balance, one must conclude that Reeve's novels reinforce the codes of conduct expected of women. The intellectual development of women is ignored in *Destination,* Reeve's work most specifically concerned with education. Frances Darnford deserved knowledge because she made good use of it by setting a good example and teaching her pupils their duty, while Miss Melcombe's accomplishments are modestly concealed, and her useful needlework receives equal if not greater praise. Reeve thus also tends to accede to the conservative position that women were most suited to the domestic sphere, and that striving for learning was at best unnecessary and at worst harmful. In *The School for Widows* Reeve gives a graphic picture of the daily unhappiness that a good woman could suffer in marriage. However, the novel never actually protests the structure of marriage but rather becomes a conduct book, showing how a wife can best accommodate herself to her unhappy lot. Rachel Strictland's praise of her husband's restrictive will also suggests that a husband's authority quite rightfully extends beyond the grave. The most demanding of the conduct book writers could find little to cavil at in the novels of Reeve.

As the titles indicate, Fanny Burney's novels—*Evelina, Camilla,* and *Cecilia*—are all focussed on a woman as the central character, and the happiness and well-being of these women are the chief concern of the action.[8] While intelligent and lively, her heroines are not

Figure 15. Portrait of Fanny Burney. Edward Burney. Used as a frontispiece to her collected works, Burney's portrait projects an image of the woman writer as a fashion plate, perhaps indicating the ambivalent feeling of Burney and other women writers toward their role. Reproduced by courtesy of the Trustees of the British Museum.

exceptionally learned. *Camilla* is, in part, a debate about women's education which offers no real solution to the proper mode but suggests as correct Mr. Tyrold's method of educating a young woman to fit her for the "doubly appendant" role she is destined to play—first daughter, then wife. This involves a careful compromise which stresses simplicity, docility, and accommodation to the world at large. However, the intelligence of Burney's heroines does mark them as different from the mindless society beauties they encounter and gives them the ability to live happily in their own company. Intelligence is also part of their appeal.

While intelligence, liveliness, and wit characterize Burney's heroines, too much learning in women is usually looked on with suspicion. In *Evelina* the "extremely clever" Mrs. Selwin is satirized as unfeminine, although the modern reader sees her only as a witty woman who answers the attacks of a group of supercilious young men in kind. A double standard seems to be applied to Mrs. Selwin's use of wit. The young men include a fop who taunts her with the observation that he has "an insuperable aversion to strength, either of body or mind, in a female." Another beau chimes in, "Egad, I'd as soon see a woman chop wood as hear her chop logic" (361). Still another adds, "A woman wants nothing to recommend her but beauty and good nature; in every other thing she is either impertinent or unnatural," and declares, "Deuce take me if ever I wish to hear a word of sense from a woman as long as I live!" Mrs. Selwin replies, "It has always been agreed that no man ought to be connected with a woman whose understanding is superior to his own," and then voices her fear that "to accommodate all this good company according to such a rule, would be utterly impracticable, unless we should choose subjects from Swift's hospital of idiots" (362).

Ignoring the deliberate provocation which prompted Mrs. Selwin's reply, Evelina deplores it, exclaiming, "How many enemies . . . does this unbounded severity excite!" Another character, with Evelina's tacit consent, acknowledges that Mrs. Selwin "has wit . . . and more understanding than half her sex put together" (343), but finds "the unbounded license of her tongue" to be intolerable "in a *woman*." Evelina herself, worried about a minor *faux pas* with Lord Orville, says, "I am inexpressibly concerned at the thought of his harboring an opinion that I am bold or impertinent, and I could almost kill myself for having given him the shadow of a reason for so shocking an idea" (72).

Burney's novels exhibit a curious ambivalence toward the proper role of women, especially in considering the natural capacity of women, and, consequently, their relationship to men. *Cecilia* could certainly be called a feminist novel; it shows strong women functioning competently on an equal, if not superior, level with men. In *Evelina* and *Camilla,* on the other hand, women are depicted as needing the help and guidance of men to correct their feminine impulsiveness and lack of judgment. *Evelina* and *Camilla* suggest that the century's insistence that a woman is always in need of a masculine protector and mentor is correct, while *Cecilia* challenges this principle, showing women as consistently wiser, more virtuous, and even more decisive.

Cecilia's position as an orphaned heiress gives her unusual independence, and in general she uses her freedom wisely. Her troubles stem not from any youthful imprudence, but from the provisions made for her by her father and her uncle. Cecilia makes her only real mistakes in judgment when she follows the advice of another man, Mr. Monckton, an old family friend. He is planning to marry her himself and gives advice which suits his own purposes rather than her welfare. It is hard to blame her harshly in this case, however, because Monckton fools everyone, and she is doing just what the conduct books would urge a wealthy young woman to do—trusting the wisdom of an experienced older man, a trusted friend of her father, rather than her own.

In every crisis, Cecilia proves very capable. When her guardian, Harrel, commits suicide in a melodramatic fashion at Vauxhall, it is she who, after her initial shock, in "a few minutes" recovers, hastens to summon "all the strength of mind" she possesses, and takes charge, acting "to the utmost stretch of her abilities and power" (III, 170). Questioning witnesses, she makes inquiries into the exact circumstances of the death, arranges for the body to be removed, and copes with the hysterical widow. Mortimer Delvile admires her conduct, exclaiming, "What a cruel task have you nobly performed! such spirit with such softness! so much presence of mind with such feeling!—but you are all excellence!" (III, 180).

At one point, thinking that marriage to Mortimer is impossible, Cecilia retires to the country, determined "to think and live for herself" (V, 138). She sets up a household "formed by rules of reason, and her own ideas of right" (V, 139). Doing good deeds and pursuing intellectual pleasures, "she had sedulously filled [her life] with occupations, and her occupations had proved fertile in keeping her mind from idleness, and in restoring it to cheerfulness" (V, 145). Cecilia shows herself capable of fashioning a happy and useful life for herself independent of marriage.

After they are married, Cecilia fully justifies Mortimer's confidence in her steadiness and good sense. When she learns that he has fought a duel with Monckton and has been dangerously wounded, the news momentarily overwhelms her, leaving her speechless, but Delvile pleads for advice, telling her he is "scarce able to think" for himself (V, 232). She suggests a practical course of action, and he responds, "I will go then without doubt: too happy to be guided by you," and "What next shall I do?" She again makes plans and decisions, and he declares, "I will go,—stay,—do which and whatever you bid me" (V, 237). Despite the shock of his news, she "was sooner in a condition for reasoning and deliberation than himself" (V, 236). The expected roles of husband and wife are here reversed, with Cecilia coping in a crisis much better than Mortimer.

While rational virtue is depicted as Cecilia's chief characteristic, a crucial scene in the novel makes it clear that Cecilia is also tenderhearted. Obeying Mortimer's mother's command, Cecilia has renounced Mortimer and retired to a quiet country life. His dog wanders into her garden and, thinking herself alone, Cecilia talks to the animal, confessing her love for its owner. When she realizes that her meanderings have been overheard by Mortimer himself, she laments that her folly has lowered her in his eyes, but he insists that, on the contrary, she is now more dear than ever. "Fortune, beauty, worth and sweetness I had the power to relinquish," he declares, "but when to these I find joined so attractive a softness . . . I can quit you no more!" (IV, 47).

Cecilia, like Burney's other novels, presents a satiric gallery of portraits of both men and women. The frivolous belles of the society in which the Harrels move are shown in all their foolishness, as are the corresponding beaus. In general, however, where characters are paired the woman is better. Mrs. Delvile is far superior to her husband. Mrs. Harrel is silly, but her husband is vicious. Miss Belafield is naturally refined, sweet, and pleasant, although she has no advantages of education, while her brother, who has been given every advantage, is worthless. Mrs. Monckton is a shrew, but Monckton is evil. Cecilia usually shows greater moral strength than Mortimer, and, especially in a crisis, is more decisive. The notions that man is intrinsically superior to woman and that a husband properly is a guide and protector are certainly called into question. The couple's financial problems are solved when Mortimer's aunt is so impressed by Cecilia's virtues that she makes Cecilia her heir, and the final praises of the novel go to the heroine. "Good and excellent young lady!" says Dr. Lyster, "the first of blessings indeed is yours in the temperance of your own mind." Whereas, all the trouble, the doctor declares, "has been the result of PRIDE and PREJUDICE" (V, 379) on the part of two men: her uncle with his egotistical will and Mr. Delvile with his self-partiality.

Both *Evelina* and *Camilla* show a different pattern. In these novels Lord Orville and Edgar Mandelbert, who, respectively, court and eventually marry the two heroines, are seen as wiser and more prudent than they. In marriage, both Evelina and Camilla will find a loving guide and protector. The heroines are intelligent, and this is part of their charm, but they are not notably capable; their errors of judgment activate the plot. Both novels, then, tend to reinforce prevailing ideas about the proper relative roles of men and women, although *Camilla* does challenge courtship customs, as discussed in chapter 3.

In both novels, in contrast to Mrs. Delvile in *Cecilia,* intelligent women have little function as advisors. Evelina's mother is dead, and she has been raised by her guardian, Mr. Villars, in country seclusion. As the subtitle of the novel, *The History of a Young Lady's Entrance into the World,* indicates, the plot chiefly concerns Evelina's experiences as she encounters society in London and later in Bristol. Her errors all stem from a lack of knowledge of form and custom; they are errors of decorum rather than judgment. She must learn prudence, however, for an impulsive action, even if entirely innocent, can destroy reputation. Mr. Villars cautions her, "Remember, my dear Evelina, nothing is so delicate as the reputation of a woman: it is, at once, the most beautiful and most brittle of all human things" (164). On her first visit to London, she is in the company of the Mirvans—Captain Mirvan, an absolute boor; Mrs. Mirvan, his perhaps too good-natured but intelligent wife; and Maria, their daughter, a virtuous and sensible young woman. Both Evelina's inexperience and Captain Mirvan's coarseness create problems for her, but in her difficulties she never turns for advice to Mrs. Mirvan, her chaperone, or to Maria, her friend, who might, one would think, serve as a valued confidante.

Mrs. Selwyn accompanies Evelina to Bristol, but, once again, Evelina almost never seeks her advice. That Evelina would turn to her guardian is, of course, understandable, but turning to an unattached young man such as Lord Orville for advice is certainly unconventional and suggests a denigration of women as a valuable source of counsel. Although Orville has made no declaration to her, and certainly has no authority over her, when he, misunderstanding the situation, objects to a planned meeting with Macartney, her half-brother, she immediately volunteers, "If your Lordship thinks there is any impropriety in my seeing him tomorrow, I am ready to give up that intention" (299). Mrs. Selwyn's opinions, in contrast, are almost never sought and resisted if offered. To counterbalance this, it should be noted, it is Mrs. Selwyn's advice, unwillingly followed by Evelina, which does bring about the eventual reconciliation with her father.

One of the most brutally satirized characters in the novel is Madame Duval, Evelina's grandmother, a model of pretentious vulgarity. She and Captain Mirvan, two of a kind, instantly become sworn enemies. Madame Duval is vain, stupid, pushy, and vulgar, but she is not cruel—her faults are largely unconscious. Captain Mirvan, on the other hand, is her match in general boorishness and adds deliberate cruelty. While Madame Duval is humiliated not once but several times, her discomfiture being presented as high comedy, the captain escapes scot-free. His many offenses against not merely decorum but common decency are never chastised.

One curious incident in *Evelina* is the race between two old women. This is agreed upon as a substitute for a phaeton race between two frivolous young men, a contest that would be dangerous to them. Instead, each is to produce a woman proved to be more than eighty to represent him in a foot race. The stakes are high, and Evelina expresses astonishment to Lord Orville "at this extraordinary method of spending so much money" (295). He reassures her that he has prevailed upon the young bloods to reduce the wager from one thousand to one hundred pounds. To do Orville justice, he has previously suggested a more humane way of settling the debt—"that the money should be his due, who, according to the opinion of the two judges, should bring the worthiest object with which to share it" (292)—but he laughingly confesses that he never expected this proposal to succeed and only offered it to make it clear that he is "no friend to gaming" (296).

At the start of the race, "the poor creatures, feeble and frightened, ran against each other, and, neither of them able to support the shock, they both fell on the ground" (312). After they are revived, they start off again; the race is finally decided when one of them falls and is unable to rise again, "too much hurt to move." Lord Orville looks "very grave" but makes no protest at any time. Evelina does "involuntarily" start to the assistance of the fallen woman but otherwise makes no comment except that "the scene was truly ridiculous." Certainly the modern reader feels that another adjective, such as cruel or vicious, would be more appropriate. The race violates all decent respect for age, a universal precept of the century, as well as concern for women as needing special care and protection. It seems to demonstrate that old women are a different category: being old makes them defective as women, while being women deprives them of the respect due to age. Old women are portrayed as intrinsically ludicrous. Lord Orville and Evelina are more distressed by the gambling involved than by the treatment of the two victims, and it seems that all the company agree that to risk harm to these poor creatures is far preferable than to risk any injury to the young men themselves. The passage is all the more shocking because it is completely gratuitous; it in no way furthers the development of the novel or significantly differentiates Orville and Evelina from the other characters.

Because *Evelina* is told in letters, the reader is fully aware of the sharp, satiric perceptions of Evelina. However, Evelina is shocked to think that she might have given any impression of being "bold," and Mrs. Selwyn is criticized for being outspoken. The novel has, in fact, a tension between the values it proposes as proper for young women and the tone of Evelina's letters. The events of the plot, however, stress the need for prudence and attention to society's conventions. The final letter is from Evelina on the day of her marriage. "All is over, my dearest Sir, and the fate of your Evelina is decided!" she writes her guardian. "This morning, with fearful joy, and trembling gratitude, she united herself for ever with the object of her dearest, her eternal affection!" (406). Evelina will now begin to carry out her previously expressed plan: "Oh Lord Orville!—it shall be the sole study of my happy life, to express, better than by words, the sense I have of your exalted benevolence, and greatness of mind!" (387).

The same pattern of the intelligent and virtuous heroine being fallible in judgment compared to the wiser hero is true of *Camilla*. Again, the errors that Camilla makes are relatively minor, and the conflicting advice given to Edgar and herself by male mentors is largely responsible for many of her difficulties. However, women in the novel are largely ineffectual and sometimes harmful. Her mother is sent off to Lisbon and is therefore absent during most of the action. Mrs. Berlington, a young woman whom Camilla likes very much but of whom Edgar disapproves, proves a bad influence when her flouting of convention, at first innocent, leads in time to vice. Mrs. Mitten, who seems a kindly helper, gets Camilla into debt. To be sure, there are foolish and wicked men in the novel as well—Sir Hugh is as impulsive and silly as any woman, while Lionel is destructive, Bellamy venal, and so on—but the characters presented as exemplars are men, the absent Mrs. Tyrold excepted. A part of her exemplary nature, in fact, is wifely submissiveness. "She never resisted a remonstrance of her husband," and "no dissent in opinion exculpated, in her mind, the least deviation from his will" (14). Even the Reverend John Sprint would approve of Camilla's mother.

Toward the end of the novel, Camilla, reflecting on her difficulties, exclaims, "Ah, Edgar! had I trusted you as I ought . . . had my confidence been as firm in your kindness as in your honour, what misery had I been saved! . . . I could then have erred no more, for I should have thought but of your approvance!" (848). Kindness has not, in fact, been Edgar's chief characteristic; he has almost uniformly put an ungenerous interpretation on Camilla's actions. He is finally convinced of her sincerity only when he accidentally receives a letter she has written when she thinks she is dying. This deathbed confession has "wholly, and even miraculously" removed every doubt, by enabling him to learn "the true feelings of her heart, as depicted at the awful crisis of expected dissolution" (898). In the light of this extraordinary evidence, Edgar voices "the most generous apologies" and "the most liberal self-blame" and asks Mr. Tyrold's "consent for a union." In their marriage "Edgar, by generous confidence, became the repository of her every thought," so that "her friends read her exquisite lot in a gaiety no longer to be feared" (913). Edgar, like Orville, will become a fond mentor.

The contradictions evident in Burney's work are symptomatic of the treatment of women by this group of women novelists.[9] One might even suggest that the tensions in *Evelina* between the energetic intelligence of Evelina, as conveyed by the style of the letters, and the precepts which the novel seems to advocate by explicit statement are emblematic of these writers. On the one hand, since being a professional writer was in itself a somewhat daring role for a woman, it might be expected that women novelists would depict notably independent women and that they would generally deplore the more restrictive conventions which governed women. Since writing a novel was evidence of some intelligence, education, and ability, it might be expected that the usual picture of women as childlike creatures needing the guidance of men would be sharply challenged in the works of women novelists. On the other hand, we are all products of our own acculturation and, given the general attitudes toward women in the century, it is not, perhaps, surprising that women writers often support the status quo, despite the example of Richardson. The more conservative, such as Sarah Fielding and Clara Reeve, may even have felt defensive, wishing to distinguish themselves from some of their more outspoken sisters, especially when much of the early writing by women was considered morally faulty. Certainly the almost universal denigration of learned ladies in these novels by women suggests some uncomfortable self-consciousness at work.

An undeniable contribution of women writers is the novels themselves, which demonstrated that women could indeed write, and which undoubtedly encouraged others to enter the field, as Jane Austen's title *Pride and Prejudice,* taken from Burney, suggests. Another related contribution of this body of work is its emphasis upon women of ordinary social status and achievement as worthy of interest in themselves. (*Destination* is the one exception here.) The happiness of the heroine is the concern of the text, not merely her effect on the well-being of men. Furthermore, moral and intellectual qualities are usually valued above mere physical beauty, although most of the heroines are also beautiful. It seems probable that reading these novels would, on balance, encourage a woman's interest in intellectual improvement—even if only to enhance her general attractiveness. Many of the heroines provide models of capable, energetic women who act in order to change their lives. They may not always succeed, but at least they are not completely passive.

Realism of characterization, not unexpectedly, is inversely related to idealization. In Sarah Fielding, for example, the resentment Cynthia displays against her authoritarian father, jealous sisters, and domineering patron is convincing. Mrs. Bilson, who never shows any anger toward her faithless husband, is not believable. Henry Fielding's Amelia also strains credibility. Exemplary real women, such as Sarah Chapone, agreed that the duties imposed on a wife were sanctioned by scripture, and therefore inviolate, but they also recognized the difficulties faced by a woman when her husband no longer deserved the obedience and respect pledged in the marriage vows. To depict women adhering resolutely to the standards of behavior expected of them is not unrealistic; many actual women did this, as we have seen above. But they usually did so at considerable cost to themselves, as the records of real women also show.

In most cases, novels by women represented a woman's view. The delineation of unhappy marriages in Lennox's *Euphemia* and Reeve's *School for Widows,* for example, certainly has the ring of the wife's experience, echoing the account of actual women such as Sarah Cowper. The dilemmas of Burney's heroines, caught up in a network of puzzling conventions they dare not flout, reflect the uncertainties of many young women. Even in Sarah Fielding's work, the difficulties of Camilla and Cynthia show the workings of society from the vantage of a woman trying to make a living for herself. The struggles of most of the heroines demonstrate the great handicap that simply being a woman represented in the eighteenth century.

While marriage is presented as the most desirable state in fiction by women (as it is also in novels by Richardson and Henry Fielding) and the patriarchal model of husbandly authority is seldom questioned, the best marriage is presented as one of loving cooperation. Husbands who have to insist on absolute authority are usually inadequate. The implicit text is that a husband who commands a greater degree of submission than a wife is willing to grant probably doesn't deserve it, since a good woman will happily comply when she recognizes the justice of a request. However, Evelina's desire for Lord Orville's guidance and Camilla's admiration of Edgar's superior judgment are usually seen as both the norm and the ideal. In marriage a good woman hopes to find a husband who will be a loving, wise guide and mentor. To honor and obey such a husband will be easy because his superior qualities will make wifely submission natural. Pairing one's heroine with a more intelligent and capable man is a way of avoiding a challenge to the conduct-book view of marriage. Burney's *Cecilia* does imply a rejection of the usual pattern of marriage, but only Richardson consistently questions the century's views on the proper relationship of husband and wife. Women novelists, however, with the exception of Clara Reeve, did insist that the ideal husband was one who will respect and admire his wife's intelligence. Mutual cooperation will then be the result. They therefore depicted more egalitarian marriages than those of Henry Fielding, whose heroines consider it heresy to question a husband's judgment.

Some of society's mores are questioned in these novels by women, most notably the double standard in sexual fidelity. While some heroines do marry reformed rakes, the men's reformation is stressed and they remain faithful after marriage. When erring husbands such as Mr. Bilson are portrayed, it is clear that their conduct produces unhappiness even though the patient wife makes no protest. Again, women novelists were less insistent than Richardson about the harm created by the double standard but considerably less forgiving than Henry Fielding, especially when sexual lapses occurred after marriage. In *Euphemia* and *The School for Widows* Lennox and Reeve gave realistic accounts of just what daily misery an unsuitable marriage could produce. Courtship customs were also attacked by women novelists, especially Scott and Burney, and all of these novelists stressed the need for careful and rational consideration of future marriage partners.

Scott is the most radically feminist of these women writers, insisting that women's incapacities are not genetic but cultural. *Leonora* demonstrates that, given the necessary education, a woman could function with great success in roles society barred to women. *Millenium Hall* shows widows and spinsters leading happy and useful lives without the aid of men. In *Cecilia* Burney also wrote a markedly feminist novel wherein the women are not only morally superior to the men but also more capable, more practical, and more decisive.

As a group, however, these women novelists cannot be called revolutionary or radical. Scott comes closest to this description, but ameliorative modification rather than wholesale reform is the more usual program suggested by this body of work. While fiction by women tended, in many ways, to reinforce prevailing opinion and custom, it did give women a voice of their own and create novels centered on their concerns. Novelists did treat subjects that were important to the lives of real eighteenth-century women. The novelists themselves also gave women models of intellectual endeavor and professional achievement, just as their heroines almost universally provided models of intelligent and capable women to emulate.

Richardson, however, remains the strongest supporter of women's equality, depicting women as intelligent, capable, and often superior to men. A truly good and wise man recognizes their parity in Richardson's fiction, while those who strive to enforce patriarchal attitudes—the Harlowes, Lovelace, the unreformed Mr. B.—are vicious. In contrast, Henry Fielding's novels cheerfully support the century's mores, admiring women who are quietly submissive and tolerating sexual waywardness in men, except for the sin of adultery, which deprives another man of his property. It has often been remarked that Henry Fielding won the battle for style over Richardson, with his omniscient narrator becoming the norm for the nineteenth-century novel. Perhaps we can also say he won the battle as to whether the novel would become a voice for rebellion or conformity.

In general, Dr. Samuel Johnson's judgment, quoted in the introduction, was correct. Novels did usually depict women who would be recognizably realistic to their actual women readers.

Sometimes their adventures might seem unusual, but their characters and personalities, their fears and aspirations, would have seemed to "exhibit life in its true state." Real women's letters and diaries often detail the same situations that are described in novels. (The similarity is striking, for example, between the letter of Mary Cowper to her husband, quoted in chapter 3, and Pamela's words to her husband in *Pamela II* when she believes him to be unfaithful, although no actual influence of one on the other is possible.) The novels also almost uniformly did "promote the cause of religion and virtue," but usually within the safe framework of received opinion. Richardson's revolutionary stance, which began the realistic novel, was not imitated by most subsequent women novelists in the century and was flatly contradicted by Henry Fielding's deep conservatism. However, in important ways the novel improved the self-image of eighteenth-century women by showing them capable of being heroines of their own stories, by admiring intelligence in women, by depicting more humane models of marriage, by condemning sexual transgressions in marriage, and by treating women as interesting and important beings in their own right. The twentieth-century feminist reader may regret that Richardson's call for radical reassessment of women's position in eighteenth-century society did not become the hallmark of the new genre; nevertheless, the novel did, on balance, become a voice for the enhancement of women's status.

NOTES

Chapter 1

1. On conduct books see Nancy Armstrong, "The Rise of the Domestic Woman," 96–141, in Nancy Armstrong and Leonard Tennenhouse, eds., *The Ideology of Conduct: Essays on Literature and the History of Sexuality* (New York: Methuen, 1987).
2. On children's literature in the century see Bette P. Goldstone, *Lessons to be Learned: A Study of Eighteenth Century Didactic Children's Literature* (New York: Lang, 1984); Mary Jackson, *Engines of Instruction, Mischief and Magic: Children's Literature in England* (Lincoln: University of Nebraska Press, 1989); Sylvia Patterson, "Eighteenth-Century Children's Literature in England: A Mirror of Its Culture," *Journal of Popular Culture* 13 (1979): 38–43; Samuel Pickering, Jr., *John Locke and Children's Books in Eighteenth Century England* (Knoxville: University of Tennessee Press, 1980).
3. See Janelle Greenberg, "The Legal Status of the English Woman in Early Eighteenth-Century Common Law and Equity," *SECC* (1975): 171–81.

Chapter 2

1. On attitudes toward learned women see Jocelyn Harris, "Sappho, Souls, and the Salic Law of Wit," 232–58, in Alan Charles Kors and Paul J. Korshin, eds., *Anticipations of the Enlightenment in England, France and Ger-*

many (Philadelphia: University of Pennsylvania Press, 1987); Sylvia H. Myers, "Learning, Virtue, and the Term 'Bluestocking,'" *SECC* 15 (1986): 279–88.

2. See Ruth Perry, *The Celebrated Mary Astell: An Early English Feminist* (Chicago: University of Chicago Press, 1986).

3. See Erica Harth, "The Virtue of Love: Lord Hardwicke's Marriage Act," *Cultural Critique* (Spring 1988): 123–54; and Christopher Lasch, "The Suppression of Marriage in England: The Marriage Act of 1754," *Salmagundi* 26 (Spring 1974): 99–104.

Chapter 3

1. On marriage settlements see Lloyd Bonfield, *Marriage Settlements, 1601–1740: The Adoption of the Strict Settlement* (Cambridge: Cambridge University Press, 1983); H. J. Habakkuk, "Marriage Settlements in the Eighteenth Century," *Transactions of the Royal Historical Society* 4th ser. 32(1950): 25–30; Eileen Spring, "The Family, Strict Settlement, and Historians," *Canadian Journal of History* 18 (December 1983): 379–98.

Chapter 4

1. The extent to which marriages were patriarchal or companionate during the period is the topic of continuing debate. I think, based upon my research, that the ideal of companionate marriage did gain strength during the century, just as the ideal of companionate courtship did. Since legal protection lagged far behind this ideal, however, the wife who had the misfortune to be married to a patriarchal husband had little or no recourse. The extent to which the ideal was embodied in actual marriages varied widely, as this chapter will demonstrate. See Ian Duffy, ed., *Women and Society in the Eighteenth Century* (Bethlehem, Pa.: Lawrence Henry Gibson Inst., 1983); John R. Gillis, *For Better, for Worse: British Marriages, 1600 to the Present* (New York: Oxford University Press, 1985); J. E. Goldthorpe, *Family Life in Western Societies; A Historical Sociology of Family Relationships in Britain and North America* (Cambridge: Cambridge University Press, 1987); Jean H. Hagstrum, *Sex and Sensibility: Ideal and Erotic Love from Milton to Mozart* (Chicago: University of Chicago Press, 1982); Susan Moller, "Patriarchy and Married Women's Property in England: Questions on Some Current Views," *ECS* 17 (1983): 121–38 (attack on Stone); Roy Porter, *English Society in the Eighteenth Century* (London: Allen Lane, 1981); Lawrence Stone, *The Family, Sex and Marriage in England, 1500–1800* (New York: Harper & Row, 1977); Randolph Trumbach, *The Rise of the Egalitarian Family: Aristocratic Kinship and Domestic Relations in Eighteenth-Century England* (New York: Academic Press, 1978).

Chapter 5

1. For a discussion of this see Ian Watt, *The Rise of the Novel* (Berkeley: University of California Press, 1965), 145.

2. See Ruth McClure, *Coram's Children: The London Foundling in the Eighteenth Century* (New Haven: Yale University Press, 1981).

Chapter 6

1. For other discussions of the treatment of women in novels of the period, see: "Women and Early Fiction," *Studies in the Novel,* ed. Jerry C. Beasley 19, no. 3 (Fall 1987): 139–44; Alice Browne, *The Eighteenth Century Feminist Mind* (Detroit: Wayne State University Press, 1987); Frances M. Clements, "The Rights of Women in the Eighteenth-Century Novel," *Enlightenment Essays* 4, iii–iv (1973): 63–70; Wallace Austin Flanders, *Structures of Experience: History, Society and Personal Life in the Eighteenth-Century British Novel* (Columbia: University of South Carolina Press, 1984).
2. See Elizabeth Bergen Brophy, *Samuel Richardson: The Triumph of Craft* (Knoxville: University of Tennessee Press, 1974), 20–24.
3. See Janet M. Todd, *Women's Friendship in Literature: The Eighteenth-Century Novel in England and France* (New York: Columbia University Press, 1980).
4. See Katharine M. Rogers, "Sensitive Feminism vs. Conventional Sympathy: Richardson and Fielding on Women," *Novel* 9 (1976): 256–70.
5. Most of the standard treatments of Richardson emphasize this aspect of his novels. See especially Elizabeth Bergen Brophy, *Samuel Richardson* (Boston: Twayne, 1987); Margaret Anne Doody, *A Natural Passion: A Study of the Novels of Samuel Richardson* (Oxford: Clarendon Press, 1974); Rita Goldberg, *Sex and Enlightenment: Women in Richardson and Diderot* (Cambridge: Cambridge University Press, 1984); Mark Kinkead-Weekes, *Samuel Richardson: Dramatic Novelist* (Ithaca: Cornell University Press, 1973); Valerie Grosvenor Myer, ed., *Samuel Richardson: Passion and Prudence* (London: Vision, 1986); and Patricia McKee, "Corresponding Freedoms: Language and the Self in *Pamela*," *ELH* 52, no. 3 (Fall 1985): 621–48.
6. For another view, see Anthony Hassall, "Women in Richardson and Fielding," *Novel* 14, no. 2 (Winter 1981): 168–74 (a reply to Katharine Rogers, cited above). See also April London, "Controlling the Text: Women in *Tom Jones*," *Studies in the Novel* 19, no. 3 (Fall 1987): 323–33; Mary Anne Schofield, "Exploring the Woman Question: A Reading of Fielding's *Amelia*," *ArielE* 16, no. 1 (January 1985) 45–57; Angela Smallwood, *Fielding and the Woman Question: The Novels of Henry Fielding and the Feminist Debate, 1700–1750* (New York: St. Martin's Press, 1989).
7. See C. Woodward, "'Feminine Virtue, Ladylike Disguise, Women of Community': Sarah Fielding and the Female I Am at Mid-Century," *Transactions of the Samuel Johnson Society of the Northwest* 15 (1984): 57–71.
8. For other treatments of Burney, see: Rose Marie Cutting, "Defiant Women: The Growth of Feminism in Fanny Burney's Novels," *SEL* 17 (Summer 1977): 519–30; Marjorie W. Dobbin, "The Novel, Women's Awareness, and Fanny Burney," *ELN* 22, no. 3 (March 1985): 42–52; Margaret A. Doody, *Frances Burney: The Life in the Works* (New Brunswick: Rutgers University Press, 1988); Susan Staves, "*Evelina;* or, *Female Difficulties,*" *MP* 73 (1976): 368–81; Kristina Straub, *Divided Fictions: Fanny Burney and Feminine Strategy* (Lexington: University Press of Kentucky, 1987).
9. For discussions of women novelists in the century and their treatment of

women see: Nancy Armstrong and Leonard Tennenhouse, "The Rise of Feminine Authority in the Novel," *Novel* 15, no. 2 (Winter 1982): 127–45; Ann Messenger, *His and Hers: Essays in Restoration and Eighteenth-Century Literature* (Lexington: University Press of Kentucky, 1986); Rosalind Miles, *The Female Form: Women Writers and the Conquest of the Novel* (London: Routledge & Kegan Paul, 1987); Felicity Nussbaum, *The Autobiographical Subject: Gender and Ideology in Eighteenth-Century England* (Baltimore: Johns Hopkins University Press, 1989); Ruth Perry, *Women, Letters and the Novel* (New York: AMS Press, 1980); Mary Anne Schofield and Cecilia Macheski, eds., *Fettr'd or Free? British Women Novelists, 1670–1815* (Athens: Ohio University Press, 1986); Patricia Spacks, *Imagining a Self: Autobiography and the Novel in Eighteenth-Century England* (Cambridge: Harvard University Press, 1976); Dale Spender, *Mothers of the Novel; 100 Good Women Writers Before Jane Austen* (New York: Pandora, 1986); Jane Spencer, *The Rise of the Woman Novelist* (Oxford: Basil Blackwell, 1986).

BIBLIOGRAPHY

Primary Sources

MANUSCRIPTS

Alden, Mary. Letters, 1740–1745. Middlesex P.R.O., 249/2617-25.

Allgood, Jane. Letters, 1715. Northumberland P.R.O., ZAL 40/12.

Allsopp, Mary. Letters, 1762. Derbyshire P.R.O., 231 M/F 211.

Amherst, Elizabeth. Letters, 1769. Kent P.R.O., U 1350, C 82.

Amynta. Letter book, 1746. Beinecke, Osborn Shelves, C 153.

Anon. Letters, c. 1700. Dorset P.R.O., NU 21.

Arundell, Mary. Letters, 1735–1737. Middlesex P.R.O., 249/2553-55.

Aspin, Lucy. Letters, 1740–1743. Middlesex P.R.O., 249/2366-71.

Baker, Elizabeth. Letters, 1726–1736. Northumberland P.R.O., ZAL 39/3.

Ball, Elizabeth. Letters, 1748. Warwickshire P.R.O., CR 136 B/1454.

Ball, Jane. Letters, 1779. Warwickshire P.R.O., CR 136 B/1457.

Bampylde, Gertrude. Letters, 1750–1754. Somerset P.R.O., DD/TB 15/16.

Banbury, Countess of (Wife of 7th Earl). Letters, 1770–1786. Hampshire P.R.O., 1 M 44/71/19, 1 M 44/70.

Barnes, "Nanny." Letters, 1768–1786. Derbyshire P.R.O., 231 M/F 217-274.

Barnston, Letitia. Letters, 1736–1745. Shropshire P.R.O., Ch 1536/5.

Barton, Mary. Journal, 1790. Northamptonshire P.R.O., YO 559.

Bell, Deborah. Journal, 1776. Friends' Library, Temp MSS 15/3.

Bishop, Betty. Diaries, 1779, 1785–1801. Friends' Library.

273

Blanchard, Margaret. Letters, 1717, 1749–1758. Durham P.R.O., D/Ch/C 23–82.

Boone, Susanna. Memoires, 1773–1789. Friends' Library.

Borda, Madam. Letters, 1742. Northumberland P.R.O., ZBL 267/4.

Boscawen, Frances. Diary, 1763. Bodleian, MS. Eng. misc. f. 71.

Bradshaigh, Dorothy. Letters, 1748–1761. Victoria and Albert, Forster Collection, XI.

Bramston, Mrs. Letters, 1788–1800. Hampshire P.R.O., 20 M 64.

Bringhurst, Hannah. Spiritual Diary, 1781–1782. Friends' Library.

Broadnax, Jane. Letters, 1666. Kent P.R.O., U 1015 C 4.

Brooke, Mary. Letters, 1788–1790. Hereford P.R.O., RC/IV/E/402–448.

Buller, Mary Carew. Letters, 1750–1754. Somerset P.R.O., DD/TB 15/16.

Butterfield, Rebekah. Diary, 1725. Friends' Library, MS Vol S 73.

Carleton, Deborah. Letters, 1774, 1778. Beinecke, Osborn Files.

Carter, Elizabeth. Letter, 1753. New York Public Library, Berg Collection.

Cartwright, Dorothy. Letters, 1684. Kent P.R.O., U 1015 C 13.

Cater, Margaret. Letters, 1773–1779. Bedfordshire P.R.O., M 10/4/19–59.

Catherall, Emma. Letters, 1731–1738. Surrey P.R.O., Loosley MSS, uncatalogued.

Cawthorne, Frances. Letters, 1770–1800. Northumberland P.R.O., 2 DE. 39/10/1–32.

Chapone, Hester Mulso. Letter, March 22 (no year). New York Public Library, Berg Collection.

Chapone, Sarah. Letters, 1749–1752. Bodleian, Ballard 43.

———. Letters, 1750–1755. Victoria and Albert, Forster Collection, XII, ii, XIII, i.

Charlton, Teresa. Letters, 1756–1782. Northumberland P.R.O., ZSW 521/1–9.

Chaytor, Ann. Letters, 1697–1701. Durham P.R.O., D/Ch/C 658–758.

Chaytor, Anne. Letters, 1673–1684. Durham P.R.O., D/Ch/C 610–657.

Chaytor, Mrs. William. Letter, 1695. Durham P.R.O., D/Ch/20.

Clark, Susanna. Letter, 1752. Somerset P.R.O., DD/TB 15/16.

Clarke, Mary. Letters, 1751–1752. Middlesex P.R.O., 1214/26.

———. Letters, n.d. Somerset P.R.O., DD/SF.

Clayfield, Arabella. Letters, 1785–1800. Berkshire P.R.O., D/ESV (B) F 11.

Coke, Mrs. Letter 34, n.d. Scrapbook: Fanny d'Arblay and friends. New York Public Library, Berg Collection.

Cole, Ann. Letters, 1727–1729. Nottinghamshire P.R.O., DDSR 212/1–2.

Congreve, Ann. Letters, 1740–1755. Staffordshire P.R.O., SNS/47/28/1, SNS/47/16/3, SNS/47/19/1, SMS/47/15/2, SMS/47/18/1.

Cornwallis, Cassandra. Letters, 1701–1719. Surrey P.R.O., Loosley MSS, uncatalogued.

Cowper, Mary. Letters, 1717–1718. Hertfordshire P.R.O., D/EP F 59.

———. Letters, 1739–1769. Norwich P.R.O., Walsingham XIV/9–16.

Cowper, Sarah. Diary, 1700–1716. Hertfordshire P.R.O., D/EP f 29–35.

Cremer, Anne. Diaries, 1795, 1796, 1798. Norwich P.R.O., WKC 6/302–304.

Darby, Abiah. Journal, 1744–1769. Friends' Library.

Dashwood, Martha. Letters, 1776. Hampshire P.R.O., 1 M 44/31.
Day, Susannah. Memoire, Diary. Friends' Library, Temp. MSS 1/9; 36/3.
Deloval, Elizabeth. Letters, 1770–1780. Northumberland P.R.O., 2 DE/39/6/1–9.
Deloval, Susanna. Letters, 1753–1783. Northumberland P.R.O., 2 DE. 39/1/1–25.
Diary of a Young Girl. Diary, 1769–1773. Essex P.R.O., D/DRU F 10.
Dighton, Arabella. Memoire, 1743. Beinecke, Osborn Shelves, C 55, 68. 3. 49.
Elliot, Philip. Letters, 1740s. Middlesex P.R.O., 1017/975–987.
Elstob, Elizabeth. Letters, 1735–1752. Bodleian, Ballard 43.
———. Letters, 1739–40. Beinecke, Osborn Shelves.
Englefield, Ann. Letters, 1754. Dorset P.R.O., D10/C38.
Everard, Isabella Eccleston. Letters, 1726–1734. Bedfordshire P.R.O., HW 86.
Farrer, Elizabeth. Letters, 1730s, 1755. Berkshire P.R.O., D/ELI C 1/233, D/ELI C 1/246.
Farrin, Jane. Letters, 1744–1791. Essex P.R.O., D/DZ g 34.
Farrin, Mary. Letters, 1757. Essex P.R.O., D/DZ g 33.
Fenton, Anastasia. Letters, 1750–1788. Staffordshire P.R.O., D (W) 1788 Box F1.
Filliter, Mary. Diary, 1799. Dorset P.R.O., D 131/4 O a.
Filmer, Amy. Letters, 1750–1768. Kent P.R.O., U 120 C 58.
Filmer, Dorothy. Letters, 1759–1768. Kent P.R.O., U 120 C 55, U 120 C 56, U 120 C 83.
Foley, Anne. Letters, 1684–1716. Hereford P.R.O., F/iv/ta/71–180.
Foley, Pen. Letters, 1724. Hereford P.R.O., F/W/Ta/153.
Foljambe, M. A. Letters, 1778. Nottinghamshire P.R.O., Foljambe MXX XI.
Fothergill, Betty. Diary, 1769–1770. Friends' Library, MS Vol S 51, Box 4 (18).
Foundling Hospital Records. Letters of petition, 1762–1772; Correspondence, 1744, 1749, 1750–1758. London County Hall P.R.O.
Fox, Mary. Letters, 1732. Staffordshire P.R.O., SMS / 47/6/12.
Fox, Sarah. Diary, 1761. Friends' Library, MS Box D.
Frampton, Elizabeth. Letters, 1755–1756. Surrey P.R.O., Loosley MSS 121/4/1–10.
Glasse, Hannah. Letters, 1744–1746. Northumberland P.R.O., Box 40/30.
Gurney, Louisa. Journals, 1797–1800. Norwich P.R.O., Q 173 B.
Hamilton, Frances. Diaries, 1779–1800. Somerset P.R.O., DD/FS Boxes 5–7.
Hanmer, Susan. Letters, 1758. Bedfordshire P.R.O., M 10/2/28.
Hayes, Phillipa. Letters, 1749–1755. Warwickshire P.R.O., L 6/1367-1376.
Helyar, Joanna. Letters, 1742–1759. Somerset P.R.O., DD/WH h 55.
Heneage, Catherine. Letters, 1774. Dorset P.R.O., D/10/C 78.
Honeywood, Dorothy. Letters, 1760s. Kent P.R.O., U 120 C 63.
Hope, Ellen. Letters, 1740–1744. Middlesex P.R.O., 249/2684-96.
Horner, Susanna. Letters, 1736. Dorset P.R.O., D 124/Box 240.
Howard, Teresa. Letters, 1759–1760. Dorset P.R.O., D10/C46.
Humphrey, Elizabeth. Letters, 1785–1805. Kent P.R.O., U 1050 C 30.
Hyde, Jane (Lady). Letters, 1707. Staffordshire P.R.O., D 868/6/26 a-d.
Isham, Elizabeth. Letters, 1706–1713. Northamptonshire P.R.O., Isham Collection.

Isham, Susannah. Letters, 1721. Northamptonshire P.R.O., Isham Collection.

Isham, Vere. Letters, 1713–1730. Northamptonshire P.R.O., Isham Collection.

Jeffreys, Frances. Letters, 1740s. Kent P.R.O., U 840, C11/1, 2–3.

Jeffreys, Maria. Letters, 1740s. Kent P.R.O., U 840, C12/1–2.

Jennings, Deborah. Letters, 1739–1754. Salop P.R.O., Ch 1536/5.

Jolliffe, Mrs. Letters, 1750. Somerset P.R.O., DD/HY Box 21.

Jurin, Mary. Letters, 1762–1763. Northumberland P.R.O., ZBL. 201.

King, Mary. Letters, 1750. Hereford P.R.O., E 31–53.

Knapton, Mary. Letters, 1750. Dorset P.R.O., D 131/17/284, D 131/22.

Knatchbull, Edward. Letters, 1780. Kent P.R.O., U 95 1 C 138.

Knollis, Mary. Letters, 1755–1780. Hampshire P.R.O., 1 M 44/30, 1 M 44/7.

Kynaston, Anne. Letter, 1750. Shropshire P.R.O., Ch 1536/5.

A Lady. Diary, 1691–1702. British Library, Add MS. 5858.

Leadbeater, Mary Shackleton. Letters, 1778–1791. Beinecke, Osborn Files.

Leake, Mary Martin. Diary, 1792–1801. Hertfordshire P.R.O., 84630.

Leigh, Mary. Letters, 1745–1748. Surrey P.R.O., Loosley MSS, uncatalogued.

Leighton, Anna Maria. Letters, 1740–1750. Salop P.R.O., Ch 1536/5.

Lennard, Anne. Letters, 1681–1689. Essex P.R.O., D/DLC 47.

Lennard, Jane. Letters, 1689–1691. Essex P.R.O., D/DLC 43/2.

Letters, c. 1700. Dorset P.R.O., NU 21.

Lettsom, Joan. Letters, 1742. Friends' Library, Temp MSS 4/14.

Levermore, Elizabeth. Diary, 1769–1801. Essex P.R.O., D/DT a F5.

Liffen, Ann. Letters, c. 1760. Norwich P.R.O., MC 7/400-401.

Maitland, Penelope. Diary, 1787–1800. Bodleian, MS. Eng. misc. e. 642–3.

Mapletoft, Edmund. Letters, 1770s. Kent P.R.O., U 1050 C 8.

Markland, E. Letters, 1728–1730. Essex P.R.O., D/DT w F 4/4/1.

Massingberd, Ann. Letters, 1668–1671. Bedfordshire P.R.O., B 652–57.

Maude, Elizabeth. Letters, 1740–1750. Surrey P.R.O., Loosley MSS, uncatalogued.

Molesworth, Mrs. Letters, 1760s. Northumberland P.R.O., ZBL. 242.

Molyneux, Jane. Letters, 1731–1759. Surrey P.R.O., Loosley MSS, 778/35/26-28, 1687/101–256.

Montagu, Elizabeth. Letters, 1730s. Hampshire P.R.O., 21 M 69/4/50.

Moore, Jenetta. Letters, 1780–1792. Hampshire P.R.O., 1 M 44/144–47.

Morris, Mary. Verse letters, 1762. Friends' Library, Temp MSS 1/35, Temp MSS 5/30.

Needham, Mary. Letters, 1740–1744. Middlesex P.R.O., 249/2662–67.

Needham, Sarah. Letters, 1739–1745. Middlesex P.R.O., 249/2584–2600.

Noble, Pye. Letters, 1769–1780. Hereford P.R.O., RC/IV/P/1–25.

Norman, Eleanora. Letters, 1760–1764. Kent P.R.O., U 310, C2.

Oakeley, Louisa. Letters, 1748. Salop P.R.O., Ch 1536/5.

Okeover, Mary. Letters, 1748–1763. Derbyshire P.R.O., 231 M/F 172–216.

Papillon, Anne. Letters, 1746–1748. Kent P.R.O., U 1015 C60.

Papillon, Elizabeth. Letters, 1746–1748. Kent P.R.O., U 1015 C60.

Papillon, Jane. Letters, 1667–1697. Kent P.R.O., U 1015 C 11.

Papillon, Mary, Jr. Letters, 1746–1748, 1770–1777. Kent P.R.O., U 1015 C 60–61.

Papillon, Mary, Sr. Letters, 1746–1747, 1760–1761. Kent P.R.O., U 1015 C 59.

Papillon, Phillip. Letters, 1684. Kent P.R.O., U 1015 C 13.

Papillon, Sarah. Letters, 1746–1748. Kent P.R.O., U 1015 C 60.

Papillon, Susannah. Letters, 1746–1748, 1758–1793. Kent P.R.O., U 1015 C 60, C 70.

Papillon, Thomas. Letters, 1666, 1672–1692. Kent P.R.O., U 1015 C10, C29.

Parker, Mary. Letters, 1760's. Kent P.R.O., U 120 C66.

Parker, Therese. Letters, 1769–1775. British Library, Add. MS 48, 218.

Pateshall, Ann. Letters, 1773–1800. Hereford P.R.O., A95/V/AB.

Pateshall, Jane. Journal, 1762. Hereford P.R.O., A95/V/35.

Peacock, Ann ("Nanny"). Letters, 1708–1713. Durham P.R.O., D/Ch/C 1016–1024.

Pern, Catherine. Letters, 1701–1775. Berkshire P.R.O., D/ESv (B) F 31.

Perrin, Sarah. Journal, 1740–1792. Derbyshire P.R.O., Accession 239, Fitzherbert Papers.

Petre, Helen. Letters, 1760. Dorset P.R.O., D/10 C28.

Phelips, Elizabeth. Letters, c. 1740. Somerset P.R.O., DD/PH 130–35, 182, 224, 229.

Plymley, Katherine. Diaries, 1791–1800. Salop P.R.O.

Polhill, Elizabeth. Letters, 1742–1743. Kent P.R.O., U 1007 C 19.

Potter, Eleanor. Letters, 1757. Essex P.R.O., D/DZg 33.

Powys, Caroline. Journals, 1767–1788. British Library, Add MS 42, 160–70.

Pratt, Charles. Letters, 1747–1765. Kent P.R.O., U 840 C1, C2.

Pratt, Elizabeth. Letters, 1747–1749, 1769–1779. Kent P.R.O., U 840, C 9/1–33, C 10.

Pratt, Mrs. John. Diary, 1767. Kent P.R.O., U 840 F 159.

Pytts, Elizabeth. Letters, 1732. Hereford P.R.O., E 69/122.

Rebow, Mary Martin. Letters, 1767–1778. Colchester Library, Washington State University.

Richards, Elizabeth Kiddle. Journal, 1760–1800. Norwich P.R.O., MS 178, T 136 B.

Richardson, Samuel. Letters, 1740–1761. Victoria and Albert, Forster Collection XI–XVI.

Robinson, Anne. Letters, 1771–1786. British Library, Add MS 48, 218.

Robinson, Emma. Letters, 1733–1743. Surrey P.R.O., Loosley MSS, uncatalogued.

Rogers, Elizabeth. Letters, 1742–1745. Middlesex P.R.O., 249/2638–55.

Rogers, Jane. Letters, 1721. Middlesex P.R.O., 249/2354–56.

Routh, Martha. Journals, 1770, 1794, 1797. Friends' Library MS.

Russel, Christian. Letters, 1750–1775. Bedfordshire P.R.O., M 10/2/94–169, M 10/4/67–124.

Savage, Sarah. Journal, 1743–1748; Letters, 1687–1734. Dr. William's Library, Henry MSS.

———. Diary, 1714–1723. Bodleian, MS. Eng. misc. e. 331.

Savile, Barbara. Letters, 1727–1729. Nottinghamshire P.R.O., DDSR 212/1–2.

Savile, Gertrude. Journal, 1721–1722, 1727–1731; Letters, 1721–1736. Nottinghamshire P.R.O., DDSR 212/10–11; DDSR 221–89.

Seward, Anna. Letters, 1782–1792. Beinecke, Osborn Shelves C 202.

Shakleton, Elizabeth. Memoire, 1780. Beinecke, Osborn Files.

Simeon, Mary. Letters, 1759–1765. Dorset P.R.O., D 10/ C 32, C 49.

Smith, Mary. Letters, 1764. Essex P.R.O., D/DM F 27/8.

Sneyd, Frances. Diaries, 1767, 1768, 1771. Warwickshire P.R.O., CR 136/A 554–56.

Sneyd, Mary. Letters, 1744–1758. Warwickshire P.R.O., L 6/1476–98.

Stamforth, Rebecca. Letters, 1734–1739. Northumberland P.R.O., ZAL. 39/6.

Stevens, Susanna. Diary, 1795–1796. Berkshire P.R.O., D/EP 7/139.

Sturge, Mary. Letters, 1780s. Oxfordshire P.R.O., Marshall XVII/i/1.

Talbot, Catherine. Journal, 1751–1753. British Library, Add MS 46, 688–690.

———. Diary, 1745. Bedfordshire P.R.O., L 31/106.

Talbot, S. Letters, 1746. Bodleian, Ballard 43.

Taylor, Marthae. Letters, 1736. Beinecke, Osborn Shelves, C 263.

Thomas, Elizabeth Amherst. Letters, 1762–1777. Kent P.R.O., C5, C 83.

Tinney, Mary. Letters, 1773–1800. Berkshire P.R.O., D/ESv (B) F 34, 35.

Tipping, Mary. Letters, 1761–1767. Bedfordshire P.R.O., M 10/4/ 135–165.

Tomlinson, Elizabeth. Letters, 1794. Essex P.R.O., D/DSr.

Trenchard, Mary. Letters, 1724–1726. Dorset P.R.O., D60/F65.

Tuke, Elizabeth. Letters, 1795. Hertfordshire P.R.O., E/ES e C 17.

Tuke, Esther Maud. Letters, 1777–1790. Hertfordshire P.R.O., D/ES e C 11.

Tuke, Sarah. Letters, 1756–1790. Hertfordshire P.R.O., D/ES e C 13.

Turner, Anna Maria. Journal, 1716–1730. Kent P.R.O., U 1015 F 30.

Turner, Elizabeth. Journal, 1658–1678. Kent P.R.O., U 1015 F 27.

Twisden, Mary Jarvis. Diaries, 1759–1767. Kent P.R.O., U 49 F 4/1–2.

Vane, Frances (Viscountess). Letters, 1750. Somerset P.R.O., DD/HY Box 21.

Vaughn, Catherine. Letters, 1761–1762. Dorset P.R.O., D10/C55.

Venner, Ursula. Letters, c. 1760. Somerset P.R.O., DD/SF/3084–86.

Vernon, Jane. Letters, 1740. Surrey P.R.O., Loosley MSS, uncatalogued.

Vernon, Lydia. Letters, 1779. Staffordshire P.R.O., SMS/47/48/4.

Vincent, Mary. Letters, 1783–1784. Northumberland P.R.O., ZBL. 238.

Wade-Gery, Hester. Diary, 1791–1797. Bedfordshire P.R.O., CRT 190/141.

Ward, Lydia. Letters, 1755. Berkshire P.R.O., D/ELi C1/246.

Warde, Anne. Letters, 1778–1780. Nottinghamshire P.R.O., Foljambe MSSX1.

Weld, Elizabeth. Letters, 1749–1765. Dorset P.R.O., D 10/C 19, C 24, C 41.

Weld, Mary. Letters, 1760–1774. Dorset P.R.O., D10/C 69, 73.

Weld, Mrs. Letters, 1751. Dorset P.R.O., D10/C37.

Wescomb, Sophia Scudamore. Letters, 1745–1758. Victoria and Albert, Forster Collection, XIV, ii, iii.

Weston, Mary. Diary, 1737. Friends' Library, MS Cupboard 5, Case 31.

Wheeler, Elizabeth. Letters, 1745–1754. Hertfordshire P.R.O., D/ES e C 6/1.

Wheeler, Elizabeth Brown. Diary, 1778–1791. Bedfordshire P.R.O., X 67/847.

Wigham, Mabel. Journal, 1721–1781. Friends' Library.

Williams, Frances. Diary, 1753. Hertfordshire P.R.O., M 299.

Williamson, Mary. Letters, 1772–1778. Bedfordshire P.R.O., M/10/4/ 282–305.

Wilson, Rachel. *Journal*, 1768–1769. Friends' Library, Temp MSS 70/1.

Woodgate, Anne. *Letters*, 1770s. Kent P.R.O., U 1050 C 8.

Woods, Margaret. *Journal*, 1771–1821. Friends' Library, Box O.

Woolrich, Anne. *Letter*, 1718. Durham P.R.O., D/Ch/C 410.

Young, Ann. *Journal*, 1758–1768; *Letters*, 1728–1790. Friends' Library.

Young, Frances. *Letters*, 1770s. Northamptonshire P.R.O., YO 551 (IV).

NONFICTION

Allestree, Richard. *The Gentleman's Calling.* London: Printed for T. Garthwait at the Little North-doore of St. Paul's, 1660.

Allestree, Richard. *The Ladies Calling.* Oxford: Printed at the Theatre, 1673.

Astell, Mary. *A Serious Proposal to the Ladies.* London: Printed for R. Wilkin at the King's Head in St. Paul's Church-Yard, 1694.

———. *Some Reflections Upon Marriage.* London: Printed for John Nutt near Stationers-Hall, 1700.

Ballard, George. *Memoires of Several Ladies of Great Britain.* Oxford: Printed by W. Jackson, for the Author, 1752.

Bell, Deborah. *A Short Journal of the Labours and Travels of Deborah Bell.* London: James Phillips, 1777.

Carroll, John, ed. *Selected Letters of Samuel Richardson.* Oxford: Clarendon Press, 1964.

Chapone, Hester Mulso. *Miscellanies in Prose and Verse.* London: Printed for E. and C. Dilly, in the Poultry, and J. Walter, Charing-Cross, 1775.

Essay in Defence of the Female Sex, An, In a Letter to a Lady. Written by a Lady. London: Printed for A. Roper at the Black Boy, and R. Clavel at the Peacock, both in Fleetstreet, 1697.

Eugenia [pseud.]. *The Female Advocate; or, A Plea for the Just Liberty of the Tender Sex, and Particularly of Married Women.* By a Lady of Quality. London: Printed for Andrew Bell at the Cross-keys and Bible in Cornhill, near Stockmarket, 1770.

Evelyn, Mary. *The Ladies Dressing Room Unlock'd.* London: Printed for R. Bently in Russel Street in Covent Garden, 1690.

Female Guardian, The; Designed to Correct some of the Foibles incident to Girls. By a Lady. London: Printed and Sold by John Marshall and Co. No. 42 Aldermary Church-Yard, in Bow Lane, 1784.

Female Jester, The; or, Wit for the Ladies. Compiled by a Lady. London: Printed for and Sold by J. Bew, No. 28, Paternoster-Row, and T. Lewis, Russel Street, Covent Garden, n.d.

Independent Chronicle. No. 14. London: Published by Robinson and Roberts, 25 Paternoster Row, 1769.

Ladies Complete Pocket Book for 1768, The. Printed for John Newbery in St. Paul's Church Yard.

Ladies Defence, The: or The Bride-Woman's Counsellor Answer'd, A Poem. Written by a Lady [Mary Chudleigh]. London: Printed for John Deeve, at Bernard's-Inn-Gate in Holborn, 1701.

Ladies Library, The. Written by a Lady. Published by Mr. Steele. London: Printed for Jacob Tonson, at Shakespeare's Head over against Catherine Street in the Strand, 1714.

Ladies Magazine, The, or Polite Companion for the Fair Sex. Vol. 1. London: Printed for F. Wilkie at the Bible in St. Paul's Church Yard, 1759–1760.

Ladies Magazine, The: or, the Universal Entertainer. Edited by Jasper Goodwill London: Printed for the Proprietor and sold at the corner of Elliot's Court Little Old Bailey, 1749–1752.

Lady's New-Year's Gift, The: or Advice to a Daughter. By a Father [Marquis of Halifax]. London: Printed and are to be sold by Randal Taylor near Stationer's Hall, 1688.

Letters from the Duchess de Crui and Others on Subjects Moral and Entertaining. By a Lady. 5 vols. London: Printed for Robson, New Bond Street; Walter, Charing Cross; and Robinson, Pater-Noster Row, 1776.

Lucas, Margaret. "An Account of the Convincement etc. of Margaret Lucas (1701–1769)." In *Autobiographical Narratives of the Convincement and other Religious Experience.* London: Charles Gilpin, 1848.

May Day; or, Anecdotes of Miss Lydia Lively, Intended to Improve and Amuse the Rising Generation. London: Printed and sold by John Marshall and Co. at No. 42, Aldermary Church-Yard in Bow Lane, 1787.

Oeconomy of Female Life, The. By a Lady. London: Printed for G. Smith, near Temple-Bar, 1751.

Polite Lady, The: or, A Course of Female Education in a Series of Letters from a Mother to her Daughter. London: Printed for J. Newbery at the Bible and Sun in St. Paul's Church-Yard, 1760.

Polite Reasoner, The: in Letters addressed to a Young Lady at Boarding School in Hoddeston, Hartfordshire. London: Printed for W. Bent, Pater-Noster Row, 1787.

Progress of a Female Mind, The. By a Lady. London: Printed for A. and C. Corbett, opposite St. Dunstan's Church, Fleetstreet, 1764.

Religious and Christian Advice to a Daughter. Written by a Lady. London: Printed for R. Robinson, at the Golden Lyon, in St. Paul's Church-Yard, 1714.

Sprint, John. *The Bride-Woman Counsellor, Being a Sermon Preached at a Wedding, May the 11th, 1699, at Sherbourn in Dorsetshire.* London: Printed by H. Hills in Blackfryars, near the Water-side, for the Benefit of the Poor, 1699.

Whipping-Tom: or a Rod for a Proud Lady. London: Printed for Sam. Briscoe, at the Bell-Savage on Ludgate Hill; also at the Sun against John's Coffee-House in Swithen's Alley, Cornhill, 1722.

Whole Duty of a Woman, The: Or a Guide to the Female Sex from the Age of Sixteen to Sixty. Written by a Lady. London: Printed for J. Guillion, against the Great James Tavern in Bishopsgate Street, 1701.

Woman as Good as the Man, The: or the Equallity of Both Sexes. Written originally in French and translated into English by A. L. London: Printed by T. M. for N. Brooks, at the Angel in Cornhill, 1677.

Woman: Sketches of the History, Genius, Disposition, Accomplishments, Employments, Customs and Importance of the Fair Sex. By a Friend to the Sex. London: Printed for G. Kearsley, No. 46, Fleet Street, 1790.

Young Lady's Companion, The; or Beauty's Looking-Glass. In a Letter of Advice from a Father to his Daughter, after the Decease of her Mother. London: Printed and sold by the Booksellers of London and Westminster, 1740.

Burney, Frances. *Camilla or A Picture of Youth.* 1796. Reprint. London: Oxford University Press, 1972.

————. *Cecilia, or Memoires of an Heiress.* London: Printed for T. Payne and Son at the Mews-Gate, and T. Cadell in the Strand, 1782.

————. *Evelina or The History of a Young Lady's Entrance into the World.* 1778. Reprint. London: Oxford University Press, 1968.

Fielding, Henry. *Amelia.* 1752. Reprint. Middletown, Ct.: Wesleyan University Press, 1983.

————. *An Apology for The Life of Mrs. Shamela Andrews.* London: Printed for A. Dodd, 1741.

————. *The History of Tom Jones, a Foundling.* 1749. 2 vols. Reprint. Middletown, Ct.: Wesleyan University Press, 1974.

————. *Joseph Andrews.* 1742. Reprint. Middletown, Ct.: Wesleyan University Press, 1967.

Fielding, Sarah. *The Adventures of David Simple.* 1744. Reprint. London: Oxford University Press, 1969.

————. *Familiar Letters between the Principal Characters in David Simple.* London: Printed for the Author, 1747.

————. *The Governess, or The Little Female Academy.* London: Printed for A. Millar, 1749.

————. *The History of Ophelia.* London: Printed for Harrison and Co., 1785.

————. *The History of the Countess of Dellwyn.* 2 vols. London: Printed for A. Millar, 1759.

————. *The Lives of Cleopatra and Octavia.* London: Printed for the Author, 1757.

Lennox, Charlotte. *Euphemia.* 4 vols. London: Printed for T. Cadell, in the Strand; and J. Evans, Paternoster Row, 1790.

————. *The Female Quixote.* 1752. Reprint. London: Oxford University Press, 1970.

————. *Henrietta.* 2 vols. London: Printed for A. Millar, in the Strand, 1758.

————. *The Life of Harriot Stuart.* 2 vols. London: Printed for J. Payne and J. Bouquet, 1751.

————. *Sophia.* 2 vols. London: Printed for James Fletcher, 1762.

Reeve, Clara. *Destination: or, Memoires of a Private Family.* 3 vols. London: Printed for T. N. Longman and O. Rees, 1799.

————. *The Old English Baron: A Gothic Story.* London: Printed for Charles Dilly, 1777.

————. *The School for Widows.* 3 vols. London: Printed for T. Hookam, 1791.

————. *The Two Mentors: A Modern Story.* London: Printed for Charles Dilly, 1783.

Richardson, Samuel. *Clarissa.* 1747–48. 4 vols. Reprint. London: Dent, 1962.

————. *Pamela.* 1740, 1741. 2 vols. Reprint. London: Dent, 1962.

————. *Sir Charles Grandison.* (1753–54) 3 vols. Reprint. London: Oxford University Press, 1972.

Scott, Sarah. *Agreeable Ugliness: or The Triumph of the Graces.* London: Printed for R. and J. Dodsley, 1754.

————. *A Description of Millenium Hall*. London: Printed for J. Newbery, 1764.

————. *The History of Cornelia*. Dublin: Printed for John Smith on the Blind-Quay, 1750.

————. *A Journey Through Every Stage of Life*. 2 vols. London: Printed for A. Millar in the Strand, 1754.

————. *The Man of Real Sensibility, or the History of Sir George Ellison*. London: Printed for Chapman Whitcomb, n.d. (1770?)

————. *The Test of Filial Duty*. London: Printed for the Author and sold by T. Carman, 1772.

Secondary Sources

————. "The Rise of the Domestic Woman." In *The Ideology of Conduct: Essays on Literature and the History of Sexuality,* edited by Nancy Armstrong and Leonard Tennenhouse. 96–141. New York: Methuen, 1987.

Armstrong, Nancy. "The Rise of Feminine Authority in the Novel." *Novel* 15, no. 2 (Winter 1982): 127–45.

Beasley, Jerry C., ed. "Women and Early Fiction." *Studies in the Novel* 19, no. 3 (Fall 1987): 239–44.

Bonfield, Lloyd. *Marriage Settlements, 1601–1740: The Adoption of the Strict Settlement*. Cambridge: Cambridge University Press, 1983.

Brophy, Elizabeth Bergen. *Samuel Richardson*. Boston: Twayne, 1987.

————. *Samuel Richardson: The Triumph of Craft*. Knoxville: University of Tennessee Press, 1974.

Browne, Alice. *The Eighteenth Century Feminist Mind*. Detroit: Wayne State University Press, 1987.

Clements, Frances M. "The Rights of Women in the Eighteenth-Century Novel." *EnlE* 4, nos. iii–iv (1973): 63–70.

Cutting, Rose Marie. "Defiant Women: The Growth of Feminism in Fanny Burney's Novels." *SEL* 17 (Summer 1977): 519–30.

Dobbin, Marjorie W. "The Novel, Women's Awareness, and Fanny Burney." *ELN* 22, no. 3 (March 1985): 42–52.

Doody, Margaret A. *A Natural Passion: A Study of the Novels of Samuel Richardson*. Oxford: Clarendon, 1974.

————. *Frances Burney: The Life in the Works*. New Brunswick, N.J.: Rutgers University Press, 1988.

Duffy, Ian. *Women and Society in the Eighteenth Century*. Bethlehem, Pa.: Lawrence Henry Gipson Inst., 1983.

Flanders, Wallace Austin. *Structures of Experience: History, Society and Personal Life in the Eighteenth-Century British Novel*. Columbia: University of South Carolina Press, 1984.

Gillis, John R. *For Better, for Worse: British Marriages, 1600 to the Present*. New York: Oxford University Press, 1985.

Goldberg, Rita. *Sex and Enlightenment: Women in Richardson and Diderot*. Cambridge: Cambridge University Press, 1984.

Goldstone, Bette P. *Lessons to be Learned: A Study of Eighteenth Century Didactic Children's Literature*. New York: Lang, 1984.

Goldthorpe, J. E. *Family Life in Western Societies; A Historical Sociology of Fam-*

ily *Relationships in Britain and North America*. Cambridge: Cambridge University Press, 1987.

Greenberg, Janelle. "The Legal Status of the English Woman in Early Eighteenth-Century Common Law and Equity." *SECC* (1975): 171–81.

Habakkuk, H. J. "Marriage Settlements in the Eighteenth Century." *Transactions of the Royal Historical Society*, 4th ser. 32 (1950): 15–30.

Hagstrum, Jean H. *Sex & Sensibility: Ideal and Erotic Love from Milton to Mozart*. Chicago: University of Chicago Press, 1982.

Harris, Jocelyn. "Sappho, Souls, and the Salic Law of Wit." In *Anticipations of the Enlightenment in England, France and Germany,* edited by Alan Charles Kors and Paul J. Korshin, 232–58. Philadelphia: University of Pennsylvania Press, 1987.

Harth, Erica. "The Virtue of Love: Lord Hardwicke's Marriage Act." *Cultural Critique* (Spring 1988): 123–54.

Hassall, Anthony. "Women in Richardson and Fielding." *Novel* 14, no. 2 (Winter 1981): 168–74.

Jackson, Mary. *Engines of Instruction, Mischief and Magic: Children's Literature in England*. Lincoln: University of Nebraska Press, 1989.

Kinkead-Weekes, Mark. *Samuel Richardson: Dramatic Novelist*. Ithaca: Cornell University Press, 1973.

Lasch, Christopher. "The Suppression of Marriage in England: The Marriage Act of 1754." *Salmagundi* 26 (Spring 1974): 99–104.

London, April. "Controlling the Text: Women in *Tom Jones*." *Studies in the Novel* 19, no. 3 (Fall 1987): 323–33.

McClure, Ruth. *Coram's Children: The London Foundling Hospital in the Eighteenth Century*. New Haven: Yale University Press, 1981.

McKee, Patricia. "Corresponding Freedoms: Language and the Self in *Pamela*." *ELH* 52, no. 3 (Fall 1985): 621–48.

Messenger, Ann. *His and Hers: Essays in Restoration and Eighteenth-Century Literature*. Lexington: University Press of Kentucky, 1986.

Miles, Rosalind. *The Female Form: Women Writers and the Conquest of the Novel*. London: Routledge and Kegan Paul, 1987.

Moller, Susan. "Patriarchy and Married Women's Property in England: Questions on Some Current Views." *ECS* 17 (1983): 121–38.

Myer, Valerie Grosvenor, ed. *Samuel Richardson: Passion and Prudence*. London: Vision, 1986.

Myers, Sylvia H. "Learning, Virtue, and the Term 'Bluestocking.'" *SECC* 15 (1986): 279–88.

Nussbaum, Felicity. *The Autobiographical Subject: Gender and Ideology in Eighteenth-Century England*. Baltimore: Johns Hopkins University Press, 1989.

Okin, Susan Moller. "Patriarchy and Married Women's Property in England: Questions on Some Current Views." *ECS* 17 (1983): 121–38.

Patterson, Sylvia. "Eighteenth-Century Children's Literature in England: A Mirror of Its Culture." *JPC* 13 (1979): 38–43.

Perry, Ruth. *The Celebrated Mary Astell: An Early English Feminist*. Chicago: University of Chicago Press, 1986.

———. *Women, Letters and the Novel*. New York: AMS Press, 1980.

Pickering, Samuel F., Jr. *John Locke and Children's Books in Eighteenth Century England*. Knoxville: University of Tennessee Press, 1980.

Porter, Roy. *English Society in the Eighteenth Century.* London: Allen Lane, 1981.

Rogers, Katharine M. "Sensitive Feminism vs. Conventional Sympathy: Richardson and Fielding on Women." *Novel* 9 (1976): 256–70.

Schofield, Mary Anne. "Exploring the Woman Question: A Reading of Fielding's *Amelia.*" *ArielE* 16, no. 1 (January 1985): 45–57.

Schofield, Mary Anne, and Cecilia Macheski, eds. *Fettr'd or Free? British Women Novelists, 1670–1815.* Athens: Ohio University Press, 1986.

Smallwood, Angela. *Fielding and the Woman Question: The Novels of Henry Fielding and Feminist Debate, 1700–1750.* New York: St. Martin's Press, 1989.

Spacks, Patricia. *Imagining a Self: Autobiography and the Novel in Eighteenth-Century England.* Cambridge: Harvard University Press, 1976.

Spencer, Jane. *The Rise of the Woman Novelist.* Oxford: Basil Blackwell, 1986.

Spender, Dale. *Mothers of the Novel: 100 Good Women Writers before Jane Austen.* New York: Pandora, 1986.

Spring, Eileen. "The Family, Strict Settlement, and Historians." *Canadian Journal of History* 18 (December 1983): 379–98.

Staves, Susan. "*Evelina;* or, *Female Difficulties.*" *MP* 73 (1976): 368–81.

Stone, Lawrence. *The Family, Sex and Marriage in England, 1500–1800.* New York: Harper & Row, 1977.

Straub, Kristina. *Divided Fictions: Fanny Burney and Feminine Strategy.* Lexington: University Press of Kentucky, 1987.

Todd, Janet M. *Women's Friendship in Literature: The Eighteenth-Century Novel in England and France.* New York: Columbia University Press, 1980.

Trumbach, Randolph. *The Rise of the Egalitarian Family: Aristocratic Kinship and Domestic Relations in Eighteenth-Century England.* New York: Academic Press, 1978.

Watt, Ian. *The Rise of the Novel.* Berkeley: University of California Press, 1965.

Woodward, C. "'Feminine Virtue, Ladylike Disguise, Women of Community': Sarah Fielding and the Female I Am at Mid-Century." *Transactions of the Johnson Society of the Northwest* 15 (1984): 57–71.

INDEX

lious, 67; and reconciliation with family, 69–72; and unforgiving family, 72–75

Elstob, Charles, 48

Elstob, Elizabeth: discussed, 47–50, 57, 219–21, 222; *An English-Saxon Homily on the Birth-day of St. Gregory*, 48, 49; *An Essay on Glory*, 49; portrait of, 48; *Rudiments of Grammar for the English-Saxon Tongue*, 49

Employment open to women, 209–26

Essay in Defence of the Female Sex, An, 29, 51–52

Evelyn, Mary, 42

Everard, John, 72–75

Fables for the Female Sex, 56

Female Advocate, The, 28, 142, 143 (ill.)

Female Guardian, The, 12

Female Jester; or Wit for the Ladies, The, 36

Fenton, Anastasia, 166, 169, 173, 213

Fielding, Henry: on adultery, 22; *Amelia*, 19, 20, 22, 39, 64–65, 77, 137, 155–58, 241–43; on beauty in women, 19, 241; believable women in, 238; courtship customs in, 107; embraced double standard, 20–22, 240–41; on forced marriage, 97; *Joseph Andrews*, 19, 21, 107, 240; on learning in women, 62–65; on marriage, 155–58; presented real life, 2–3; runaway heroines of, 77–78; on runaway marriage, 137; *Shamela*, 22; *Tom Jones*, 19, 20, 21, 62–64, 77–78, 97, 239; traditional view of women in, 238–41; as voice for conformity, 266; women ruled by emotion in, 242; on women's friendships, 241

Fielding, Sarah: *The Adventures of David Simple*, 55, 75, 97, 164–65, 209, 243, 244; criteria for inclusion of, 3; on double standard, 20, 39; *Familiar Letters between the Principal Characters in David Simple*, 165, 243, 244, 245; on forced marriage, 97; *The Governess, or the Little Female Academy*, 55, 243, 246; *The History of the Countess of Dellwyn*, 56, 97, 165, 243, 245; *The History of Ophelia*, 76, 207, 243; intelligent women in, 244; *The Lives of Cleopatra and Octavia*, 243; on marriage, 164–66, 244–45, 246; and runaway daughters, 75–76; on women's learning, 55; women trying to earn a living in, 209

Filmer, Mary, 101

Flanders, Wallace Austin, 271*n*

Fleet, the, 69, 70

Foley, Anne, 111

Foley, Pen, 188

Foljambe, Mary, 169

Fothergill, Betty, 119–27

Fothergill, John, 119

Foundling Hospital, 168, 171, 214, 223

Fox, Mary, 173

Fox, Sarah, 16, 113, 114, 117

Fox, Stephen, 68

Gentleman's Calling, The, 7

Gillis, John, 270*n*

Goldberg, Rita, 271*n*

Goldstone, Bette, 269*n*

Goldthorpe, J. E., 270*n*

Governess, post of, 222–23

Grainger, Frances, 41

Grainger, Sarah, 224

Gravelot, 154

Green, Valentine, 53

Greenberg, Janelle, 269*n*

Gretna Green, 67

Habakkuk, H. J., 270*n*

Hagstrum, Jean, 270*n*

Hale, Elizabeth, 215

Halifax, Marquis of, 42

Hamilton, Frances, 227

Hanmer, Susan, 115

Harris, Jocelyn, 269*n*

Watt, Ian, 270n
Weekly Intelligencer, 85
Wheatly, Francis, 220
Wheeler, Elizabeth, 107
Wheeler, Joshua, 117–18
Whole Duty of a Woman, The: Or a Guide to the Female Sex from the Age of Sixteen to Sixty, 11–12, 107, 147
Widows: discussed, 198–99, 223–32; employment of, 223–26; in fiction, 199, 232; financial problems of, 226–27; independent, 227–28; legal status of, 38; and possibilities of interesting life, 230–31; remarriage of, 10, 228–30; should retire from world, 10
Wilder, William, 224
Wingrove, Elizabeth, 224
Wives: avoided jealousy, 144; bound to obedience, 27, 144; discussed, 139–97; fidelity absolute duty of, 10; financial protection for, 174–76; ignored sexual promiscuity in husband, 148; legal protection for, 146; and moral welfare of household, 10; patience of, 144, 147, 150; physical abuse of, 173–74; subject to husband's wishes, 28–30; used conciliation, 148, 149
Woman: Sketches of the History, Genius, Disposition, Accomplishments, Employments, Customs and Importance of the Fair Sex, 33

Woman as Good as the Man, The: or The Equallity of Both Sexes, 32, 52
Women: education of, 9, 33–36, 42–54; equality of, 32–33; and friendship, 183–84; ideal attributes of, 8–13; influences on, 6; importance of beauty in, 13–16; and law, 82–83; learned women in fiction, 54–66; need to be guarded, 9; passions more keen and violent, 12; politics as concern of, 12; private and domestic as proper sphere of, 12, 13; ruled by charm, 12; submissive selflessness of, 11; souls of, equal to men's, 9
Women's role: in becoming preacher, 32; diffidence, 30; domesticity, 11; and double standard, 19–20, 27; general view of, 38–39 (in novels, 39–40); *Genesis,* 26–27; inequality culturally imposed on, 30, 32–33; subjection, 9
Women writers: and denigration of learned ladies, 264; and double standard, 265; and marriage, 265; not radical, 266; represented women's point of view, 264; somewhat daring role of, 263; tended to support status quo, 263
Woodgate, Anne, 111–12
Woodward, C., 271n
Woolrich, Anne, 211
Wright, Mary, 223